THE
AMERICAN HERITAGE®
ABBREVIATIONS
DICTIONARY

THIRD EDITION

THE
AMERICAN HERITAGE®
ABBREVIATIONS
DICTIONARY

THIRD EDITION

Houghton Mifflin Harcourt
BOSTON • NEW YORK

ISBN-13: 978-0-618-85747-0
ISBN-10: 0-618-85747-8

Visit our website: www.hmhbooks.com

Library of Congress Cataloging-in-Publication Data
The American heritage abbreviations dictionary.-- 3rd ed.
    p. cm.
  ISBN-13: 978-0-618-62123-1
  ISBN-10: 0-618-62123-7
  1. Acronyms--United States. 2. Americanisms--Dictionaries. 3.
Abbreviations, English. I. Title: Abbreviations dictionary. II. Houghton
Mifflin Company.
  PE2839.A457 2005
  423'.15--dc22
                                        2005010764

Manufactured in Singapore

TWP 10 9 8 7 6 5 4 3 2

EDITORIAL AND PRODUCTION STAFF

Senior Editor, Project Director
Steven Kleinedler

Vice President, Managing Editor
Christopher Leonesio

Associate Editors
Nicholas A. Durlacher
Uchenna Ikonné

Assistant Editor
Peter Chipman

Art and Production Supervisor
Margaret Anne Miles

Database Production Supervisor
Christopher Granniss

Production Associate
Katherine M. Getz

Production Assistance
Tracy Duff

Text Design
Melodie Wertelet

Compiler, First Edition
Robert S. Wachal

PREFACE

The rate at which new abbreviations proliferate in English sky-rocketed throughout the second half of the 20th century and continues unabated into the 21st. This explosion of terms is reflected in the abundance of new material in *The American Heritage Abbreviations Dictionary*, Third Edition. With almost 20,000 entries and meanings, this revised work includes:

Internet Chatroom Abbreviations
FCOL for crying out loud
POS parent over shoulder

Professional Baseball and Football Teams
NYY New York Yankees
CAR Carolina Panthers

Sports Terminology
GDP ground into double plays
IFK indirect free kick

Three-letter Airport Codes for Major US and International Airports:
CLE Cleveland Hopkins International Airport
YYZ Pearson International Airport, Toronto, Canada

Colleges and Universities
CWRU Case Western Reserve University
LSU Louisiana State University

Constellations
PEG Pegasus
UMA Ursa Major

Vehicular Country Identification Codes
A Austria
CDN Canada

Hundreds of New and Up-To-Date Abbreviations
DHS Department of Homeland Security
TAS time addressable storage

The American Heritage Abbreviations Dictionary, Third Edition, lists not only terms commonly encountered in newspaper ads, but also those encountered in specialized fields, whose language is often underrepresented in general dictionary. This Dictionary serves as a quick and easy reference for abbreviated terms that Americans may encounter in a multitude of situations. In addition to wide coverage of spheres of interest, the *Abbreviations Dictionary* also has a broad range of abbreviation types. These include:

Acronyms
scuba self-contained underwater breathing apparatus

Blends
napalm naphthene + palmitate

Clippings
delts deltoid muscles

Defined Terms
ABC's the basics

Foreign Terms
op. cit. opere citato (in the work cited)

Initialisms
NIH National Institutes of Health

Mnemonic Devices
HOMES Huron, Ontario, Michigan, Erie, Superior

Numericals
B4N bye for now

Phonetic Initialisms
EZ easy

Respellings
biz business

Symbols
Na sodium

Truncations
adv. adverb

A NOTE ON STYLING

Abbreviations vary widely in their style of punctuations, capitalization, and internal spacing. Following the contemporary trend toward less frequent use of periods, entries in *The American Heritage Abbreviations Dictionary*, Third Edition, are generally shown without periods, except for truncations and terms that require or almost always appear with punctuation. Abbreviations used in Internet domain names are listed with a preceding period (.com, .edu, .br, .ne).

A

a absent

A accusative; ace; across; adenine; alto; American Stock Exchange; ammeter; ampere; angstrom; area; Asian (as in personal ads); *Baseball* assist; Austria (international vehicle ID)

a. acre; adjective; *Latin* anno (in the year); *Latin* annus (year); anode; answer; *Latin* ante (before); anterior; artery

A2 Ann Arbor [Michigan]

A2LA American Association for Laboratory Accreditation

aa Afar (language); author's alteration

AA Academy of Aphasia; Acts of the Apostles; administrative assistant; adverse action; Alcoa Inc.; Alcoholics Anonymous; Alzheimer's Association; antiaircraft; Armed Forces Americas (except Canada); Associate in Arts; atomic absorption

aa. arteries

AAA abdominal aortic aneurysm; American Arbitration Association; antiaircraft artillery; Area Agencies on Aging

AAAA American Academy of Anesthesiologists Assistants

AAAAI American Academy of Allergy, Asthma, and Immunology

AAAC American Academy of Ambulatory Care

AAACN American Academy of Ambulatory Care Nursing

AAAD American Athletic Association of the Deaf (now

USADSF: United States of America Deaf Sports Federation); antiaircraft artillery defense

AAAE American Association of Engineers

AAAH American Association of Alternative Healers

AAAHC Accreditation Association for Ambulatory Health Care

AAAI American Association for Artificial Intelligence

AAAL American Academy of Arts and Letters; American Association of Applied Linguistics

AAALAC Association for Assessment and Accreditation of Laboratory Animal Care International

AAAM advanced air-to-air missile; American Association of Aircraft Manufacturers

AAANA American Academy of Ambulatory Nursing Administration

AAAOM American Association of Acupuncture and Oriental Medicine

AAAP Association of Administrators in Academic Pediatrics

AAARRO Association of Administrators in Academic Radiology and Radiation Oncology

AAAS American Association for the Advancement of Science

AABA American Anorexia/Bulimia Association

AABB American Association of Blood Banks

AABH Association of Ambulatory Behavior Healthcare

AABIC Association for the Advancement of Brain Injured Children

AABP American Association of Bovine Practitioners

AABT Association for the Advancement of Behavior Therapy

AAC AIDS Action Council

A.A.C. *Latin* anno ante Christum (the year before Christ)

AACA Antique Automobile Club of America

AACAP American Academy of Child and Adolescent Psychiatry

AACC American Association for Clinical Chemistry

AACCR American Association of Central Cancer Registries

AACD American Academy of Cosmetic Dentistry

AACDP American Association of Chairs of Departments of Psychiatry

AACE American Association for Cancer Education; American Association of Clinical Endocrinologists

AACMHP American Association of Community Mental Health Center Psychiatrists

AACN American Association of Colleges of Nursing; American Association of Critical-Care Nurses

A.A.C.N. *Latin* anno ante Christum natum (the year before the birth of Christ)

AACOM American Association of Colleges of Osteopathic Medicine

AACOMAS American Association of Colleges of Osteopathic Medicine Applications Service

AACP American Academy for Child Psychoanalysts; American Academy of Clinical Psychiatrists; American Association of Colleges of Pharmacy; American Association of Community Psychiatrists

AACPDM American Academy for Cerebral Palsy and Developmental Medicine

AACPM American Association of Colleges of Podiatric Medicine

AACPMAS American Association of Colleges of Podiatric Medicine Application Service

AACPR American Association of Cardiovascular and Pulmonary Rehabilitation

AACR American Association for Cancer Research

AACS American Academy of Cosmetic Surgery

AACT American Academy of Clinical Toxicology

AACVPR American Association of Cardiovascular and Pulmonary Rehabilitation

Aad α-aminoadipic acid

AAD American Academy of Dermatology; Attitude Anomaly Detector

AADA American Academy of Dramatic Arts

AADB American Association of the Deaf-Blind

AADE American Association of Dental Editors; American Association of Diabetes Educators

AADEP American Academy of Disability Evaluating Physicians

AADGP American Academy of Dental Group Practice

AADPRT American Association of Directors of Psychiatric Residency Training

AADT annual average daily traffic

AADS American Association of Dental Schools

AAE African American English; Agriculture and Applied Econmics

AAED American Academy of Esthetic Dentistry

AAEE American Association of Electrical Engineers; American Academy of Environmental Engineers

AAEM American Academy of Emergency Medicine; American Academy of Environmental Medicine

AAEP American Association of Equine Practitioners

AAES American Association of Engineering Societies

AAETS American Academy of Experts in Traumatic Stress

AAF Army Air Forces; as a friend

AAFA Alliance Against Fraud in Advertising; Asthma and Allergy Foundation of America

AAFES Army and Air Force Exchange Service

AAFP American Academy of Family Physicians; American Association of Feline Practitioners

AAFPRS American Academy of Facial Plastic and Reconstructive Surgery

AAFS Academy of Ambulatory Foot Surgery; American Academy of Forensic Sciences

AAFT Alliance Against Fraud in Telemarketing

AAGHP American Association

of General Hospital Psychiatrists

AAGL American Association of Gynecologic Laparoscopists

AAGP American Association of Geriatric Psychiatry

AAGT Association for the Advancement of Gestalt Therapy

AAH Academy on Architecture for Health; Alliance for Alternatives in Healthcare

AAHA American Animal Hospital Association; American Association of Homes for the Aging

AAHC Alliance for Alternative Health Care; American Association of Healthcare Consultants

AAHE American Association for Health Education

AAHFP American Academy of Health and Fitness Professionals

AAHKS American Association of Hip and Knee Surgeons

AAHM American Association for the History of Medicine

AAHN American Association for the History of Nursing

AAHP American Association of Health Plans

AAHPERD American Alliance for Health, Physical Education, Recreation, and Dance

AAHPM American Academy of Hospice and Palliative Medicine

AAHS American Association for Hand Surgery

AAHSA American Association of Homes and Services for the Aging

AAHSL Association of Academic Health Sciences Libraries

AAHSLD Association of Academic Health Sciences Library Directors

AAI American Association of Immunologists

AAID American Academy of Implant Dentistry

AAIHDS American Association of Integrated Healthcare Delivery Systems

AAIM Association for Applied Interactive Multimedia

AAIP Association of American Indian Physicians

AAIR Asthma and Allergy Information and Research

AAK asleep at keyboard

AAKP American Association of Kidney Patients

AALA American Association for Laboratory Accreditation

AALAS American Association for Laboratory Animal Science

AALL American Association of Law Libraries

AALNC American Association of Legal Nurse Consultants

AALS Association of American Law Schools

AAM air-to-air missile; American Academy of Microbiology

AAMA American Academy of Medical Acupuncture; American Apparel Manufacturers Association

AAMC Association of American Medical Colleges

AAMCN American Association of Managed Care Nurses

AAMD American Academy of Medical Directors

AAMFT American Association for Marriage and Family Therapy

AAMI Association for the Advancement of Medical Instrumentation

AAMN American Assembly for Men in Nursing

AAMOF as a matter of fact

AAMOI as a matter of interest

AAMR American Association on Mental Retardation

AAMRO American Association of Medical Review Officers

AAMS Association of Air Medical Services

AAMSG Asian American Medical Student Group

AAMSI American Association for Medical Systems and Informatics

AAMT American Association for Medical Transcription

AAN American Academy of Neurology; American Academy of Nursing

AANA American Association of Nurse Anesthetists

A & A astronomy and astrophysics

A & E Arts and Entertainment

a & h accident and health

A & M agricultural and mechanical

A & O alert and oriented

A & P anterior and posterior; [Great] Atlantic and Pacific Tea Company; avant-pop

A and R artists and repertory

AANE American Association of Nurse Executives

AAN/MA Allergy and Asthma Network/Mothers of Asthmatics

AANN American Association of Neuroscience Nurses

AANNT American Association

of Nephrology Nurses and
Technicians

AANP American Academy of
Nurse Practitioners; American
Association of Naturopathic
Physicians; American Associa-
tion of Neuropathologists

AANS American Association of
Neurological Surgeons

AANWR Alaskan Arctic National
Wildlife Refuge

AAO American Academy of
Ophthalmology; American
Academy of Optometry; Ameri-
can Academy of Osteopathy;
American Association of Ortho-
dontists

A-A-O awake-alert-oriented

AAoA American Alliance of
Aromatherapy

AAOA Association of Academic
Orthopedic Administrators

AAOB American Association for
Oral Biologists

AAOHN American Association
of Occupational Health Nurses

AAO-HNS American Academy
of Otolaryngology-Head and
Neck Surgery

AAOM American Association of
Oriental Medicine

AAOMS American Association
of Oral and Maxillofacial Surgeons

AAON American Association of
Office Nurses

AAOP American Academy of
Orthotists and Prosthetists

AAOS American Academy of
Orthopaedic Surgeons

AAP affirmative action plan;
American Academy of Pedi-
atrics; American Academy of
Periodontology; American

Academy of Psychoanalysis;
American Academy of Psy-
chotherapists; Association for
Academic Psychiatry; Association for the Advancement of
Psychoanalysis; Association for
the Advancement of Psy-
chotherapy; Association of Academic Physiatrists; Association
of American Physicians; Association of American Publishers

AAPA American Academy of
Physician Assistants

AAPAA American Association of
Psychiatrists in Alcoholism and
Addictions

AAPB Association for Applied
Psychophysiology and Biofeedback

AAPC American Association of
Pastoral Counselors

AAPCC American Association of
Poison Control Centers

AAPCO Association of American
Pesticides Control Officers

AAPD American Academy of Pediatric Dentistry; American Association of People with
Disabilities

AAPH Asian-Americans in Public Health; Association for the
Advancement of Private Health

AAPHO American Association
of Physician Hospital Organizations

AAPHR American Association
of Physicians for Human Rights

AAPL American Academy of
Psychiatry and the Law

AAPM American Academy of
Pain Management

AAPMR American Academy of
Physical Medicine and Rehabilitation

AAPOS American Association for Pediatric Ophthalmology and Strabismus

AAPPO American Association of Preferred Provider Organizations

AAPS American Association of Pharmaceutical Scientists; American Association of Plastic Surgeons; Association of American Physicians and Surgeons

AAPSA American Academy of Psychoanalysis

AAPSC American Association of Psychiatric Services for Children

AAPSS American Academy of Political and Social Sciences

AAPT Association for the Advancement of Psychotherapy

AAR against all risks; Alliance for Aging Research; at any rate

AAR8 at any rate

a.a.r. against all risks

AARC Alliance for Acid Rain Control; American Association for Respiratory Care

AARDA American Autoimmune Related Diseases Association

AARP American Association of Retired Persons

AARS automated aircraft reporting system

AART American Association for Respiratory Therapy

AAS American Association of Suicidology; American Astronautical Society; American Astronomical Society; anabolic-androgenic steroid(s); Associate in Applied Sciences

AASA American Association of Surgical Administrators

AASCIN American Association of Spinal Cord Injury Nurses

AASCU American Association of State Colleges and Universities

AASH adrenal androgen-stimulating hormone; American Association for the Study of Headache

AASK Adopt A Special Kid

AASLD American Association for the Study of Liver Diseases

AASP American Association for Social Psychiatry; American Association of Swine Practitioners

AAST American Association for the Surgery of Trauma

AAT Animal-Assisted-Therapy Teams

AATA American Art Therapy Association; American Association of Thoracic Surgeons

AATBS Association for Advanced Training in Behavioral Sciences

AAU Amateur Athletic Union

AAUI Apple Attachment Unit Interface

AAUP American Association of University Professors

AAUW American Association of University Women

AAV adeno-associated virus; amphibious assault vehicle; Association of Avian Veterinarians

AAVA American Association of Veterinary Anatomists

AAVC American Association of Veterinary Clinicians

AAVE African American Vernacular English

AAVI American Association of Veterinary Immunologists

AAVMC American Association of Veterinary Medical Colleges

AAVSO American Association of Variable Star Observers

AAWP American Association of Working People

AAWR American Association for Women Radiologists

AAWV American Association of Wildlife Veterinarians

ab Abkhazian

Ab antibody

AB able-bodied [seaman]; about (shortwave transmission); airbase; airman basic; Alberta; *Latin* Artium Baccalaureus (Bachelor of Arts); at bats (baseball)

ab. about; abbreviation

ABA abscisic acid; American Badminton Association; American Bankers Association; American Bar Association; American Basketball Association; American Booksellers Association

ABAA Antiquarian Booksellers Association of America

ABAJ American Bar Association Journal

ABB American Brotherhood for the Blind

Abb. abbess; abbot

abbr. abbreviate; abbreviation

abbrev. abbreviate; abbreviation

ABC American Broadcasting Company; American-born Chinese

ABCC American Board of Clinical Chemistry

ABC's the alphabet; the basics

ABD all but dissertation

abd. abdicated; abdomen; abdominal

ABDC Association of Birth Defect Children

abdom. abdomen; abdominal

ABDR aircraft battle damage repair

ABE Lehigh Valley International Airport (Allentown, PA)

ABEDA Arab Bank for Economic Development in Africa

ABEM American Board of Emergency Medicine

ABEND abnormal end of task

ABES Alliance for Balanced Environmental Solutions

ABFP American Board of Forensic Psychiatry

ABG arterial blood gas

ABHES Accrediting Bureau of Health Education Schools

ABI Abilene Regional Airport; acquired brain injury

ABIH American Board of Industrial Hygiene

ABIM American Board of Internal Medicine

ab init. *Latin* ab initio (from the beginning)

ABJS Association of Bone and Joint Surgeons

ABL airborne laser; atmospheric boundary layer

abl. ablative

abl. absol. ablative absolute

ABLE Association for Biology Laboratory Education

ABM antiballistic missile

ABMC American Battle Monuments Commission

ABMCM American Board of Managed Care Medicine

ABMM American Board of Medical Management

ABMR Academy of Behavioral Medicine Research

ABMS American Board of Medical Specialties

ABMT autologous bone marrow transplantation

ABMTR Autologous Blood and Marrow Transplant Registry

abn airborne

ABN abnormal

ABNF Association of Black Nursing Faculty in Higher Education

ABNS American Board of Nursing Specialties

ABO annular beam oscillator

A-bomb atomic bomb

ABOMBI American Board of Minor Brain Injury

Aborig. Aboriginal

ABP American Board of Pediatrics; androgen binding protein; arterial blood pressure

Abp. archbishop

ABPA allergic bronchopulmonary aspergillosis

ABPN American Board of Psychiatry and Neurology

ABPP American Board of Professional Psychology

ABPS American Board of Plastic Surgery

ABQ Albuquerque International Airport

ABR aeroballistic rocket; American Bankruptcy Reports; area border router; available bit rate

abr. abridged; abridgment

abs abdominal muscles; absolute temperature

ABS American Board of Surgery; Animal Behavior Society; antilock braking system

abs. absent; absolute; absolutely; abstract

ABSA American Biological Safety Association

abs. feb. *Latin* absente febre (when fever is absent)

absol. absolute; absolutely

abstr. abstract

ABT about (shortwave transmission); American Ballet Theatre

abt. about

ABTA American Brain Tumor Association

ABTP American Board of Transcultural Psychiatry

ABTRES Abatement and Residual Forecasting Model

ABV above (shortwave transmission)

abv. above

ABVD adriamycin, bleomycin, vinblastine, and dacarbazine

ABYC American Boat & Yacht Council

Ac actinium; Acts of the Apostles

AC adult contemporary; air conditioning; alternating current

ac. acre; air-cool

a.c. *Latin* ante cibum (before meals)

A.C. *Latin* anno Christi (the year of Christ); appellate court; Army Corps; Athletic Club

a/c account; account current; air conditioning

A/C aircraft

ACA American Camping Association; American Canoe Association; American Casting Association; American Chiropractic Association; American Collectors Association; American Counseling Association; Amputee Coalition of America

AC/A accommodative convergence/accommodation ratio

ACAAI American College of Allergy, Asthma, and Immunology

acad. academic; academy

ACAI American College of Allergy and Immunology

ACAM American College for Advancement in Medicine

ACAPN Association for Child and Adolescent Psychiatric Nurses

ACAT/H Academy of Clinical and Applied Thrombosis/Hemostasis

ACATS airborne chromatograph for atmospheric trace species

ACB American Council of the Blind; armored cavalry brigade; Association of Clinical Biochemists

ACBM Asbestos-Containing Building Material

ACC Air Combat Command; ambulatory care center; American College of Cardiology; anthropogenic climate change; Atlantic Coast Conference; Arab Cooperation Council

acc. accelerate; acceleration; accept; accompanied; according; account; accusative

ACCC Association of Community Cancer Centers

ACCD American Coalition of Citizens with Disabilities

ACCEL American College of Cardiology Extended Learning

ACCESS Architectural and Transportation Barriers Compliance Board

ACCH Association for the Care of Children's Health

ACCI American Council on Consumer Interests

ACCINTNET Air Combat Command Intelligence Network

ACCME Accreditation Council for Continuing Medical Education

accomp. accompaniment

ACCP American College of Chest Physicians; American College of Clinical Pharmacy

accrd. accrued

ACCRI Wright's Anaesthesia and Critical Care Resources on the Internet

ACCT *French* Agence de Coopération Culturelle et Technique (Agency for Cultural and Technical Cooperation)

acct. account; accountant

accum. accumulate

accus. accusative

ACD acid-citrate-dextrose; alt + control + delete; American College of Dentists; automatic call distribution; automatic call distributor

ACDA Arms Control and Disarmament Agency

AC/DC alternating current/direct current; bisexual

ACDS Association for Children with Down Syndrome

ACE access control entry; American Council on Education; angiotensin-converting enzyme; Army Corps of Engineering

ACEC American Consulting Engineers Council; Area of Critical Environmental Concern

ACEDB A Caenorhabditis Elegans Database

ACEHSA Accrediting Commission on Education for Health

Services Administration

ACEI angiotensin-converting enzyme inhibitor

ACEP American College of Emergency Physicians

ACES adaptation controlled environment system

acet. acetone

ACF access control field; Administration for Children and Families; Albedo Correction Factor; Asian Christian female

ACFE American College of Forensic Examiners

ACFP American College of Osteopathic Family Physicians

acft aircraft

ACG American College of Gastroenterology

ac-g accelerator globulin

ACGE Accreditation Council for Gynecologic Endoscopy

ACGIH American Conference of Governmental Industrial Hygienists

ACGME Accreditation Council for Graduate Medical Education

ACGP American College of General Practitioners in Osteopathic Medicine and Surgery

ACh acetylcholine

ACH Association for Computers and the Humanities; automated clearing house

ACHA American College Health Association; American College of Hospital Administrators

ACHE American College of Healthcare Executives; American Council for Headache Education

achiev. achievement

ACHIS Association of Consumer Health Information Specialists

ACHNE Association of Community Health Nursing Educators

ACHR Advisory Committee on Health Research

AC/HR aircraft per hour

ACHRE Advisory Committee on Human Radiation Experiments

ACHSA American Correctional Health Services Association

ACIC Aeronautical Charting and Information Center

ACICS Accrediting Council for Independent Colleges and Schools

ACID aircraft identification

ACIDS American College of Integrated Delivery Systems

ACIP Advisory Committee for Immunization Practices

ack. acknowledge; acknowledgment

ACK acknowledgment; Nantucket Memorial Airport

ack emma A.M. (*Latin* ante meridiem—before noon)

ACL Analytical Chemistry Laboratory; anterior cruciate ligament

ACLAD American Committee on Laboratory Animal Diseases

ACLAM American College of Laboratory Animal Medicine

ACLI American Council of Life Insurance

ACLM American College of Legal Medicine

ACLs Alternate Concentration Limits

ACLS advanced cardiology life support; American Council of Learned Societies

ACLT actual calculated landing time

ACLU American Civil Liberties Union

ACM asbestos-containing material; Asian Christian male; Association for Computing Machinery

ACMCM American College of Managed Care Medicine

ACME Advisory Committee on the Marine Environment

ACMHA American College of Mental Health Administration

ACMHS Asian Community Mental Health Services

ACMP Advisory Committee on Marine Pollution; American College of Medical Physics

ACMPD American Council on Marijuana and other Psychoactive Drugs

ACMPE American College of Medical Practice Executives

ACMQ American College of Medical Quality

ACMS advanced cost management systems

ACN Association for Comprehensive NeuroTherapy

ACNM American College of Nuclear Medicine; American College of Nurse-Midwives

ACNP American College of Neuropsychiatrists; American College of Nuclear Physicians; American College of Nurse Practitioners

ACNPP American College of Neuropsychopharmacology

ACO Association of Commissioned Officers

ACOE Army Corps of Engineers

ACOEM American College of Occupational and Environmental Medicine

ACOG American College of Obstetricians and Gynecologists

ACOM American College of Occupational Medicine

ACOOG American College of Osteopathic Obstetricians and Gynecologists

ACOPS Advisory Committee on Protection of the Sea

ACOR Association of Cancer Online Resources

ACP African, Caribbean, and Pacific Countries; American College of Physicians; American College of Psychiatrists; Association for Child Psychoanalysis

ACPA American Chronic Pain Association; American College of Psychoanalysts

ACPE American College of Physician Executives; American Council on Pharmaceutical Education

ACPM American College of Prehospital Medicine; American College of Preventive Medicine

ACPOC Association of Children's Prosthetic-Orthotic Clinics

ACPPD average cost per patient day

ACPS acrocephalosyndactyly

acpt. acceptance

acq acquire

ACQIP Ambulatory Care Quality Improvement Program

ACR American College of Radiology; American College of Rheumatology; armored cavalry regiment

ACRM American Congress of

Rehabilitation Medicine

ACRO American College of Radiation Oncology

ACRP Association of Clinical Research Professionals

ACRR American Council on Race Relations

ACRS accelerated cost recovery system

ACS American Cancer Society; American Chemical Society; American College of Surgeons; asynchronous communications server

ACSA American Center for Social Awareness

ACSH American Council on Science and Health

ACSM American College of Sports Medicine

ACSMA American Canine Sports Medicine Association

ACSN Aspartame Consumer Safety Network

A/cs pay. accounts payable

ACSR *Annual Cancer Statistics Review*

A/cs rec. accounts receivable

acst. acoustic

ACSUS AIDS Cost and Services Utilization Survey

ACSW Academy of Certified Social Workers

ACT a trademark for a standardized college entrance examination (originally American College Test); American Conservatory Theater; Waco Regional Airport

act. acting; action; active; actively; actor; actual; actuary

A.C.T. Australian Capital Territory

ACTe anodal closure tetanus

actg. acting

ACTH adrenocorticotropic hormone

ACTION American Council to Improve Our Neighborhoods

ACTIS AIDS Clinical Trials Information Service

ACTIVE advanced controls technology for integrated vehicles

ACTS asbestos contractor tracking system

ACT-UP AIDS Coalition to Unleash Power

ACU Association of Clinicians for the Underserved; Attitude Control Unit

ACURP American College of Utilization Review Physicians

ACUS Administrative Conference of the United States

acv actual cash value

ACV air-cushion vehicle

ACVA American College of Veterinary Anesthesiologists

ACVD arteriosclerotic cardiovascular disease

ACVIM American College of Veterinary Internal Medicine

ACVM American College of Veterinary Microbiologists

ACVP American College of Veterinary Pathologists; American College of Veterinary Radiology

ACVRD arteriosclerotic cardiovascular renal disease

ACVS American College of Veterinary Surgeons

ACW alternating continuous waves

ACWA American Clean Water Association

ACYF Administration for Children, Youth, and Families

ad advertisement

AD active duty; air-dried; Alzheimer's disease; athletic director; average deviation

ad. adapter; adverb

.ad Andorra

a.d. after date; *Latin* ante diem (before the day); autograph document

A.D. *Latin* anno Domini (in the year of our Lord); *Latin* auris dexter (right ear)

A/D arrival/departure

A-D analog to digital

ADA American Dental Association; American Diabetes Association; American Dietetic Association; Americans for Democratic Action; Americans with Disabilities Act; assistant district attorney

ADAA Anxiety Disorders Association of America

ADACS Attitude Determination and Control Subsystem

ADAD *Alzheimer Disease and Associated Disorders*

ADAM Animated Dissection of Anatomy for Medicine

ADAMHA Alcohol, Drug Abuse and Mental Health Administration

Adapt American Disabled for Attendant Programs Today

adapt. adaptation; adapted by

ADARA American Deafness and Rehabilitation Association

ADAS airborne data acquisition system

adb accidental death benefit

ADB African Development Bank; Asian Development Bank

ADBB all done, bye-bye

ADC advanced developing country; aide-de-camp; Aid to Dependent Children; Air Defense Command; Alzheimer's Disease Center; analog to digital converter

ADCC antibody-dependent cell-mediated cytotoxicity

ADCP acoustic Doppler current profiler

ADD Administration on Developmental Disabilities; attention deficit disorder

add. addendum; addition

ADDA [National] Attention Deficit Disorder Association

addn. addition

addnl. additional

ADDS American Digestive Disease Society

Ade adenine

ADE Array Drive Electronics

ADEAR Alzheimer's Disease Education and Referral Center

ADEC Association of Death Education and Counseling

ADF adapter description file; automatic direction finder

ADFS Alternative Delivery and Financing System

ADH antidiuretic hormone

ADHA American Dental Hygienists Association

ADHD attention deficit hyperactivity disorder

ADHF American Digestive Health Foundation

adhib. *Latin* adhibendus (to be administered)

ad inf. *Latin* ad infinitum (to infinity)

ad init. *Latin* ad initium (at the beginning)

ad int. *Latin* ad interim (in the meantime)

ADIOS Asian Dust Input to the Oceanic System

ADIZ air defense identification zone

adj. adjectival; adjective; adjunct; adjutant

Adjt. adjutant

ADL activities of daily living; Anti-Defamation League

ad lib *Latin* ad libitum (at pleasure, speak without notes or script—that is, an unscripted comment)

ad loc. *Latin* ad locum (to, or at, the place)

ADM add/drop multiplexer; admiral

adm. administration; administrative; administrator; admission

ADMD Administration Management Domain

admin. administration; administrator

admov. *Latin* admove (apply)

ADMSEP Association of Directors of Medical Student Education in Psychiatry

adn adenoid

ADN Advanced Digital Network; any day now; Associate Degree in Nursing

ADOL Adolescence Directory Online

AdoMet S-adenosyl-L-methionine

ADP adenosine diphosphate; automatic data processing

ADPANA Alcohol and Drug

Problems Association of North America

ADPCM adaptive differential pulse code modulation

ADPE automated data processing equipment

ADR address (shortwave transmission); adverse drug reaction; American depository receipt; automatic dialogue replacement

A.D.R. alternative dispute resolution; asset depreciation range

ADRC Alzheimer's Disease Research Center

ADRDA Alzheimer's Disease and Related Disorders Association

ADS alternative delivery systems; American Dialect Society

ads. *Latin* ad sectam (at the suit of)

a.d.s. autograph document, signed

ad sat *Latin* ad saturatum (to saturation)

ADSC active duty service commitment

ADSL asynchronous digital subscriber line.

ADSS Alcohol and Drug Services Study

ADT Alaska Daylight Time; Atlantic Daylight Time; average daily traffic

ADTA American Dance Therapy Association

ADTe anodal duration tetanus

adv. advance; adverb; *Latin* adversus (against); advertisement; advisory

Adv. Advent; advocate

ad val. *Latin* ad valorem (in proportion to the value)

advb. adverbial; adverbially

advs. adverbs; *Latin* adversus (against)

advt. advertisement

ADWAS Abused Deaf Women's Advocacy Services

ADZ advise (shortwave transmission)

ae Avestan

AE account executive; adult education; American English; Armed Forces Europe; atomic energy

ae. *Latin* aetatis (at the age of)

.ae United Arab Emirates

A.E. aeronautical engineer; aeronautical engineering; astronautical engineer; astronautical engineering

AEA Actors Equity Association; Atomic Energy Act

AEC Atomic Energy Commission

AECLP alliance to end childhood lead poisoning

AECOPD acute exacerbations of COPD

AECT Association for Educational Communications and Technology

AED Automatic External Defibrillator; United Arab Emirates—dirham (currency)

AEDC Arnold Engineering Development Center

AEDS Atomic Energy Detection System

Ae.E aeronautical engineer; aeronautical engineering

AEF American Enuresis Foundation; American Expeditionary Force

aeg. *Latin* aequalis (equal, equals)

AEGIS AIDS Education Global

Information System

AEHF American Environmental Health Foundation

AEIDC Arctic Environmental Information and Data Center

AEK all electric kitchen

AELDS Advanced Earth Location Data System

AEM acoustic emission monitoring

AEOS advanced electro-optical system

AEP Association of Emergency Physicians

aeq. *Latin* aequalis (equal)

AERA American Educational Research Association

AERC Association of Ecosystem Research Centers

aero. aeronautical; aeronautics

AEROCE Atmosphere/Ocean Chemistry Experiment

aerodyn. aerodynamics

aeron. aeronautics

aeronaut. aeronautics

AERS Association of Educators in Radiological Sciences

AES Adlai E. Stevenson; advanced encryption standard

AESA Association of Environmental Scientists and Administrators

AESOP Airborne Experiment to Study Ozone Production

aet. *Latin* aetatis (at the age of, aged)

aetat. *Latin* aetatis (at the age of, aged)

AEW airborne early warning

AEWC Alaska Eskimo Whaling System

af Afrikaans

AF acre-feet; after (shortwave

transmission); air force; Anglo-French; Arthritis Foundation; Asian female; atrial fibrillation; audio frequency; autofocus

af. affix

Af. Afghani; Afghanistan; Africa; African; Afrikaans

.af Afghanistan

AFA Adoptive Families of America; Associate in Fine Arts; Afghanistan—afghani (currency); American Forestry Association

AFAA Air Force Audit Agency

AFAIAA as far as I am aware

AFAIAC as far as I am concerned

AFAICR as far as I can recall

AFAICT as far as I can tell

AFAIK as far as I know

AFAIR as far as I recall

AFAIU as far as I understand

AFAIUI as far as I understand it

AFAM Ancient Free and Accepted Masons

AFAP as far as possible

AFAR American Federation for Aging Research

AFB air force base; American Foundation for the Blind

AFBCMR Air Force Review Board for Correction of Military Records

AFBF American Farm Bureau Federation

AFC adult foster care; American Football Conference; automatic flight control; automatic frequency control; away from computer

AFCA area fuel consumption allocation

AFCARA Air Force Civilian Ap-

pellate Review Agency

AFCEE Air Force Center for Environmental Excellence

AFCR American Federation for Clinical Research (now **AFMR**: American Federation for Medical Research)

AFCS automatic flight control system

AfDB African Development Bank

AFDBA Armed Forces Dental Benefit Association

AFDC Aid to Families with Dependent Children

AFDF African Development Fund

AFED Alliance to Fight Eating Disorders

AFESD Arab Fund for Economic and Social Development

AFEWES Air Force Electronic Warfare Effectiveness Simulator

aff. affairs; affectionate; affirmative; affix

affd. affirmed

affg. affirming

afft. affidavit

Afg. Afghanistan

AFG Afghanistan (international vehicle ID)

AFGE American Federation of Government Employees

Afgh. Afghanistan

AFGIHS Air Force Geographic Information Handling System

AFGWC Air Force Global Weather Center

AFH anterior facial height

AFI American Film Institute; American Forest Institute

A-fib atrial fibrillation

AFICC Academy of Forensic and

Industrial Chiropractic Consultants

AFIP Armed Forces Institute of Pathology

AFIPS American Federation of Information Processing Societies

AFIS American Forces Information Service

AFIT Air Force Institute of Technology

AFK away from keyboard

Afk. Afrikaans

AFL American Federation of Labor; American Football League

AFL-CIO American Federation of Labor and Congress of Industrial Organizations

AFM American Federation of Musicians; audio frequency modulation

AFMA American Film Marketing Association

AFMC Air Force Material Command

AFMR American Federation for Medical Research

AFN American Forensic Nurses

AFO ankle-foot orthosis

AFOS [National Weather Service] Automation of Field Operations and Services

AFOSI Air Force Office of Special Investigations

AFOSR Air Force Office of Scientific Research

AFP acute flaccid paralysis; alpha-fetoprotein

AFPA Association of Family Practice Administrators

AFPC Armed Forces Policy Council

AFPEO Air Force Program Executive Office

AFPPS American Forces Press and Publications Service

AFQT Armed Forces Qualification TEST

Afr. Africa; African

AFRCE Air Force Regional Civil Engineers

AFRES Air Force Reserves

Afrik. Afrikaans

AFRRI Armed Forces Radiobiology Research Institute

AFRTS Armed Forces Radio and Television Service

AFS American Field Service; American Folklore Society

AFSAA Air Force Studies and Analysis Agency

AFSC Air Force Specialty Code; Armed Forces Staff College

AFSCF Air Force Satellite Control Facility

AFSCME American Federation of State, County, and Municipal Employees

AFSCN Air Force Satellite Control Network

AFSFC Air Force Space Forecasting Center

AFSOC Air Force Special Operations Command

AFSPC Air Force Space Command

AFT American Federation of Teachers

aft. afternoon

AFTA American Family Therapy Association

AFTAD Analysis-Forecast Transport and Diffusion

AFTN Aeronautical Fixed Telecommunications Network

AFTRA American Federation of Television and Radio Artists

AFUD American Foundation for Urologic Disease

AFV alternate fuel vehicle

AFY acre-feet per year

ag agricultural; agriculture

Ag antigen; silver

AG adjutant general; again (shortwave transmission); attorney general

Ag. August

.ag Antigua and Barbuda

a.g. above ground (for example, as applied to an outdoor pool)

A.G. *German* Aktiengesellschaft (joint-stock company, that is, incorporated)

AGA Amateur Gymnastics Association; American Gastroenterological Association

AGAC American Guild of Authors and Composers

AGARD [NATO] Advisory Group for Aerospace Research and Development

AGBAD Alexander Graham Bell Association for the Deaf

AGC advanced graduate certificate; automatic gain control

AGCA automatic ground-controlled approach

AGCM atmospheric general circulation model

agcy. agency

AGD Academy of General Dentistry

A.G.Dec. Attorney General's Decisions

AGE acute gastroenteritis

Ag.E. agricultural engineer; agricultural engineering

agent-n agent-noun

AGFS Aviation Gridded Forecast System

AGGG [World Climate Program] Advisory Group on Greenhouse Gases

AGHE Association for Gerontology in Higher Education

AGI adjusted gross income

AGL above ground level

AGLP Association of Gay and Lesbian Psychiatrists

AGM air-to-ground missile

AGN active galactic nucleus; again (shortwave transmission)

AGO American Gastroenterological Organization

AGP accelerated graphics port

AGPA American Group Practice Association; American Group Psychotherapy Association

AGPAM American Guild of Patient Account Management

AGpO Academy of Gp Orthodontics

agr. agreement; agricultural; agriculture

A/G ratio albumin-globulin ratio

agri. agricultural; agriculture

agric. agricultural; agriculture

AGRICOLA Agricultural Online Access

agron. agronomy

AGS American Geriatrics Society

AGSD Association for Glycogen Storage Disease

AGSG Alliance of Genetic Support Groups

AGSN Ambiguous Genitalia Support Network

AGSS attitude ground support system

agt. agent; agreement

AGU American Geophysical Union

AH *American Health*; assisted hatching

A.h. ampere-hour

A.H. *Latin* Anno Hebraico (in the Hebrew year); *Latin* Anno Hegirae (in the year of the Hegira)

A-h ampere-hour

AHA American Heart Association; American Historical Association; American Hospital Association; American Hyperlexia Association

AHAF American Health Assistance Foundation

AHC Association of Academic Health Centers

AHCA American Health Care Association

AHCPR Agency for Healthcare Policy and Research

AHD arteriosclerotic heart disease

AHDL analog hardware descriptive language

AHEAD Association on Higher Education and Disability

AHEC Area Health Education Center

AHERA Asbestos Hazard Emergency Response Act

AHF antihemophilic factor

AHFS American Hospital Formulary Service

AHFS DI American Hospital Formulary Service Drug Information

AHG antihemophilic globulin

AHI American Health Institute; Animal Health Institute; at-home insemination

AHILA Association for Health Information and Libraries in Africa

AHIMA American Health Information Management Association

AHIP Academy of Health Information Professionals

AHL American Hockey League

AHM Academy for Healthcare Management

AHMA American Holistic Medical Association

AHME Association for Hospital Medical Education

AHNA American Holistic Nurses' Association

AHP Academy of Hospice Physicians; Accountable Health Plan; Association for Humanistic Psychology

AHQ Air Headquarters; Army Headquarters

AHR Association for Health Records

AHRA American Healthcare Radiology Administrators

AHRC Association for the Help of Retarded Children

AHRIS Automated Health Research Information System

AHRQ Agency for Healthcare Research and Quality

AHS Academy of Health Sciences; American Humane Society

AHSR Association for Health Services Research

AHTA American Horticultural Therapy Association

AHVMA American Holistic Veterinary Medical Association

ai airborne intercept

AI adapter interface; Amnesty International; aortic insufficiency; artificial insemination; artificial intelligence; Associate Investigator

.ai Anguilla

a.i. *Latin* ad interim (in the meantime)

AIA American Iatrogenic Association; American Institute of Architects; Asbestos Information Association

AIAA American Institute of Aeronautics and Astronautics

AIBD Association of International Bond Dealers (now **ISMA**: International Securities Market Association)

AIBS American Institute of Biological Sciences

AIC American Institute of Chemists

AICPA American Institute of Certified Public Accountants

AICR American Institute for Cancer Research

AID Agency for International Development

AIDS acquired immune deficiency syndrome

AIDSLINE AIDS Information Online

AIDSTRIALS AIDS clinical trials

AIF audio interchange format

AIFF audio interchange file format

AIG assistant inspector general

AIH homologous artificial insemination

AIHA American Industrial Hygiene Association; American International Health Alliance

AIHC American Industrial Health Council

AIHCE American Industrial Hygiene Conference and Exposition

AIHS Academy for International Health Studies

AILC adult independent living center

AILD angioimmunoblastic lymphadenopathy with dysproteinemia

aIle alloisoleucine

AIM American Indian Movement

AIN American Institute of Nutrition

AIO Advances in Osteoporosis

AIP American Institute of Physics

Aipac American Israel Public Affairs Committee

AIPP American Institute for Psychotherapy and Psychoanalysis

AIR American Institutes for Research

AIRMoN Atmospheric Integrated Research Monitoring Network

AIRS Aerometric Information Retrieval System

AIRST advanced infrared search and track

AIS alarm indication signal; American Institute of Stress; automated information security

AISB as I said before

AISC [National Environmental Satellite, Data, and Information Service] Assessment and Information Services Center

AISE as I said earlier

AISI American Iron and Steel Institute; as I see it

AIT assembly, integration, and test; atomic international time

AIUI as I understand it

AIUM American Institute of Ultrasound in Medicine

AIV assembly-integration-verification; aviation impact variable

AJ adjust (shortwave transmission); anti-jam

AK Alaska

a.k. ass kisser

aka also known as

a/k/a also known as

AKA above knee amputation

AKC American Kennel Club

AK-47 *Russian* avtomat Kalashnikova 1947 (Kalashnikoff automatic [rifle] 1947)

AKL Auckland [NZ] International Airport

AKNF Adair-Koshland-Némethy-Filmer model

AJAO American Juvenile Arthritis Organization

AJCC American Joint Committee on Cancer

Al aluminum

AL Alabama; Albania (international vehicle ID); American League; American Legion; Anglo-Latin; artificial life

al. alcohol; alcoholic

.al Albania

a.l. autograph letter

ALA alpha-linolenic acid; American Library Association; American Lung Association; Association for Laboratory Automation

Ala. Alabama; alanine

ALAD Academic Librarians Assisting the Disabled

ALADI *Spanish* Asociación Latinoamericana de Integración (Latin American Integration Association)

Al-Anon Alcoholics Anonymous [Family Group]

ALARA as late as reasonably achievable; as low as reasonably achievable

ALARM air-launched antiradiation missile

Alas. Alaska

ALB Albany International Airport

Alb. Albania; Albanian; Albany; Alberta

alb. albumen

Alba. Alberta

ALBM air-launched ballistic missile

alc. alcohol; alcoholic

ALCA American Lock Collectors Association

Alcan Alaska-Canada

alch. alchemy

ALCI appliance leakage circuit interrupter

ALCM air-launched cruise missile

ALCS American League Championship Series

ALD adrenoleukodystrophy

Ald. alderman; alderwoman

ALDS American League Division Series

ALE additional living expense

ALEC American Legislative Exchange Council

ALERT Allergy to Latex Education and Resource Team

ALEXIS array of low energy

x-ray imaging sensors

ALF American Liver Foundation; assisted living facility

ALFA Association for Low Flow Anaesthesia

ALG antilymphocyte globulin

alg. algebra

Alg. Algeria; Algerian

ALGOL Algorithmic-Oriented Language

ALH advanced liquid hydrogen

ALI American Law Institute

ALICE all-purpose lightweight individual carrying equipment

A-life artificial life

ALJ administrative law judge

alk. alkali; alkaline

alky. alkalinity

ALL acute lymphocytic leukemia; Albania—lek

allo allegro

ALLSA Allergy Society of South Africa

allus. allusion; allusively

alm alarm

ALOS average length of stay

ALP American Labor Party

alp. alpine

ALPA Air Line Pilots Association

ALPCA Auto License Plate Collectors Association

alpha alphabetical

alphanumeric alphabetical and numerical

ALPO Association of Lunar and Planetary Observers

ALR American Law Reports

ALS advanced life support; amyotrophic lateral sclerosis

a.l.s. autograph letters, signed

ALSA Amyotrophic Lateral Sclerosis Association

ALSC Association of Literary Scholars and Critics

ALSP atmosphere and land surface processes

Alt alternate

ALT alanine aminotransferase

alt. alteration; altered; alternate; altitude; alto

Alta. Alberta

ALTA American Land Title Association

alter. alteration

alt. hor. *Latin* alternis horis (every other hour)

altm. altimeter

ALU arithmetic logic unit

alum alumna; alumnae; alumni; alumnus

alum. aluminum

alw. allowance

ALW arch-loop-whorl system

am Amharic; ammeter

Am americium; Amos

AM amplitude modulation; *Latin* Artium Magister (Master of Arts); Asian male

Am. America; American

.am Armenia

a.m. *Latin* ante meridiem (before noon)

A.M. airmail; *Latin* anno mundi (in the year of the world); *Latin* ante meridiem (before noon)

AMA against medical advice; Amarillo International Airport; American Management Association; American Medical Association; American Motorcycle Association

AMA EIB American Medical Association Enterprise Information Base

AMAHC Accreditation Manual for Ambulatory Health Care

AMAP American Medical Accreditation Program

amb. ambassador; ambiguous; ambulance

AMC American Maritime Cases; American Mining Congress; American Movie Classics; antecedent moisture condition; Atlantic Marine Center

AMCHAM American Chamber of Commerce

AMCHP Association of Maternal and Child Health Programs

AMCLD active matrix liquid crystal display

AMCP Association of Managed Care Providers

AMCRA American Managed Care and Review Association

AMD acid mine drainage; age-related macular degeneration; Armenia—dram (currency)

amd. amended

AMDA American Medical Directors Association

AMDRFM advanced monolithic digital radio frequency memory

Ame America; American

AmE American English

AME African Methodist Episcopal

AMED Allied and Alternative Medicine

AMEDS Army Medical Service

Amer. America; American

AmerF. American French

AmerInd American Indian

AMERSA Association for Medical Education and Research in Substance Abuse

AmerSp. American Spanish

Ameslan American Sign Language

Amex American Stock Exchange

AmEx American Express

AMF Arab Monetary Fund

AmFAR American Foundation for AIDS Research

AMGA American Medical Group Association

AMGO Association of Manager of Gynecology and Obstetrics

AMHA Association of Mental Health Administrators

AMHC Association of Mental Health Clergy

AMHCA American Mental Health Counselors Association

AMHF American Mental Health Foundation

AMHL Association of Mental Health Librarians

AMHPA Assembly of Mental Healthcare Practice Administrators

AMI acute myocardial infarction

AMIA American Medical Informatics Association

AMIA-IWG American Medical Informatics Association-Internet Working Group

AMM antimissile missile; Queen Alia International Airport (Amman, Jordan)

ammo ammunition

Amn airman

AMN American Mobile Nurses

AMNH American Museum of Natural History

Amoco American Oil Company

AMORC Ancient Mystical Order Rosae Crucis

amort. amortization

AMOS Automated Meteorological Observing System

amp ampere; amplifier

AMP adenosine monophosphate; Association for Molecular Pathology

AMPAS Academy of Motion Picture Arts and Sciences

amp hr ampere-hour

ampl. *Latin* amplus (large)

AMPRO American Medical Peer Review Organization

AMRA American Medical Record Association

AMRAAM advanced medium-range air-to-air missile

AMRC Association of Medical Research Charities

AMRIID Army Medical Research Institute of Infectious Diseases

AMRTA Alchemical Medicine Research and Teaching Association

AMS Agricultural Marketing Service; American Mathematical Society; American Meteorological Society; Amsterdam-Schiphol Airport; Army Map Service; auditory memory span

AMSA American Medical Society on Alcoholism and Other Drug Dependencies; American Medical Student Association

AMSAODD American Medical Society on Alcoholism and Other Drug Dependencies

AMSAT [Radio] Amateur Satellite [Corporation]

AmSECT American Society of Extra-Corporal Technology

AMSN Academy of Medical-Surgical Nursing

AMSO American Medical Specialty Organization

AMSSM American Medical Society for Sports Medicine

AMSU Advanced Microwave Sounding Unit

AMT alternative minimum tax

amt. amount

AMTA American Massage Therapy Association

AMTEC Association for Media and Technology in Education

Amtrak National Railroad Passenger Corporation (from "American track")

amu atomic mass unit

AMU Arab Maghreb Union

AMWA American Medical Women's Association; American Medical Writers Association

AN airman, Navy; Anglo-Norman; Associate in Nursing

an. above named; *Latin* anno (in the year); annual; annotated; *Latin* ante (before)

.an Netherlands Antilles

ANA Administration for Native Americans; American Newspaper Association; American Nurses Association; Anaheim Angels; antinuclear antibody; Association of National Advertisers

ANAC Association of Nurses in AIDS Care

anal. analogous; analogy; analysis; analytic

ANAP anionic neutrophil activating peptide

anat. anatomical; anatomist; anatomy

ANC African National Congress; Army Nurse Corps; Ted Stevens Anchorage International Airport

anc. ancient

AnCC anodal closure contraction

ANCC American Nurses Credentialing Center

ANCS Automated Nautical Charting System

AND Andorra (international vehicle ID); Andromeda

and. andante

And. Andorra; Andorran

ANDA abbreviated new drug application

ANDP Association of Neuroscience Departments and Programs

AnDTe anodal duration tetanus

ANEC American Nuclear Energy Council

anes. anesthesia

ANF American Nurses Foundation; atrial natriuretic factor

ANG Air National Guard; Netherlands Antilles—guilder

ang. angiogram; angle; angular

Ang. Angola; Angolan

Angl. Anglican; Anglicized

Anglo *Spanish* angloamericano (Anglo-American)[that is, White North American of non-Hispanic descent]

Anglo-Ind. Anglo-Indian

Anglo-Ir. Anglo-Irish

angst angstrom

ANHS American Natural Hygiene Society

anhyd. anhydrous

anhydr. anhydrous

ANICA Atmospheric Nutrient Input to Coastal Areas [Project]

anim. animato

ANL Argonne National Laboratory; automatic noise limiter

ANMA American Naturopathic Medical Association

ann. annals; annual; annotated; annuity

ANNA American Nephrology Nurses' Association

anniv. anniversary

annot. annotated; annotation; annotator

AnOC anodal opening contraction

anon. anonymous

ANOVA analysis of variance

ANP atrial natriuretic peptide

ANPA American Newspaper Publishers Association

ANPACC Advanced Nursing Practice in Acute and Critical Care

ANR American Negligence Reports; Americans for Nonsmokers' Rights; another (shortwave transmission); automatic network routing

ANRC American National Red Cross

ANRED Anorexia Nervosa and Related Eating Disorders

ANRF Americans for Nonsmokers' Rights Foundation

ANS Advanced Network Services; American Name Society; aquatic nuisance species; autonomic nervous system

ans. answer

ANSI American National Standards Institute

ANT antenna (shortwave transmission); Antlia (constellation)

ant. antenna; anterior; antiquarian; antiquity; antonym

Ant. Antarctica

ANTA American National Theatre and Academy

anthol. anthology

anthro anthropology

anthrop. anthropological; anthropology

anthropol. anthropological; anthropology

antiq. antiquarian; antiquary; antiquities; antiquity

ANTS Antenna Subsystem

ANTU alpha-naphthylthiourea

ANUG acute necrotizing ulcerative gingivitis

Anzac Australia and New Zealand Army Corps

ANZUS Australia—New Zealand—United States Security Treaty

AO aorta

.ao Angola

a/o account of; and others

AOA Administration on Aging; American Optometric Association; analysis of alternatives; angle of attack

AOARD Asian Office of Aerospace Research and Development

AOASM American Osteopathic Academy of Sports Medicine

AOB alcohol on breath

AOBGP American Osteopathic Board of General Practice

AOC anodal opening contraction

A.O.C. *Latin* anno orbis conditi

(the year of the creation of the world)

AOCA American Osteopathic College of Anesthesiologists

AOCE attitude and orbit control electronics

AOCMS attitude and orbit control measurement system

AOCOOHNS American Osteopathic Colleges of Ophthalmology and Otolaryngology, Head and Neck Surgery

AOCPM American Osteopathic College of Preventive Medicine

AOCR American Osteopathic College of Radiology

AOCS attitude and orbit control system

AOD aerosol optical depth

AODM adult onset diabetes mellitis

AODME Association of Osteopathic Directors and Medical Educators

AOEC Association of Occupational and Environmental Clinics

AOFAS American Orthopaedic Foot and Ankle Society

AOFLA Atlantic Offshore Fish and Lobster Association

AOH Ancient Order of Hibernians

AOHA Administrators in Oncology/Hematology Assembly; American Osteopathic Hospital Association

AOHP Association of Occupational Health Professionals

AOIPS Atmospheric and Oceanographic Information Processing System

A-OK all OK (perfect)

AOL America Online

AOML Atlantic Oceanographic and Meteorological Laboratory

AON all or none; Angola—new kwanza (currency)

AONE American Organization of Nurse Executives

A-1 first class (excellent)

A-one first class (excellent)

A1C airman first class

A1NA Alpha1 National Association

AOO American Oceanic Organization

AOPA American Orthotic and Prosthetic Association

AOPR Americans for Open Planetary Research

AOR advice of rights; album-oriented radio; album-oriented rock; at own risk

aor. aorist

AORN Association of Operating Room Nurses

AOS Academic Orthopaedic Society; acquisition of signal; American Otological Society

AOSB Arctic Ocean Science Board

AOSP Atmospheric and Ocean Sciences Program

AOSSM American Orthopaedic Society for Sports Medicine

AOSW Association of Oncology Social Work

AOT anyone out there?; astronomical observation template

AOTA American Occupational Therapy Association

AOTF American Occupational Therapy Foundation

AOU American Ornithologists Union

AP access point; adjective

phrase; advanced placement; airplane; air police; American plan; antipersonnel; aorticopulmonary; Armed Forces Pacific; Associated Press

ap. apothecary

Ap. Apostle; April

a.p. additional premium; author's proof

A-P anteroposterior

A/P account paid; accounts payable; authority to pay; authority to purchase

APA Administrative Procedure Act; all points addressable; also printed as; American Paralysis Association; American Philological Association; American Philosophical Association; American Podiatry Association; American Psychiatric Association; American Psychological Association

APACHE acute physiology and chronic health evaluation

APAMSA Asian Pacific Medical Student Association

APAOG Association of Physician Assistants in Obstetrics and Gynecology

APAP Association of Physician Assistant Programs

A-part alpha particle

APB all points bulletin

APC alien property custodian; armored personnel carrier; aspirin, phenacetin, and caffeine

A-P-C adenoidal-pharyngeal-conjunctival

APCA Air Pollution Control Association

APCD Air Pollution Control District

A.P.C.N. *Latin* anno post Christum natum (the year after the birth of Christ)

APDA American Parkinson's Disease Association

APDIM Association of Program Directors in Internal Medicine

APDR Association of Program Directors in Radiology

APDU Application Protocol Data Unit

APE acute pulmonary edema

APEC Asia Pacific Economic Co-operation

APER Air Pollution Emissions Report

aper. aperture

APEX Arctic Polynya Experiment

APF animal protein factor; Asian professional female

APG Aberdeen Proving Grounds; ambulatory patient group

APH American Printing House [for the Blind]

aph. aphetic

APhA American Pharmaceutical Association

APHA American Public Health Association

aphet. aphetic; aphetized

APHIS [United States Department of Agriculture] Animal and Plant Health Inspection Service

APHS American Pseudo-obstruction and Hirschsprung's Disease Society

API antecedent precipitation index; application program interface; Asian and Pacific Islander

APIC American Political Items Collectors; Association for Pro-

fessionals in Infection Control and Epidemiology

APID Application Identification

APL American Poetry and Literacy [Project]; Applied Physics Laboratory; A Programming Language

Apl. April

APLS Antiphospholipid Syndrome

APM Academy of Psychosomatic Medicine; antenna pointing mechanism; Asian professional male; Association of Professors of Medicine

APMA American Podiatric Medical Association; American Preventive Medical Association

APME Attitude Pointing Mechanism Electronics

APMR Association for Physical and Mental Rehabilitation

APNA American Psychiatric Nurses Association

apo apoenzyme; apolipoprotein

APO Army Post Office

Apoc. Apocalypse; Apocrypha

apo-E apolipoprotein-E

APON Association of Pediatric Oncology Nurses

app [software] application

APP approved

app. apparatus; apparently; appendix; applied; appoint; appointed; apprentice

APPA American Professional Practice Association; American Psychopathological Association; American Public Power Association

APPAP Association of Postgraduate Physician Assistant Programs

appar. apparent; apparently

APPC Advanced Program-to-Program Communication

App. Ct. appellate court

appd. approved

appl. appliances; applied

applicand. *Latin* applicandus (to be applied)

APPM Association for Psychoanalytic and Psychosomatic Medicine

appmt. appointment

APPN Advanced Peer-to-Peer Networking

appr. approximate; approximately

appro. approval

approx. approximate; approximately

appt. appoint; appointment

apptd. appointed

appx. appendix

appy. appendectomy

APR annual percentage rate

Apr. April

A.P.R.C. *Latin* anno post Roman conditam (year after the foundation of Rome)

APS American Pain Society; American Peace Society; American Philatelic Society; American Philosophical Society; American Physical Society; American Physiological Society; American Protestant Society; American Psychosomatic Society; Apus (constellation)

APSA American Political Science Association; American Psychoanalytic Association

APSF Anesthesia Patient Safety Foundation

APT admissions per thousand; advanced personnel testing; apartment

apt. apartment

APTA American Physical Therapy Association

aPTT activated partial thromboplastin time

apu auxiliary power unit

APWA American Public Welfare Association; American Public Works Association

apx. appendix; approximate; approximately

APY annual percentage yield

AQ as quoted

aq. aqua; *Latin* aqua (water); aqueous

.aq Antarctica

aq. bull. *Latin* aqua bulliens (boiling water)

aq. dest. *Latin* aqua destillata (distilled water)

AQDM air quality display model

aq. ferv. *Latin* aqua fervens (hot water)

aq. frig. *Latin* aqua frigida (cold water)

AQL acceptable quality level; Aquila (constellation)

AQMP air quality maintenance plan; air quality management plan

AQR Aquarius

AQSM air quality simulation model

AQU Aquarius

ar Arabic

Ar argon

AR account receivable; accounts receivable; anal retentive; annual return; answer (shortwave transmission); Arkansas; army regulation

ar. arrival; arrive

Ar. Arabia; Arabic; Aramaic

.ar Argentina

a.r. all risks

A.R. *Latin* anno Regni (in the year of the reign)

A/R account receivable; accounts receivable

ARA American Railway Society; Academy of Rehabilitative Audiology; American Rheumatism Association; Ara (constellation)

Arab. Arabia; Arabian; Arabic

Arabsat Arab Satellite Communications Organization

AraC cytosine arabinoside

Aram. Aramaic

ARAMIS American Rheumatism Association Medical Information System

ARARs applicable, relevant, or appropriate requirements

ARAT atmospheric research and remote sensing plane

arb arbitrageur

ARB *Accounting Research Bulletin*

ARBIAS Alcohol Related Brain Injury Association

arc archive

ARC Addiction Research Center; advance readers copy; AIDS-related complex; amateur radio club; American Red Cross; [National Aeronautics and Space Administration] Ames Research Center; Appalachian Regional Commission

Arc. Arcade; Arctic

ARCA Automobile Racing Club of America

arc cos arc cosine

arc cot arc cotangent

arc csc arc cosecant

arch. archaic; archaism; archery; archipelago; architect; architectural; architecture; archives

Arch. archbishop

archaeol. archeological; archeology

Archbp. archbishop

Archd. archdeacon

Arch.E. architectural engineer

archit. architecture

archt. architect

ARCS assessment and remediation of contaminated sediments

arc sec arc secant

arc sin arc sine

ARCSS Arctic System Science [Program]

arc tan arc tangent

ARD acute respiratory disease

ARDMS American Registry of Diagnostic Medical Sonographers

ARDS adult respiratory distress syndrome

AREP [United Nations] Atmospheric Research and Environment Program

ARF acute renal failure; Addiction Research Foundation

arg. argent; *Latin* arguendo (for the sake of the argument, in the course of the argument)

Arg. Argentina; Argentine; Argentinean

ARGOS advanced research and global observation satellite

ARHP Association of Reproductive Health Professionals

ARI Aries; Arizona Cardinals;

Arizona Diamondbacks; Arthritis and Rheumatism International

ARIA advanced range instrumented aircraft

aristo aristocrat

arith. arithmetic

Ariz. Arizona

Ark. Arkansas

ARL [National Oceanic and Atmospheric Administration] Air Resources Laboratory; Arctic Research Laboratory; Association of Research Libraries

ARM adjustable rate mortgage; Alien Resistance Movement; antiradiation missile; Armenia (international vehicle ID)

Arm. Armenia; Armenian

ARMA Association of Records Managers and Administrators International; autoregressive moving average

ARN Arlanda International Airport (Stockholm, Sweden); Association of Rehabilitation Nurses

ARNA American Radiological Nurses Association

ARNMD Association for Research in Nervous and Mental Disease

ARO after receipt of order; Army Research Office; Association for Research in Otolaryngology

ARP Address Resolution Protocol; air-raid precautions; Argentina—peso

ARPA Advanced Research Projects Agency

ARPANET Advanced Research Projects Agency Network

ARPO Acid Rain Policy Office

ARPS Advanced Regional Prediction System

ARq authentication request

arr. arranged; arrangement; arranger; arrival; arrived

arrgt. arrangement

ARRS American Roentgen Ray Society

ARRT American Registry of Radiologic Technologists

ARs authentication response

ARS Agricultural Research Service; Agricultural Restructuring Scenario; Archive Retrieval System; autonomously replicating sequence

ART airborne radiation thermometer; assisted reproductive technology

art. article; artificial; artillery

ARTCC air route traffic control center

ARTEMIS Advanced Research Testbed for Medical Informatics

ARTS automated radar terminal system

arty. artillery

ARU audio response unit

ARV AIDS-related virus; American Revised Version

ARVIN Army of the Republic of Vietnam

ARVO Association for Research in Vision and Ophthalmology

A.R.V.R. *Latin* anno Regni Victoriae Reginae (in the year of the reign of Queen Victoria)

ARZ auto-restricted zone

as Assamese

As arsenic

AS air speed; American Samoa; Anglo-Saxon; antisubmarine; Associate in Science

As. Asia; Asian

.as American Samoa

A.S. *Latin* auris sinister (left ear)

A/S account sales; after sight; at sight

A's [Oakland] Athletics

ASA Acoustical Society of America; American Schizophrenia Association; American Society of Andrology; American Society of Anesthesiologists; American Society on Aging; American Standards Association; Autism Society of America

ASAA American Sleep Apnea Association

ASAE American Society of Association Executives

ASAIO American Society for Artificial Internal Organs

ASAM American Society of Addiction Medicine

ASAM PPC American Society of Addiction Medicine Patient Placement Criteria

ASAP American Society for Adolescent Psychiatry; American Society of Adults with Pseudo-Obstruction; as soon as possible

ASAPS American Society for Aesthetic Plastic Surgery

ASAR advanced synthetic aperture radar

ASAT American Society of Alternative Therapists; antisatellite

ASATT American Society of Anesthesia Technologists and Technicians

ASB American Society of Biomechanics; Associated Services for the Blind

asb. asbestos

ASBCD American Society of Bookplate Collectors and Designers

ASBM air-to-surface ballistic missile

ASBMB American Society for Biochemistry and Molecular Biology

ASBO antisocial behavior disorder

ASBS American Society for Bariatric Surgery

asc ascending

ASC American Society of Cinematographers

ASCAD atherosclerotic coronary artery disease

ASCAP American Society of Composers, Authors, and Publishers

ASCB American Society for Cell Biology

ASCE American Society of Civil Engineers

ASCI Accelerated Strategic Computing Initiative; American Society of Clinical Investigation

ASCII American Standard Code for Information Interchange

ASCLS American Society for Clinical Laboratory Science

ASCN American Society for Clinical Nutrition

ASCO American Society of Clinical Oncology

ASCOT American Share Coalition on Transplantation

ASCP American Society of Clinical Pathologists

ASCPT American Society for Clinical Pharmacology and Therapeutics

ASCRS American Society of Cataract and Refractive Surgery

ASCS Agricultural Stabilization and Conservation Service

ASCU Association of State Colleges and Universities

ASCVD arteriosclerotic cardiovascular disease

ASCVRD arteriosclerotic cardiovascular renal disease

ASD American Society for the Deaf; atrial septal defect

ASDA American Sleep Disorders Association

ASDAR aircraft-to-satellite data relay system

AsDB Asian Development Bank

ASDC American Society for Deaf Children

ASDS American Society of Dermatologic Surgery

ASDVS American Society of Directors of Volunteer Services

ASE airborne support equipment; American Stock Exchange; available solar energy

ASEAMS Association of South-East Asian Marine Scientists

ASEAN Association of Southeast Asian Nations

ASEP American Society of Exercise Physiologists

ASER American Society of Emergency Radiology

ASES American Shoulder and Elbow Surgeons

ASF African swine fever; American Schizophrenia Foundation

ASFIS Aquatic Sciences and Fisheries Information System

asg. assigned; assignment

asgd. assigned

ASGE American Society for Gas-

trointestinal Endoscopy

asgmt. assignment

ASGPA Assembly of Surgical Group Practice Administrators

ASGPI Association of Sea Grant Program Institutes

ASGPP American Society of Group Psychotherapy and Psychodrama

ash Additional Sponsors House

ASH Action on Smoking and Health; American Society of Hematology; American Society of Hypertension; asymmetric septal hypertrophy

ASHA American School Health Association; American Social Health Association; American Speech-Language and Hearing Association

ASHCMPR American Society for Health Care Marketing and Public Relations

ASHCRM American Society of Health Care Risk Managers

ASHCSP American Society for Healthcare Central Service Personnel

ASHD arteriosclerotic heart disease

ASHE American Society for Healthcare Engineering

ASHES American Society for Healthcare Environmental Services

ASHET American Society for Healthcare Education and Training

ASHFSA American Society for Hospital Food Service Administrators

ASHG American Society of Human Genetics

ASHHRA American Society for

Healthcare Human Resources Administration

ASHI American Society for Histocompatibility and Immunogenetics

ASHMM American Society for Hospital Materials Management

ASHNR American Society of Head and Neck Radiology

ASHNS American Society for Head and Neck Surgery

ASHOE Airborne Southern Hemisphere Ozone Expedition

ASHP American Society of Health-System Pharmacists

ASHRM American Society for Healthcare Risk Management

ASI air speed indicator

ASIA American Spinal Injury Association

ASIC application-specific integrated chip; application-specific integrated circuit

ASID American Society of Interior Designers

ASIDIC Association of Information and Dissemination Centers

ASIG American Special Interest Group

ASIM American Society of Internal Medicine

ASIP American Society of Investigative Pathology

ASITN American Society of Interventional and Therapeutic Neuroradiology

ASL age/sex/location?; American Sign Language; American Soccer League; atmospheric surface layer

ASLA American Society of Landscape Architects

ASLEF Associated Society of Locomotive Engineers and Firemen

ASLME American Society of Law, Medicine, and Ethics

ASLO American Society of Limnology and Oceanography

ASM air-to-surface missile; American Society for Microbiology

asm. assembly

AsMA Aerospace Medical Association

ASME American Society of Mechanical Engineers

ASMI American Sports Medicine Institute

ASMIC American Society of Military Insignia Collectors

ASMP American Society of Media Photographers

ASMS Ambulatory Surgery Management Society; American Society for Mohs Surgery

ASMT American Society of Medical Technologists

Asn asparagine

ASN abstract syntax notation; American Society of Nephrology; American Society of Neuroradiology; Army service number

ASNC American Society of Nuclear Cardiology

ASNE American Society of Newspaper Editors

ASNR American Society of Neuroradiology

ASNS American Society for Nutritional Sciences

ASNT American Society for Neural Transplantation

ASO administrative services only

ASORN American Society of Ophthalmic Registered Nurses

ASOS American Society of Outpatient Surgeons; Automated Seismological Observation System; [National Oceanic and Atmospheric Administration] Automated Surface Observing Systems

Asp aspartic acid

ASP American selling price; American Society for Photogrammetry and Remote Sensing; American Society of Parasitologists; Association of Subspecialty Professors

ASPAN American Society of PeriAnesthesia Nurses

ASPCA American Society for the Prevention of Cruelty to Animals

ASPCC American Society for the Prevention of Cruelty to Children

ASPEN American Society for Parenteral and Enteral Nutrition

ASPET American Society for Pharmacology and Experimental Therapeutics

ASPH Association of Schools of Public Health

ASPI advanced small computer systems interface

ASPNR American Society of Pediatric Neuroradiology

ASPP American Society of Psychoanalytic Physicians

ASPR Armed Services Procurement Regulations

ASPRS American Society of Plastic and Reconstructive Surgery

ASPRSN American Society of Plastic and Reconstructive Surgical Nurses

ASPS advanced sleep phase syndrome

ASR airport surveillance radar; air-sea rescue; automatic speech recognition; available solar radiation

ASRAAM advanced short-range air-to-air missile

ASRM advanced solid rocket motor; American Society for Reproductive Medicine

ASRS Association of Students of the Radiologic Sciences

ASRT American Society of Radiologic Technologists

ass. assistant; association

assem. assembly

ASSH American Society for Surgery of the Hand

assim. assimilated; assimilation

assn. association

assoc. associate; associated; association

ASSP aerosol scattering spectrometer probe; approved species-specific protocol

ASSR Autonomous Soviet Socialist Republic

asst. assistant

asstd. assisted; assorted

assy. assembly

Assyr. Assyrian

AST Alaska Standard Time; Atlantic Standard Time

ASTA American Society of Travel Agents

ASTC Association of Science and Technology Centers

ASTDN Association of State and Territorial Directors of Nursing

ASTE Association of State and Territorial Epidemiologists

ASTHO Association of State and Territorial Health Officials

ASTM American Society for Testing and Materials

ASTMH American Society of Tropical Medicine and Hygiene

ASTP American Society of Transplant Physicians; Army Specialized Training Program

ASTREX Advanced Space Structures Technology Research Experiment

ASTRO American Society for Therapeutic Radiology and Oncology

astrol. astrologer; astrological; astrology

astron. astronomer; astronomical; astronomy

astronaut. astronautics

ASTS American Society of Transplant Surgeons

ASU Arizona State University

ASV American Standard Version

ASW antisubmarine warfare

asym. asymmetric; asymmetrical

aT attotesla

At ampere-turn; astatine

AT achievement test; advanced technology; air temperature; antitank; Atlantic Time; automatic transmission

at. airtight; atmosphere; atomic; attorney

.at Austria

ata atmosphere absolute

ATA advanced technology attachment; Air Transport Association; American Telemedicine Association; American Tinnitus Association; American Tunaboat Association

ATAD atmospheric transport and dispersion [model]

ATAF Allied Tactical Air Forces

ATAGS advanced technology anti-G suit

AT&T American Telephone and Telegraph Company

ATB antibiotic

ATC air traffic control; Air Transport Command

ATCC American Type Culture Collection

ATCP Antarctic Treaty Consultative Parties

ATCSCC air traffic control system command center

ATCT airport traffic control tower

ATDRS advanced tracking and data relay satellite

ATE automatic test equipment

ATEGG Advanced Turbine Engine Gas Generator

ATF automatic transmission fluid; Bureau of Alcohol, Tobacco, and Firearms

ath Agreed to House

ath. athletic; athletic; athletics

ATH Athens [Greece] International Airport

athl. athlete; athletic; athletics

aThr allothreonine

ATIRCM advanced threat infrared countermeasures

ATL adult T-cell leukemia; adult T-cell lymphoma; Atlanta Braves; Atlanta Falcons; William B. Hartsfield International Airport (Atlanta, GA)

Atl. Atlantic

ATLA American Trial Lawyers Association

ATLAS [National Aeronautics and Space Administration] Atmospheric Laboratory for Applications and Science

atm atmosphere

ATM Adobe Type Manager; asynchronous transfer mode; at the moment; automated teller machine; automatic teller machine

ATMCH Association of Teachers of Maternal and Child Health

ATMI American Textile Manufacturers Institute

atmos. atmosphere; atmospheric

ATMS Advanced Traffic Management System

ATN acute tubular necrosis; Aeronautical Telecommunications Network

at. no. atomic number

ATNR asymmetrical tonic neck reflex

ATOC Acoustic Thermography of Ocean Climate

ATP adenosine triphosphate; Association for Transpersonal Psychology

ATPase adenosine triphosphatase

ATPM Association of Teachers of Preventive Medicine

ATR air turbo rocket; automatic target recognition

ATRA Assistive Technology Resource Alliance

ats Agreed to Senate

ATS against the spread; alternate to suspension; American Temperance Society; American Thoracic Society; American Tract Society; American Transport Service; Austria—schilling

ATSDR Agency for Toxic Substances and Disease Registry

ATSL along the same line

ATSR along-track scanning radiometer

att. attached; attachment; attention; attorney

ATTF air toxics task force

Att. Gen. attorney general

attn. attention

attr attractive

attrib. attribute; attributed to; attributive; attributively

Atty. attorney

att'y. attorney

Atty. Gen. Attorney General

ATV all-terrain vehicle

ATWC Alaska Tsunami Warning Center

at. wt. atomic weight

Au gold

AU astronomical unit

au. author

.au Australia

a.u. angstrom unit

A.U. *Latin* auris uterque (each ear, both ears)

AUA American Unitarian Association; American Urological Association

AUAA American Urologic Association Allied

AUC area under curve

A.U.C. *Latin* ab urbe condita (from the founding of the city [of Rome in 753? B.C.]); anno urbis conditae (in the year from the founding of the city [of Rome in 753? B.C.])

aud audience

AUD Australia—dollar

aud. audit; auditor; audition

augm. augmentative

aug. augmentative; augmented

Aug. August

AUH Abu Dhabi International Airport

AUI attachment unit interface

AUM air-to-underwater missile

AUP acceptable use policy

AUPHA Association of University Programs in Health Administration

AUQ *French* Association des urologues du Québec (Quebec Urological Association)

AUR ambulatory utilization review; Association of University Radiologists; Auriga

AURP AppleTalk Update-based Routing Protocol

AUS Army of the United States; Austin-Bergstrom International Airport; Australia (international vehicle ID)

Aus. Australia; Australian; Austria; Austrian

Aust. Australia; Australian; Austria; Austrian

Austl. Australia; Australian

Austral. Australasia; Australasian; Australia; Australian

auth. authentic; author; authority; authorized

Auth. Ver. Authorized Version

auto automobile

auto. automatic; automotive

AUTOCAP Automotive Consumer Action Program

Autodin Automatic Digital Network

AUV autonomous underwater vehicle

AUX auxiliary; auxiliary verb

aux. auxiliary; auxiliary verb

aux. v. auxiliary verb

AV arteriovenous; atrioventricular; audiovisual; Authorized Version; average variability

av. avenue; average; avoirdupois

Av. Avestan

a.v. *Latin* ad valorem (in proportion to the value)

A/V *Latin* ad valorem (in proportion to the value); audiovisual

A-V arteriovenous; atrioventricular; audiovisual

AVA antiovarian antibody

AVACI Academy of Veterinary Allergy and Clinical Immunology

avail. available

AVC AIDS Volunteer Clearinghouse; American Veterans Committee; automatic volume control

AVCA American Veterinary Chiropractic Association

AVD alternate voice/data; atrioventricular dissociation

AVDA American Venereal Disease Association

avdp. avoirdupois

AVE atrioventricular extrasystole

Ave. avenue

Avest. Avestan

AVF all-volunteer force; arteriovenous fistula; Aruba—florin (currency)

AVFI Action on Violence and Family Intervention

AVG ambulatory visit group

avg. average

avgas aviation gasoline

AVH Academy of Veterinary Homeopathy

AVHRR advanced very high-resolution radiometer

AVI audio-video interleave

AVIR Association of Vascular and Interventional Radiographers

AVIRIS airborne visible and infrared imaging spectrometer

AVL available

avlbl. available

AVLINE AudioVisuals Online

AVM arteriovenous malformation

AVMA American Veterinary Medical Association

AVMF American Veterinary Medical Foundation

avn. aviation

A-V node [cardiac] atrioventricular node

AVP antiviral protein; arginine vasopressin; Wilkes-Barre/Scranton International Airport

AVR aortic valve replacement

AVSC Access to Voluntary and Safe Contraception

A-V shunt arteriovenous shunt

AVSL Association of Vision Science Librarians

A-V valves [cardiac] atrioventricular valves

AW aircraft warning; Articles of War; automatic weapon

.aw Aruba

a.w. actual weight; all water

AWACS airborne warning and control system

AWAKE Alert, Well, and Keeping Energetic Network

AWARDS Automated Weather Acquisition and Retrieval Data System

AWD all-wheel drive

AWG American wire gauge

AWGTHTGTATA are we going to have to go through all this again?

AWHFY are we having fun yet?

AWHONN Association of Women's Health, Obstetric, and Neonatal Nurses

AWHP Association for Worksite Health Promotion

AWIPS Advanced Weather Interactive Processing System

AWIPS-90 Advanced Weather Interactive Processing System for the 1990s

AWIS Association for Women in Science

awk awkward

AWL absent with leave

AWOL absent without leave

AWP any will provider; average wholesale price

AWRA American Water Resources Association

AWT advanced wastewater treatment

AWW average weekly wage

AWWA American Water Works Association

AX ask (shortwave transmission)

ax. axiom; axis

AXAF Advanced X-ray Astrophysics Facility

AXBT airborne expendable bathythermograph

AXCP airborne expendable current profiler

AXP American Express Co.

ay Aymara

AY any (shortwave transmission)

AYC American Youth Congress

AYG anything (shortwave transmission)

AYH American Youth Hostels

AYM any more (shortwave transmission)

AYOR at your own risk

AYT are you there?

az Azerbaijani

AZ Arizona; Azerbaijan (international vehicle ID)

az. azimuth; azure

.az Azerbaijan

AZE Azerbaijan

AZM Azerbaijan—manat (currency)

AZO Kalamazoo/Battle Creek International Airport

AZT azidothymidine

B

b bit; barn

B baryon number; bass; be (shortwave transmission); Belgium (international vehicle ID); billion; bishop; Black (as in personal ads); boron; byte; magnetic flux density

b. base; book; born; breadth; brother

B. bacillus; Baumé scale; bay; Bible

B2B back to basics; business to business

B2C business to consumer

B2W back to work

ba Bashkir

Ba barium; Baruch

BA Bachelor of Arts; bare ass; batting average; Boeing Co.; British Academy; budget authority

ba. bathroom

.ba Bosnia-Herzegovina

BAA Bachelor of Applied Arts

BAAE Bachelor of Aeronautical and Astronautical Engineering

Bab. Babylonian

BAC blood alcohol concentration; born again Christian; by any chance

BACER Biological and Climatological Effects Research

back-form back-formation

BACT Best Available Control Technology

bact. bacteria; bacterial; bacteriology

bacteriol. bacteriology

BAD *French* Banque africaine de développement (African Development Bank)

BADEA *French* Banque Arabe pour le Développement Économique en Afrique (Arab Bank for Economic Development in Africa)

BADT best available demonstrated technology

BAE Bachelor of Aeronautical Engineering; Bachelor of Agricultural Engineering; Bachelor of Architectural Engineering; Bachelor of Art Education; Bachelor of Arts in Education; Bureau of Agricultural Economics; Bureau of Ethnology

BAEd Bachelor of Arts in Education

BAeE Bachelor of Aeronautical Engineering

BAEE Bachelor of Arts in Elementary Education

BAER brainstem auditory evoked response

BAF bunker adjustment factor

BAFO best and final offer

BAG busting a gut [laughing]

BAg Bachelor of Agriculture

BAgE Bachelor of Agricultural Engineering

BAgEco Bachelor of Agricultural Economics

BAgr Bachelor of Agriculture

BAgSc Bachelor of Agricultural Science

Ba. Is. Bahama Islands

BAJour Bachelor of Arts in Journalism

BAK Bosnia and Herzegovina—convertible mark

.bak backup file

BAL Baltimore Orioles; Baltimore Ravens; blood alcohol level; British Anti-Lewisite

bal. balance; balcony

balc balcony

Balt. Baltic; Baltimore

Balto-Slav. Balto-Slavic; Balto-Slavonic

BAM Bachelor of Applied Mathematics; Bachelor of Arts in Music; Brooklyn Academy of Music

BAMusEd Bachelor of Arts in Music Education

BANANA build absolutely nothing anywhere near anybody

B & B bed-and-breakfast; benedictine and brandy

B & D bondage and discipline; bondage and domination

B & E breaking and entering

B & F building and facilities

B & L building and loan

B & M bricks and mortar

B & O Baltimore and Ohio

B & P bid and proposal

B & S bourbon and soda; brandy and soda

b & w black and white

BAO Boulder Atmospheric Observatory

BaP benzo(a)pyrene

BAP benefits analysis program

Bap. Baptist

BAPMoN [United Nations] Background Air Pollution Monitoring Network

bapt. baptized

Bapt. Baptist

BAR Browning Automatic Rifle

bar. barometer; barometric; barrel

Bar. Baruch

BAr Bachelor of Architecture

Barb. Barbados

bar-b-q barbecue

BArch Bachelor of Architecture

BARF best available retrofit facility

barit. baritone

BARM block acceptance reporting mechanism

BART Bay Area Rapid Transit; best available retrofit technology

Bart. baronet

BAS Bachelor of Agricultural Science; Bachelor of Applied Science; block acquisition sequence

bas. basal

BASc Bachelor of Agricultural Science; Bachelor of Applied Science

BASIC Beginner's All-Purpose Symbolic Instruction Code

BAT Bachelor of Arts in Teach-

ing; best available technology
bat. battalion; battery
BATEA best available technology economically achievable
BATF Bureau of Alcohol, Tobacco, and Firearms
batt. battalion; battery
BAU business as usual
Bav. Bavaria; Bavarian
BAW bulk acoustic wave
bb ball bearing; base on balls
BB B'nai B'rith; small shot pellet (from "ball bearing")
bb. books
.bb Barbados
b.b. bail bond
BBA Bachelor of Business Administration
BBB Better Business Bureau; bundle branch block
BBC British Broadcasting Corporation
BBD Barbados—dollar
BBE Bachelor of Business Education
BBFN bye-bye for now
BBIAB be back in a bit
BBIAF be back in a flash
BBIAM be back in a minute
BBIAS be back in a second
BBL be back later
bbl. barrel
BBN bye-bye now
BBQ barbecue
BBS bulletin board service; bulletin board system
BBT basal body temperature
bc blind copy
Bc committed burst
BC Bachelor of Chemistry; because (shortwave transmission); bias contrast; board certified; British Columbia

B.C. before Christ; Breeders Cup
b/c because
B/C bill for collection
BCA Boys' Clubs of America
BCAOCS Bureau of Consular Affairs Overseas Citizens Services
BC/BS Blue Cross and Blue Shield
BCBSA Blue Cross and Blue Shield Association
bcc blind carbon copy
BCCA Beer Can Collectors Association
BCD binary coded decimal
BCE Bachelor of Chemical Engineering; Bachelor of Civil Engineering; Banque Centrale Européenne; book club edition
B.C.E. Before the Common Era
B cell bone-marrow-derived cell
BCF bioconcentration factor; Black Christian female; [The] Breast Cancer Fund
bcf. billion cubic feet
BCG bacillus Calmette-Guérin vaccine
BCh Bachelor of Chemistry
BChE Bachelor of Chemical Engineering
BCHSM Board of Certified Healthcare Safety Management
bci binary-coded information
BCI *Biotechnology Citation Index*; broadcast interference (shortwave transmission); Bureau of Criminal Investigation
BCIC Breast Cancer Information Clearinghouse
BCIE *Spanish* Banco Centroamericano de Integración Económico (Central American

Bank for Economic Integration)

BCIS Breast Cancer Information Service

BCL Bachelor of Canon Law; Bachelor of Civil Law; Batch Command Language; broadcast listener (shortwave transmission)

BCM Black Christian male

BCMD *Blood Cells, Molecules, and Diseases*

bcn beacon

BCN Barcelona International Airport

BCNU be seeing you

BComSc Bachelor of Commercial Science

BCP Best Current Practices; bioconcentration potential; birth control pill; Book of Common Prayer

BCPL Basic Combined Programming Language

BCPT best conventional pollutant technology

BCS Bachelor of Chemical Science; Bachelor of Commercial Science

BCT breast-conserving therapy

bd bundle

BD Bachelor of Divinity; Bangladesh (international vehicle ID); bank draft; bomb disposal

bd. baud; board; bond; bound

.bd Bangladesh

b/d barrels per day

B/D bank draft; bills discounted; brought down

BDA Bachelor of Domestic Arts; Bachelor of Dramatic Art; bomb damage assessment

BDB big dumb booster

BDC bottom dead center

BDDD [Division of] Birth Defects and Developmental Disabilities

bde. brigade

BDEAC *French* Banque de Développement des États de l'Afrique Centrale (Central African States Development Bank)

bd. ft. board foot

bdg. binding

BDL Bradley International Airport (Hartford, CT)

bdl. bundle

bdle. bundle

BDMP Birth Defects Monitoring Program

BDR battery discharge regulator

bdrm. bedroom

bdry boundary

Bds Barbados

BDS Bachelor of Dental Surgery; Barbados (international vehicle ID); bomb disposal squad

bds. bound in boards

BDSA Business and Defense Services Administration

BDSc Bachelor of Dental Science

BDSRA Batten Disease Support and Research Association

BDT Bangladesh—taka (currency)

BDU battle dress uniform

Bdx. Bordeaux

bdy. boundary

Bdy. Burgundy

be Belorusian

Be beryllium; excess burst

BE Bachelor of Education; Bachelor of Engineering; barium enema; board eligible; Board of Education

.be Belgium

B/E bill of entry; bill of exchange

Bé Baumé scale

BEA Bureau of Economic Analysis

BEAM biology, electronics, aesthetics, and mechanics (robotics)

BEC Bureau of Employees' Compensation

bec. because

BECN backward explicit congestion notification

BECO booster engine cutoff

BEd Bachelor of Education

BEE Bachelor of Electrical Engineering

beemer BMW car

beep borough president

BEF Belgium—franc

bef. before

BEG big evil grin

beg. begin; beginning

BEH benign essential hypertension; Bureau of Education for the Handicapped

BEI butanol-extractable iodine

BEJ best expert judgment

Bel. Belgian; Belgium

Belg. Belgian; Belgium

BEM Bachelor of Engineering of Mines; bug-eyed monster

BEMT Bureau of Health Professions Education and Manpower Training

ben *Latin* bene (well)

Benelux Belgium, the Netherlands, and Luxembourg

Beng. Bengal; Bengali

BEng Bachelor of Engineering

BEngr Bachelor of Engineering

BEngSci Bachelor of Engineering Science

BEP Bachelor of Engineering Physics; Bureau of Engraving and Printing

BER basic electrical rhythm; bit error rate

Ber. Is. Bermuda Islands

BERT bit error rate tester

BES Bachelor of Engineering Science

bet. between

BET Black Entertainment Television

betw. between

BeV billion electron volts

BEV Black English Vernacular

BEZS bandwidth efficient zero suppression

bf boldface

BF before (shortwave transmission); Black female; boyfriend; Burkina Faso (international vehicle ID)

.bf Burkina Faso (formerly Upper Volta)

b.f. board-foot

B/F brought forward

BFA Bachelor of Fine Arts

BFD big fucking deal

BFF best friend forever

BFF best friend for life

BFL Meadows Field (Bakersfield, CA)

BFN bye for now

bfo beat frequency oscillator

BFOQ bona fide occupational qualification

B4N bye for now

BFS Aldergrove International Airport (Belfast, Northern Ireland)

bft biofeedback training
bg Bulgarian
BG brigadier general; Bulgaria (international vehicle ID)
bg. background; bag
.bg Bulgaria
<BG> big grin
BGen brigadier general
BGH bovine growth hormone
BGI *French* Bureau Gravimétrique International (International Gravimetric Bureau)
B-girl bar girl
BGL Bulgaria—lev (currency)
b.g.l. below ground level
BGP bone Gla protein; Border Gateway Protocol
BGR Bangor International Airport
BGS Bachelor of General Studies; balanced groundwater scenario
BGSU Bowling Green State University
bgt. bought
bh Bihari
Bh Belize (international vehicle ID); bohrium
BH bill of health; black hole; both (shortwave transmission)
.bh Bahrain
B/H bill of health
BHA Bankcard Holders of America; butylated hydroxyanisole
BHC benzene hexachloride
BHCDA Bureau of Health Care Delivery and Assistance
BHD Bahrain—dinar
bhd. bulkhead
BHI Better Hearing Institute
BHL Bachelor of Hebrew Letters; Bachelor of Hebrew Literature
BHM Birmingham [AL] International Airport
Bhn. Brinell hardness number
BHNM bowels have not moved
bhp brake horsepower
BHPr Bureau of Health Professions
BHRD Bureau of Health Resources Development
BHSI Bicycle Helmet Safety Institute
BHT butylated hydroxytoluene
Bhu. Bhutan
bi Bislama
Bi bisexual; bismuth
BI background information; bodily injury; built-in
.bi Burundi
BIA Brain Injury Association; Bureau of Indian Affairs
BIAC Business and Industry Advisory Committee
BiAF bisexual Asian female
BiAM bisexual Asian male
BIB Board for International Broadcasting
bib. biblical
Bib. Bible; biblical
BiBF bisexual Black female
bibl. biblical
bibliog. bibliographer; bibliography
bibliogr. bibliography
BiBM bisexual Black male
BIC business information center
BICBW but I could be wrong
BID Bachelor of Industrial Design; *Spanish* Banco Interamericano de Desarrollo (Inter-American Development

Bank); buoyancy induced dispersion

b.i.d. *Latin* bis in die (twice a day)

BIE Bachelor of Industrial Engineering

BIF Bank Insurance Fund; basis in fact; before I forget; Burundi—Burundi franc

BiFET bipolar field effect transistor

Big A AIDS; Atlanta; Atlas ICBM; Big Apple (New York City)

Big B Baltimore

Big BX Big Base Exchange (United States of America)

Big C cancer; Chicago; cocaine

Big D death; defense; Denver; Detroit; Dallas; LSD

Big H heart attack; heroin

Big M marriage; Memphis; morphine

Big Mo [political campaign] momentum

Big O opium; orgasm

Big P Pentagon building

Big PX Big Post Exchange (United States of America)

Big Q San Quentin prison

Big T Tampa; Tucson

Big V Las Vegas; Vietnam

BIH Bosnia & Herzegovina (international vehicle ID)

BiHF bisexual Hispanic female

BiHM bisexual Hispanic male

BiJF bisexual Jewish female

BiJM bisexual Jewish male

BIL Billings Logan [MT] International Airport; brother-in-law

bil. or **bilat.** bilateral

bin binary

BIND Berkeley Internet Name Domain

BinHex binary hexadecimal

binos binoculars

bio biographical summary; biology

BIO Biotechnology Industry Organization

bio. biology

biochem. biochemistry

biog. biographer; biographical; biography

biol. biological; biologist; biology

BIOMASS Biological Investigations of Marine Antarctic Systems and Stocks

BIOS Basic Input/Output System

biotech biotechnology

BIOYA blow it out your ass

BIOYIOP blow it out your input/output port

BIP band interleaved by pixel; bit interleaved parity

BIPS billion instruction per second

BIS Bank for International Settlements; Brain Injury Society

Bish. Bishop

BIST built-in self-test

bisync Binary Synchronous Communication Protocol

bit binary digit

BIT built in test

BitBlt bit-block transfer

BITE built-in test equipment

BITNET Because It's Time Network

BITNIC BITNET Network Information Center

BITS building integrated timing supply

BIU bus interface unit
BiWF bisexual White female
BiWM bisexual White male
biz business
BJ biceps jerk (reflex); blowjob
.bj Benin
B.J. Bachelor of Journalism
BJA Bureau of Justice Assistance
BJM bones, joints, muscles
BJS Bureau of Justice Statistics
bk black
Bk berkelium
BK because
Bk. bank; book
bka better known as
BKA below knee amputation
bkbndr. bookbinder
bkcy. bankruptcy
bkfst. breakfast
bkg. banking; bookkeeping
bkgd. background
BKK Bangkok International Airport
bklr. black letter
bkpg. bookkeeping
bkpr. bookkeeper
bkpt. bankrupt
bks. barracks
bkt. basket; bracket
bl. bale; barrel; black; block; blue
BL Bachelor of Laws; Bachelor of Letters; Bachelor of Literature
B/L bill of lading
BLA Bachelor of Landscape Architecture; Bachelor of Liberal Arts
BLAB Biomedical Library Acquisitions Bulletin
BLB Blind Leading the Blind Foundation

bld. blood; boldface
bldg. building
BLDG building
bldr. builder
BLE Brotherhood of Locomotive Engineers
BLIPS Benthic Layer Interactive Profiling System
B-list bozo list
BLit *Latin* Baccalaureus Litterarum (Bachelor of Letters, Bachelor of Literature)
BLitt *Latin* Baccalaureus Litterarum (Bachelor of Letters, Bachelor of Literature)
blk. black; block; bulk
BLLRS Blood Lead Laboratory Reference System
BLM Bureau of Land Management
BLMRCP Bureau of Labor Management Relations and Cooperative Programs
Blnd blond
BLOB very large binary file (from "binary large object")
blog weblog
BLS Bachelor of Library Science; basic life support; Berkeley Linguistics Society; Bureau of Labor Statistics
BLT bilateral lung transplantation; bacon, lettuce, and tomato [sandwich]
blt. built
Blu blue
BLV bovine leukemia virus
Blvd. boulevard
B lymphocyte bone marrow—derived lymphocyte
BLZ Belize
BM Bachelor of Medicine; Bachelor of Music; basal me-

tabolism; Black male; bone marrow; bowel movement; British Museum

bm. beam

.bm Bermuda

b.m. board measure

BMD Bermuda—dollar; bone mineral density

BMDO Ballistic Missile Defense Organization

BME Bachelor of Mechanical Engineering; Bachelor of Mining Engineering; Bachelor of Music Education

BMEd Bachelor of Music Education

BME/RAPD Biomedical Engineering and the Research to Aid Persons with Disabilities

BMES Biomedical Engineering Society

BMet Bachelor of Metallurgy

BMEWS Ballistic Missile Early Warning System

BMHATK banging my head against the keyboard

BMHATW banging my head against the wall

BMI body mass index; Broadcast Music Incorporated; Central Illinois Regional Airport (Bloomington-Normal, IL)

BMJ *British Medical Journal*

BMOC big man on campus

BMR basal metabolic rate

BMRC Bureau of Meteorology Research Center

BMS baby-making sex; Bachelor of Marine Science

BMT Bachelor of Medical Technology; ballistic missile technology; Brooklyn-Manhattan Transit

BMus Bachelor of Music

BMW *German* Bayerische Motoren Werke (Bavarian Motor Works)

BMX bicycle motocross

bn Bengali; Bangla

BN Bachelor of Nursing; bank note; Bureau of Narcotics

Bn. baron; battalion

.bn Brunei Darussalam

BNA British North America; Bureau of National Affairs; Nashville International Airport

BND Brunei—Darussalam dollar

bnd. bound

BNDD Bureau of Narcotics and Dangerous Drugs

BNF big name fan

BNNRC Behavioral Neurogenetics and Neuroimaging Research Center

BNS Bachelor of Naval Science

bo Tibetan

BO back order; best offer; body odor; box office; branch office; broker's office; buyer's option

.bo Bolivia

B/O best offer

BOA basic ordering agreement; beginning of activity

BOAD *French* Banque Ouest Africaine de Développement (West African Development Bank)

boatel hotel in a marina

BOB best of breed; Bolivia—boliviano; Bureau of the Budget

BOBW best of both worlds

Boc t-butoxycarbonyl

BOC Bureau of the Census

BOD bandwidth on demand; biochemical oxygen demand; biological oxygen demand; board of directors

BOD5 biological oxygen demand—5 days

BOF basic oxygen furnace; beginning of file

BOG El Dorado International Airport (Bogotá, Colombia)

BOHICA bend over, here it comes again

BOI Boise Air Terminal/Gowen Field

BOJ Bank of Japan

bol bolus

BOL beginning of life; Bolivia (international vehicle ID)

Bol. Bolivia; Bolivian

BOM beginning of message; Bureau of Mines; business office must; Sahar International Airport (Mumbai, India)

BOMC Book-of-the-Month Club

BOO Bootes (constellation)

BOOP bronchiolitis obliterans with organizing pneumonia

BOP basic oxygen process; blatant other promotion (that is, blatant promotion of work of others); [Federal] Bureau of Prisons

BOPF basic oxygen process furnace

BOQ Bachelor Officers' Quarters

Bor. borough

BOREAS Boreal Ecosystem-Atmosphere Study

BOS Boston Red Sox; Logan International Airport (Boston, MA)

bot small computer program (from "robot")

BOT back on topic; beginning of tape; Board of Trade

bot. botanical; botanist; botany; bottle; bottom

Boul. boulevard

BOW bag of waters (the amniotic sac in pregnancy)

bp boiling point

BP Bachelor of Pharmacy; Bachelor of Philosophy; barometric pressure; basis point; bills payable; blood pressure; borough president

bp. baptized; birthplace

Bp. bishop

BPA Black Psychiatrists of America; Bonneville Power Administration

BPC biomass production chamber

bpd barrels per day

BPD bronchopulmonary dysplasia

BPd Bachelor of Pedagogy

Bpdu bridge protocol data unit

BPE Bachelor of Physical Education

BPF Black professional female

BPh Bachelor of Philosophy

BPH benign prostatic hypertrophy

BPharm Bachelor of Pharmacy

BPHC Bureau of Primary Health Care

BPhil Bachelor of Philosophy

bpi bits per inch; bytes per inch

bpl birthplace

BPL broadband over power lines

bpm beats per minute

BPM Black professional male; business proccess management

BPO bargain purchase option; blanket purchase order

BPOE Benevolent and Protective Order of Elks

BPR bypass ratio

bps bits per second; bytes per second

BPSK binary phase shift keying

BPT best practicable technology; Jefferson County Airport (Beaumont/Port Arthur, TX)

BPTC best practicable control technology

BPV bipolar violation

BPW Business and Professional Women

BPX base performance index

Bq becquerel

br bedroom; Breton

Br bromine; brown

BR bedroom; bills receivable; Brazil (international vehicle ID)

br. branch; brief

Br. Britain; British; brother

.br Brazil

B.R. *Latin* Bancus Regis (King's Bench); *Latin* Bancus Reginae (Queen's Bench)

B/R bills receivable

bra brassiere

BRA basic rate access

brat bratwurst

Braz. Brazil; Brazilian

BrazPg. Brazilian Portuguese

BRB be right back

BRC Biennial Report on Carcinogens

BRCA Brotherhood of Railway Carmen of America

BRCA1 breast cancer 1 (gene)

brd board

BRDF bidirectional reflectance distribution function

BrDu bromodeoxyuridine

BRE Bachelor of Religious Education; business reply envelope

Bret. Breton

brev. brevet

BRF Brain Research Foundation

BRFSS Behavioral Risk Factor Surveillance System

brg. bearing; bridge

BRHR Basic Research and Human Resources

BRI basic rate interface; brain response interface

brig brigade

Brig. brigadier

Brig. Gen. brigadier general

Brit person from Great Britain

Brit. Britain; British

Britcom British sitcom

brkfst breakfast

brl barrel

BRL Brazil—Brazilian real (currency)

brlp. burlap

Brn brown

BRN Bahrain (international vehicle ID)

bro [soul] brother

Bro. brother

bronc bronco

bros. brothers

BRP bathroom privileges

BRS Brotherhood of Railway Signalmen

brt. bright; brought

BRT Brotherhood of Railroad Trainmen

BRU battery reconditioning unit; battery regulation unit; Brunei (international vehicle ID); Zaventem Airport (Brussels, Belgium)

BRV Bravo (cable TV)

brwnstn brownstone (that is, townhouse)

bs Bosnian

BS Bachelor of Science; Bahamas (international vehicle ID); balance sheet; Bar Sirach; bill of sale; blood sugar; bowel sounds; breath sounds; bullshit

.bs Bahamas

b/s bill of sale

BSA Bachelor of Science in Agriculture; body surface area; Boy Scouts of America

BSAA Bachelor of Science in Applied Arts

BSAE Bachelor of Science in Aeronautical Engineering

BSArch Bachelor of Science in Architecture

BSBA Bachelor of Science in Business Administration

BSC Bachelor of Science in Commerce; base station controller; Biological Sciences Center; binary synchronous communication

BSc Bachelor of Science

BSC Bachelor of Science in Commerce; base station controller; Biological Sciences Center; binary synchronous communication

BSCE Bachelor of Science in Civil Engineering

BSCh Bachelor of Science in Chemistry

BScN Bachelor of Science in Nursing

BSCs Business Service Centers

BSD Bachelor of Science in Design; Bahamas—dollar

BSE Bachelor of Science in Education; Bachelor of Science in Engineering; bovine spongiform encephalopathy

BSEc Bachelor of Science in Economics

BSEC Black Sea Economic Co-operation Zone

BSEcon Bachelor of Science in Economics

BSEd Bachelor of Science in Education

BSEE Bachelor of Science in Electrical Engineering; Bachelor of Science in Elementary Education

BSEng Bachelor of Science in Engineering

BSER brainstem evoked response

BSFor Bachelor of Science in Forestry

BSFS Bachelor of Science in Foreign Service

bsh. bushel

BSHA Bachelor of Science in Health Administration

BSHE Bachelor of Science in Home Economics

BSHEc Bachelor of Science in Home Economics

BSI British Standards Institution

BSIE Bachelor of Science in Industrial Engineering

BSJ Bachelor of Science in Journalism

bsk. basket

bskt. basket

BSL Bachelor of Sacred Literature; Bachelor of Science in Law; Bachelor of Science in Linguistics

Bs/L bills of lading

BSLS Bachelor of Science in Library Science

BSM Bachelor of Sacred Music

BSME Bachelor of Science in Mechanical Engineering

BSMT Bachelor of Science in Medical Technology; basement

bsmt. basement

BSN Bachelor of Science in Nursing; backward sequence number

BSNA Bachelor of Science in Nursing Administration

BSO benzene soluble organics; Boston Symphony Orchestra

BSOD blue screen of death

BSOT Bachelor of Science in Occupational Therapy

BSP Bachelor of Science in Pharmacy; blatant self-promotion

BSPA Bachelor of Science in Public Administration

BSPE Bachelor of Science in Physical Education

BSPH Bachelor of Science in Public Health

BSPhar Bachelor of Science in Pharmacy

BSPharm Bachelor of Science in Pharmacy

BSPHN Bachelor of Science in Public Health Nursing

BSPT Bachelor of Science in Physical Therapy

BSR Back Surface Reflection

BSRF Borderlands Science Research Foundation

BSRN [United Nations] Baseline Surface Radiation Network

BSS Bachelor of Social Science; balanced salt solution; base station subsystem

BSSE Bachelor of Science in Secondary Education

BSSS Bachelor of Science in Social Science

BST Bachelor of Sacred Theology; bovine somatotropin

BSW Bachelor of Social Work

BT Bachelor of Theology; bacillus thuringiensis; bathythermograph; bleeding time; brightness temperature; burst tolerance

bt. boat; bought

Bt. baronet

.bt Bhutan

B.t. Bacillus thuringiensis

BTA Board of Tax Appeals; but then again

BTAICBW but then again I could be wrong

BTAIM be that as it may

BTDT been there, done that

BTDTGTS been there, done that, got the T-shirt

BTE Bachelor of Textile Engineering

BTEX benzene, toluene, ethylbenzene, xylene

bth bathroom

BTh Bachelor of Theology

BTL bilateral tubal ligation

btl. bottle

BTN between (shortwave transmission); Bhutan—ngultrum (currency)

btn. button

BTO big-time operator

BTR Baton Rouge Metropolitan Airport/Ryan Field; better (shortwave transmission)

BTRS Behavior Therapy and Research Society

btry. battery

BTS Bureau of Transportation Statistics

BTSOOM beats the shit out of me

Btss. baronetess

btty battery

Btu British thermal unit

BTV Burlington [VT] International Airport

BTW by the way

btwn. between

BTX beacon transmitter; brevotoxins

BU Boston University

bu. bureau; bushel

Bucks. Buckinghamshire

Bud Budweiser [beer]

BUD Ferihegy Airport (Budapest, Hungary)

BUF Buffalo Bills; Buffalo-Niagara International Airport

BUFR Binary Universal Form for Representation

bul. bulletin

Bulg. Bulgaria; Bulgarian

bull. bulletin

BUMED United States Navy Bureau of Medicine and Surgery

BUN blood urea nitrogen

BUR Burbank Glendale Pasadena Airport; Myanmar (international vehicle ID)

bur. bureau; buried

Bur. Burma; Burmese

burb suburb

Burm. Burmese

bus. business

bush. bushel

bute butethol

.bv Bouvet Island

b.v. book value

B.V. Blessed Virgin

BVA Board of Veterans Appeals

BVD Bradley, Voorhees & Day (A trademark used for undershirts and underpants. This trademark sometimes occurs in print with a final 's.)

BVE Black Vernacular English

BVI Better Vision Institute; British Virgin Islands

BVM Blessed Virgin Mary

BVP blood volume pulse

BVR beyond visual range

bvt. brevet

bw bandwidth; birth weight

BW bacteriological warfare; biological warfare; black and white

.bw Botswana

B/W black and white

B'way Broadway

bwd. backward

BWDIK but what do I know?

BWG big wide grin; Birmingham Wire Gauge

BWI Baltimore-Washington International Airport; British West Indies

BWK big wet kiss

BWP Botswana—pula (currency)

BWR boiling water reactor

Bx biopsy

BX Base Exchange

bx. box

bxd. boxed

BY budget year

.by Belarus

b.y. billion years

BYKT but you knew that

BYKTA but you knew that already

BYO bring your own [food and drink]

BYOB bring your own booze; bring your own bottle

byp. bypass

BYR Belarus—ruble

BYU bayou; Brigham Young University

Byz. Byzantine
Bz benzene; benzoyl
BZ busy
.bz Belize
BZD Belize—dollar; benzodiazepine

C

c candle; carat; charm quark; circumference; constant; cubic
C carbon; capacitance; Celsius; center; centigrade; charge; charm; Christian (as in personal ads); Citigroup Inc.; cloudy; cocaine; complement; conjugation; consonant; coulomb; couple(s) (as in personal ads); Cuba (international vehicle ID); cytosine; 100; see (shortwave transmission); yes (shortwave transmission)
c. capacity; cent; centavo; centime; centimo; chapter; *Latin* circa (in approximately, about); *Latin* congius (gallon); copy; copyright; *Latin* cum (with); cup
C. cape; Celtic; century; Chancellor
C2C consumer to consumer
C3I Command, Control, Communications, and Intelligence
ca Catalan; carcinoma; *Latin* circa (in approximately, about)
Ca calcium; cancer
CA California; Central America; chartered accountant; chronological age; Cocaine Anonymous; collision avoidance
.ca Canada
c/a capital account; credit account; current account

C/A central air conditioning
CA-125 cancer antigen 125 test
CAA Civil Aeronautics Administration; Clean Air Act; computer-aided architecture
CAADE Commission on Accreditation/Approval for Dietetics Education
CAAP Children's AIDS Awareness Project
cab cabernet
CAB Civil Aeronautics Board; coronary artery bypass
cab. cabin; cabinet; cable
CABG coronary artery bypass graft
CABS Current Awareness in Biological Sciences
cab sav cabernet sauvignon
CAC central air conditioning; [National Oceanic and Atmospheric Administration] Climate Analysis Center; Coalition for America's Children; Connection Admission Control
CAC&F Coalition for Asian-American Children and Families
CaCC cathodal closure contraction
CACGP Committee on Atmospheric Chemistry and Global Pollution
CACM Central American Common Market
CAD Canada—dollar; carbohydrate addict's diet; computer-aided design; coronary artery disease
CADA Central Asian Development Agency
CAD/CAM computer-aided design/computer-aided manufacturing

CADD computer-aided design and drafting

CADS Clinical Administrative Data Service

CaDTe cathodal duration tetanus

CAE Caelum (constellation); Columbia [SC] Metropolitan Airport; computer-aided engineering

CAEC Center for Analysis of Environmental Change

CAEHR Center for the Advancement of Electronic Health Records

CAeM [United Nations] Commission for Aeronautical Meteorology

CAEN computer-aided engineering network

CAEU Council of Arab Economic Unity

CAF Canadian Armed Forces; Cooley's Anemia Foundation; cost and freight

CAFE corporate average fuel economy

CAgM [United Nations] Commission for Agricultural Meteorology

CAGR compound annual growth rate; cumulative annual growth rate

CAGS Certificate of Advanced Graduate Study

CAH congenital adrenal hyperplasia

CAHD coronary artery heart disease

CAHSA Congenital Adrenal Hyperplasia Support Association

CAI computer-aided instruction

CAIR Comprehensive Assessment Information Rule

CAK Akron-Canton Regional Airport

cal calibration; calorie (large calorie); calorie (mean calorie); calorie (small calorie)

CAL computer-aided learning

cal. calendar; caliber

Cal. California

calc. calculate; calculus

CALGB Cancer and Leukemia Group B

Calif. California

CALM Children Affected with Lymphatic Malformations

CALResCo Complexity and Artificial Life Research Concept for Self-Organizing Systems

CALS/CE Computer-aided Acquisition and Logistic Support/Concurrent Engineering [Program]

CAM Camelopardalis (constellation); Cameroon (international vehicle ID); computer-aided manufacturing

cam. camouflage

Cam. Cambridge

Camb. Cambridge

camcorder video camera recorder

CAMEO computer-aided management of emergency operations

CAMH Comprehensive Accreditation Manual for Hospitals

CAMI Civil Aeromedical Institute

CAMIS Center for Advanced Medical Informatics at Stanford; computer-assisted minimally invasive surgery

cAMP cyclic adenosine monophosphate

CAMP continuous air monitoring program; cyclophosphamide doxorubicin methotrexate procarbazine

campanol. campanology

CAMS Chinese American Medical Society

CAN cancer (constellation)

can. canceled; cancellation; canon; canto

Can. Canada; Canadian

Canad. Canadian

canc. canceled; cancellation

CANCERLIT Cancer Literature

CanCom Women's Cancer Information Project

C & DH command and data handling

C & F cost and freight

C & GC [National Oceanic and Atmospheric Administration] Climate and Global Change Program

C & GS [National Oceanic and Atmospheric Administration Office of] Charting and Geodetic Services

C & I cost and insurance

c & lc capitals and lower case

C & S culture and sensitivity

c & sc capitals and small capitals

C & SS card and socket services

C & W country and western

Can. F. Canadian French

Can. Fr. Canadian French

Cant. Canterbury; Canticle of Canticles; Cantonese

Cantab. *Latin* Cantabrigiensis (of Cambridge)

CAO chief accounting officer; chief administrative officer;

chronic airflow obstruction

CaOC cathodal opening contraction

CaOCl cathodal opening clonus

cap capsule

CAP Capricorn; Capricornus (constellation); Civil Air Patrol; carcinoma of prostate; community-acquired pneumonia; computer-aided publishing

cap. capacity; capital; capitalize; foolscap

CAPA Critical Aquifer Protection Area

CAPCO Custom Academic Publishing Company

CAPD continuous ambulatory peritoneal dialysis

CAPHIS Consumer and Patient Health Information Section

caps capital letters

CAPS Center for AIDS Prevention Studies; Center for Analysis and Prediction of Storms; Chinese American Physicians Society

caps. capsule

caps & lc capitals and lower case

caps & sc capitals and small capitals

Caps Lock capital letter lock key

CAPT captain

Capt. captain

CAR Carina (constellation); Carolina Panthers; computer-assisted retrieval

car. carat; cargo

carb carburetor; carbohydrate

carb. carbohydrate; carbon; carburetor

carbo carbohydrate

Card player on St. Louis Cardinals baseball team
Card. cardinal
CARE Cooperative for American Relief Everywhere; Cooperative for American Relief to Europe; Ryan White Comprehensive AIDS Resources Emergency Act
ca. resp. *Latin* capias ad respondendum (take the body to answer, that is, hold a defendant for court appearance)
CARF Commission on Accreditation of Rehabilitation Facilities
Caricom Caribbean Community
carp. carpenter; carpentry
carr. carrier
CART Championship Auto Racing Team; cocaine- and amphetamine-regulated transcript
CAS Cassiopeia (constellation); Center for Automotive Safety; Certificate of Advanced Study; collision-avoidance system; cost accounting standards
cas. castle; casualty
CASA computer-assisted sperm motion analysis
ca. sa. *Latin* capias ad satisfaciendum (jail the defendant)
CASE computer-aided software engineering
cass cassette
cast broadcast
CAST Center for Applied Special Technology
cat cataract
CAT Caterpillar Inc.; clear air turbulence; computerized axial tomography
cat. catalog; catapult; catechism
Catal. Catalan

cath catheter
cath. cathode
Cath. cathedral; Catholic
CATI computer-aided telephone interviewing
CATLINE Catalog Online
CATS cheap access to [outer] space
CATT Computer Assisted Technology Transfer
CATV community antenna television
CAU carbon absorption unit
Cauc. American of European origin; Caucasian
CAUS Citizens Against UFO Secrecy
caus. causative
CAUSES Child Abuse Unit for Studies, Education, and Services
CAV cyclophosphamide doxorubicin vincristine
cav. cavalry; caveat; cavity
c.a.v. *Latin* curia advisari vult (the court will be advised, will consider, will deliberate)
CA virus croup-associated virus
CAV PE cisplatin etoposide alternating with CAV
CAVU ceiling and visibility unlimited
CAW certificate authority workstation
caz OK (from "casual")
cb centibar
Cb columbium (no longer in scientific use)
CB chronic bronchitis; citizens band; construction battalion; cornerback
C.B. common bench
c/b carry back

CBA central business area; collective bargaining agreement; cost-benefit analysis

CBBB Council of Better Business Bureaus

CBC Canadian Broadcasting Corporation; complete blood count

CBD cash before delivery; central business district; common bile duct

CBE Commander of the Order of the British Empire

CBEL *Cambridge Bibliography of English Literature*

CBF cerebral blood flow; coronary blood flow

CBG corticosteroid-binding globulin

CBHP Community Breast Health Project

CBI China, Burma, India; computer-based instruction; confidential business information; cumulative book index

Cbl cobalamin

CBL come back later; computer-based learning; convective boundary layer

CBM *Current Bibliographies in Medicine*

CBMT *Clinical Bulletin of Myofascial Therapy*

CBMTS Chemical and Biological Medical Treatment Symposia

CBN *Cancer Biotherapeutics Newsletter*; Christian Broadcasting Network

cbn. carbine

CBO collateralized bond obligation; Community-based Organization; Congressional Budget Office

CBOD carbonaceous biochemical oxygen demand

CBOE Chicago Board of Options Exchange

CBOS Chesapeake Bay Observing System

CBOT Chicago Board of Trade

CBP card balance protection; Customs and Border Protection

CBPP contagious bovine pleuropneumonia

CBR chemical, bacteriological, and radiological; chemical, biological, and radiological; constant bit rate; cost-benefit ratio

CBS Columbia Broadcasting System

CBSO City of Birmingham Symphony Orchestra

CBSS Council of the Baltic Sea States

CBT Chicago Board of Trade; computer-based training

CBW chemical and biological warfare

Cbz carbobenzoxy

cc carbon copy; contributor's copy; cubic centimeter

Cc cirrocumulus

CC Canadian Club; chief complaint; circuit court; civil code; closed-captioned; credit cards [accepted]

cc. centuries; chapters; copies

.cc Cocos (Keeling) Islands

C.C. criminal case

CCA Career College Association; Children's Craniofacial Association; Circuit Court of Appeals

CCAD Center for Computer Aided Design

CCAFS Cape Canaveral Air Force Station

CCAM collision and contamination avoidance maneuver

CCAMLR Convention of the Conservation of Antarctic Marine Living Resources

CC & R covenants, conditions, and restrictions

CCAP Center for Clean Air Policy

CCB configuration control board

CCC Civilian Conservation Corps; Commodity Credit Corporation

CCCC Conference on College Composition and Communication

CCCF Candlelighters Childhood Cancer Foundation

CCCID Center for Children with Chronic Illness and Disability

CCCO Committee on Climate Changes and the Oceans

CCCT clomiphene citrate challenge test

CCD charge-coupled device; Confraternity of Christian Doctrine; Consortium for Citizens with Disabilities

CCDM *Control of Communicable Diseases in Man*

CCE carbon-chloroform extract; Council on Chiropractic Education

CCEA Cabinet Council on Economic Affairs

CCF Cooperative Commonwealth Federation of Canada

CCFA Crohn's and Colitis Foundation of America

CCG collectible card game

CCGP Commission for Certification in Geriatric Pharmacy

CCH connections per circuit hour

CCHS congenital central hypoventilation syndrome

CCI chronic coronary insufficiency

CCID Community Colleges for International Development

CCIP continuously computed impact point

CCITT *French* Comité Consultatif International Télégraphique et Téléphonique (International Consultative Committee on Telecommunications and Telegraphy, now **ITU-T**)

CCJ county court judgment

CCK cholecystokinin

cckw. counterclockwise

CCl [United Nations] Commission for Climatology

CCL close circuit loop; Couple to Couple League for Natural Family Planning

C.Cls. Court of Claims

CCM community climate model; counter-countermeasure

CCN conclusion (shortwave transmission); Cooperative Caring Network

CCNS Concerned Citizens for Nuclear Safety

CCNY City College of New York

CCO complete/coordinated care organization

CCOL [United Nations] Coordinating Committee on the Ozone Layer

CCOM control center operations manager

CCP Campus Custom Publishing; Code of Civil Procedure

CCR cloud cover radiometer; Commission on Civil Rights;

Creedence Clearwater Revival

CCRF Children's Cancer Research Fund

CCRIS Chemical Carcinogenesis Research Information System

CCS command and control subsystems; combined chiefs of staff

CCSC Cemetery Consumer Service Council

CCSDS Consultive Committee for Space Data Systems

CCSM control center systems manager

CCSR Center for Climate System Research

CCT clomiphene challenge test; closed cranial trauma

CCTe cathodal closure tetanus

CCTP Clean Coal Technology Program

CCTR Cochrane Controlled Trials Register

CCTV closed-circuit television

CCU coronary care unit; critical care unit

CCW command and control warfare; counter clockwise

ccw. counterclockwise

CCWCP Coordinating Committee for the World Climate Program

cd candela

Cd cadmium

CD certificate of deposit; cesarean delivery; civil defense; cluster of differentiation; collision detection; compact disc; cycle day

cd. cord

c.d. cash discount

C/D carried down; certificate of deposit

CDA Certified Dental Assistant; command and data acquisition; confidential data agreement

CDB Caribbean Development Bank

CDBG Community Development Block Grant

CDC Centers for Disease Control and Prevention; century date change; [National Oceanic and Atmospheric Administration] Climate Diagnostics Center; Connected Device Configuration

CDC NAC Centers for Disease Control and Prevention National AIDS Clearinghouse

CDC WONDER Centers for Disease Control and Prevention Wide-ranging Online Data for Epidemiologic Research

CDD certificate of disability for discharge

CDDI copper distributed data interface

CDE cyclophosphamide doxorubicin etoposide

CD-E compact disc-erasable

CDEM Continuous Dynode Electron Multiplier

CDER Center for Drug Evaluation and Research

CDEV [Macintosh] control panel device

CDF Celiac Disease Foundation; channel definition format; Children's Defense Fund; Children's Dream Foundation; common data format; Congo—Congolese franc

CDFC Cloud Depiction and Forecast System

cdg commanding

CDG Roissy Charles de Gaulle International Airport (Paris, France)

CDGS carbohydrate deficient glycoprotein syndrome

CDGSFN Carbohydrate-Deficient Glycoprotein Syndrome Family Network

cdh Committee Discharged House

CDHF central data handling facility

CDI capacitive deionization

CD-I compact disc—interactive

CDIAC [United States] Carbon Dioxide Information Analysis Center

CDIM Clerkship Directors in Internal Medicine

CdLS Cornelia de Lange Syndrome Foundation

CDM climatological dispersion model; comprehensive data management

CDMA code division multiple access

CDMS cost development management system

CDMU central data management unit

CDN Canada (international vehicle ID)

Cdn. Canadian

cDNA complementary deoxyribonucleic acid

CDNS Climatological Data National Summary

CDP census designated place; certificate in data processing; cytidine 5c-diphosphate

CDPC Communicable Disease Prevention and Control

CDP-choline cytidine diphosphocholine

CDPD cellular digital packet data

CDP-glyceride cytidine diphosphoglyceride

CDP-sugar cytidine diphosphosugar

cds Committee Discharged Senate

CDR collateralized depository receipt; commander; critical design review

CD-R compact disc—recordable

CDRD Cutaneous Drug Reaction Database

CDRH Center for Devices and Radiological Health

CDRL contract data requirements list

CD-ROM compact disc—read-only memory; consumer device, rendered obsolete in months

CDRR Coalition for the Medical Rights of Women

CD-RW compact disc—read-write

CDS coronal diagnostic spectrometer

CDT Central Daylight Time

CDVIK Computerized Disease Vector Identification Keys

ce Chechen

Ce cerium

CE communications engineer; Council of Europe

c.e. *Latin* caveat emptor (let the buyer beware); compass error

C.E. chemical engineer; Church of England; civil engineer; Common Era; [United States Army] Corps of Engineers; counterespionage

CEA carcinoembryonic antigen;

cost-effectiveness analysis;
Council of Economic Advisers

CEAM Center for Exposure Assessment Modeling

CEAO *French* Communauté Économique de l'Afrique de l'Ouest (West African Economic Community)

CEBBI Center for Enhancement of the Biology/Biomaterial Interfaces

CEC cation exchange capacity; Commission for Environmental Cooperation

CED Committee for Economic Development; Council on Education of the Deaf

CEDDA [National Oceanic and Atmospheric Administration] Center for Experiment Design and Data Analysis

CEDR Comprehensive Epidemiologic Data Resource

CEEAC *French* Communauté Économique des États de l'Afrique centrale (Economic Community of Central African States)

CEEB College Entry Examination Board

CEES Committee on Earth and Environmental Sciences

CEG continuous edge graphics

CEHN Children's Environmental Health Network

CEI Central European Initiative

cel celluloid

Cel. Celsius

celeb celebrity

CELIAS Charge, Element, and Isotope Analysis System

cell cellular; celluloid

cell phone cellular telephone

Cels. Celsius

CELSS closed ecological life support system; controlled environment life support system

Celt. Celtic

cem. cement; cemetery

CEMA Council for Mutual Economic Assistance

CEMF counterelectromotive force

CEMS Continuous Emission Monitoring System

CEMSCS Central Environmental Satellite Computer System

CEN Centaurus (constellation)

cen. center; central; century

Cen. Cenozoic

CENR Committee on Environment and Natural Resources

cent. centigrade; central; *Latin* centum (hundred); century

Cent. central

CENTO Central Treaty Organization

CEO chief executive officer

CEOS Committee on Earth Observation Satellites

CEP Cepheus (constellation); Committee on Environmental Protection

CEPGL *French* Communauté Économique des Pays des Grands Lacs (Economic Community of the Great Lakes Countries)

CEPN Certification Examination for Practical and Vocational Nurses

CEPN-LTC Certification Examination for Practical and Vocational Nurses in Long-Term Care

CEPP Chemical Emergency Preparedness Program

CEPPO Chemical Emergency Preparedness and Prevention Office

CEQ Council on Environmental Quality

CER coordinated ecosystem research

CERA catcher's earned run average

CERCLA Comprehensive Environmental Response, Compensation, and Liability Act (also called "Superfund")

CERCLIS Comprehensive Environmental Response, Compensation, and Liability Information System

CERES California Environmental Resources Evaluation System

CERI Center for Environmental Research Information

CERN *French* Conseil Européen pour la Recherche Nucléaire (European Organization for Nuclear Research, now known as the European Laboratory for Particle Physics)

cert certain; certainly

cert. certificate; certified; certiorari

cert. den. certiorari [writ] denied

certif. certificate; certificated

cerv cervical

CES Center for Epidemiologic Studies; Consumer Electronics Show

CES-D Center for Epidemiologic Studies Depression Scale

CET Central European Time; Cetus (constellation)

CETA Comprehensive Employment and Training Act

cet. par. *Latin* ceteris paribus (other things being equal)

CEU continuing education unit

Cf californium

CF call forwarding; cardiac failure; center field; center fielder; control function; conversion factor; cystic fibrosis

cf. calfskin; *Latin* confer (compare)

.cf Central African Republic

c.f. cost and freight

C/F carried forward

CfA [Harvard-Smithsonian] Center for Astrophysics

CFA Campus Freethought Association; Cat Fanciers' Association; Chartered Financial Analyst; Commission of Fine Arts; Consumer Federation of America; Craniofacial Foundation of America

CFC chlorofluorocarbon

cfd cubic feet per day

CFD computational fluid dynamics

CFDA Catalog of Federal Domestic Assistance

CFE contractor-furnished equipment

CFF critical fusion frequency; Cystic Fibrosis Foundation

CFG Camp Fire Girls

cfh cubic feet per hour

CFH Council on Family Health

CFHI Child Family Health International

c.f.i. cost, freight, and insurance

CFIDS chronic fatigue immune dysfunction syndrome

CFIDSAA Chronic Fatigue and Immune Dysfunction Syndrome Association of America

CFIT controlled flight into terrain

CFL Canadian Football League

cfm cubic feet per minute

CFM chlorofluoromethane; confirm (shortwave transmission)

CFO cancel former order; chief financial officer

C4 Command, Control Communication, and Computer Systems

C4I Communication, Command, Control, Computer, and Intelligence

CFP call for proposals; Certified Financial Planner

CFR *Code of Federal Regulations*; computerized facial recognition

CFRBCS Cooperative Family Registry for Breast Cancer Studies

CFRP carbon fiber reinforced plastic

cfs cubic feet per second

CFS chronic fatigue syndrome

CFSAN Center for Food Safety and Applied Nutrition

cfsm cubic feet per second per square mile

CFSS certified fragrance sales specialist

CFT complement fixation test

c. ft. cubic feet

CFTC Commodity Futures Trading Commission

CFV call for voting

cg centigram

CG cloud to ground; coast guard; commanding general; complete games; computer graphics; consul general;

Contadora Group

.cg Republic of the Congo

c.g. center of gravity

CGA color graphics adapter; color graphics array

CGAP Cancer Genome Anatomy Project

CGCP [National Oceanic and Atmospheric Administration] Climate and Global Change Program

CGEAN Council on Graduate Education for Administration in Nursing

CGI common gateway interface; computer-generated imaging; computer graphics interface

CGIAR Consultative Group on International Agricultural Research

CGL complete game losses

cgm. centigram

cGMP cyclic guanosine 3c,5c-monophosphate

CGMS Coordination Group for Meteorological Satellites

CGMW Commission for the Geological Map of the World

CGRP calcitonin gene-related peptide

cgs centimeter-gram-second system

CGS Committee on Geological Sciences

ch chain; Chamorro; check

Ch Christian (as in personal ads); Chronicles

CH central heating; clearinghouse; compass heading; conference host; courthouse; customhouse; Switzerland (international vehicle ID)

ch. champion; chapter; check; child; children; church

Ch. Champion; channel; chaplain; chief; China; Chinese; church

.ch Switzerland

CHA Chamaeleon (constellation); Lovell Field Airport (Chattanooga, TN)

CHAANGE Center for Help for Anxiety/Agoraphobia through New Growth Experience

CHAART Center for Health Applications of Aerospace Related Technologies

CHADD Children and Adults with Attention Deficit Disorder

Chal. Chaldean

Chald. Chaldean

CHAMP Comprehensive Healthcare Analysis and Management Program

Champ. champion

CHAMPUS Civilian Health and Medical Program of the Uniformed Services

CHAMPVA Civilian Health and Medical Program of the Veterans Administration

Chan. Channel

Chanc. Chancellor

CHAP Community Health Accreditation Program

chap. chapter

Chap. chaplain

char. character; characteristic; charity; charter

chard chardonnay

CHARM Coupled Hydrosphere—Atmosphere Research Model

CHART continuous hyperfractionated accelerated radiotherapy

CHAS Center for Health Administration Studies

Chas. Charles

CHASER Congenital Heart Anomalies—Support, Education, and Resources

CHASP Community Health Accreditation and Standards Program

ChB *Latin* Chirurgiae Baccalaureus (Bachelor of Surgery)

CHC Chicago Cubs; choke coil; community health center

CHCC Coalition for Healthier Cities and Communities

CHCE Center for Healthcare Ethics

ChD *Latin* Chirurgiae Doctor (Doctor of Surgery)

CHD congenital heart disease; coronary heart disease

CHDCT Coalition for Heritable Disorders of Connective Tissue

CHDF Children's Health Development Foundation

Ch.E. chemical engineer; chemical engineering

CHEC Children's Health Environmental Coalition

CHEJ Center for Health, Environment and Justice

CHEL *Cambridge History of English Literature*

chem chemistry (academic course)

chem. chemical; chemist; chemistry

Chem.E. chemical engineer; chemical engineering

CHEMID chemical identification

CHEMLINE Chemical Dictionary Online

chemo. chemotherapy

CHES certified health education specialist

66 | Ches.

Ches. Cheshire
CHESS Community Health and Environmental Surveillance System
CHF congestive heart failure; Switzerland—franc
ChFC Chartered Financial Consultant
C-HFET complementary heterostructure field effect transistor
chg. change; charge
chgd. changed; charged
Chgo. Chicago
Chi Chicago
CHI Chicago Bears; Consumer Health Information
CHID Combined Health Information Database
CHIM Center for Healthcare Information Management
CHIME College of Healthcare Information Management Executives
CHIN Children's Health Information Network; Community Health Information Network
Chin. Chinese
CHIP Community Health Information Partnerships
CHIPS Clearing House Interbank Payments Systems
chirurg. *Latin* chirurgicalis (surgical)
CHITA Community Health Information Technology Alliance
Chi Town Chicago
Ch.J. chief justice
chk. check
CHL crown—heel length
chl. chloroform
CHLC Cooperative Human Linkage Center

chm. chairman; checkmate
CHMIS Community Health Management Information Systems
chmn. chairman
CHMR Center for Health Management Research
CHO carbohydrate
choc. chocolate
CHOICE Center for Humanitarian Outreach and Intercultural Exchange
CHOICES Children's Healthcare Options Improved through Collaborative Efforts and Services
chol. cholesterol
chor. choreographed by; choreographer
chp. chairperson
CHPA community health purchasing alliances
chpn. chairperson
CHQ Corps Headquarters
chr chrome
CHR [National] Center for Human Reproduction; contemporary hit radio
Chr. Christ; Christian; Chronicles
Chr. Ch. Christian Church
CHRIS Chemical Hazards Response Information System
christie christiania (skiing)
christy christiania (skiing)
Chr.L Christian Latin
chron. chronicle; chronological; chronology
Chron. Chronicles
chronol. chronological; chronology
CHRP common hardware reference platform

CHS Charleston [SC] International Airport

chug chug-a-lug

Chunnel [English] Channel Tunnel

chutist parachutist

Ci cirrus; curie

CI certificate of insurance; confidence interval; Côte d'Ivoire (international vehicle ID); counterintelligence

.ci Côte d'Ivoire

c.i. cost and insurance

C.I. Cayman Islands; Channel Islands

CIA cash in advance; Central Intelligence Agency; Culinary Institute of America

CIAA Central Intercollegiate Athletic Association

cib. *Latin* cibus (food)

CIBL convective internal boundary layer

CIC commander in chief; completely in the canal; Consumer Information Center

CICA Competition in Contracting Act

CICS Cooperative Institute for Climate Studies

CID Choice in Dying; Criminal Investigation Department; Eastern Iowa Airport (Cedar Rapids, IA)

CIDEM Center for Inherited Disorders of Energy Metabolism

CIDI Composite International Diagnostic Interview

CIDP chronic inflammatory demyelinating polyneuropathy

CIDR Center for Inherited Disease Research

CIDS Computer Information Delivery Service

Cie *French* Compagnie (Company)

CIEA Committee on International Ocean Affairs

CIEP Coastal Energy Impact Program

CIESIN Consortium for International Earth Science Information Network

CIF Chicago Improv Festival; cost, insurance, and freight

CIFAR Cooperative Institute for Arctic Research

CIHI Center for International Health Information

CIIT Chemical Industry Institute of Toxicology

CILER Cooperative Institute for Limnology and Ecosystems Research

CIM computer input microfilm; computer-integrated manufacturing

CIMAS Cooperative Institute for Marine and Atmospheric Studies

CIMMS Cooperative Institute for Mesoscale Meteorological Studies

cIMP cyclic inosine 3,5-monophosphate

CIMRS Cooperative Institute for Marine Resources Studies

CIMS chemical ionization mass spectrometer

CIMSS Cooperative Institute of Meteorology Satellite Studies

CIN Cincinnati Bengals; Cincinnati Reds; Circumcision Information Network

Cin. Cincinnati

CIN-BAD Chiropractic Information Network—Board Action Databank

C in C commander in chief

CINC commander in chief

CINDI Center for Integration of Natural Disaster Information

cinemat. cinematography

CIO chief information officer; Congress of Industrial Organizations

CIOMS Council for International Organizations of Medical Sciences

CIP cataloging in publication

CIPR Center for Imaging and Pharmaceutical Research

CIR Circinus (constellation); Consumptive Irrigation Requirement; Crop Irrigation Requirement

cir. circle; circuit; circular; circumference

CIRA Cooperative Institute for Research in the Atmosphere

circ circumcised

circ. circle; circuit; circular; circulation; circumference

circum. circumference

CIRES Cooperative Institute for Research in Environmental Sciences

CIS Cancer Information System; carcinoma in situ; Commonwealth of Independent States

CISC complex instruction set computer

CISS Community Integrated Service Systems

CIT California Institute of Technology; Carnegie Institute of Technology; circumstellar imaging telescope; computer integrated telephony

cit. citation; cited; citizen; citrate

CITD Center for International Trade Development

cite citation

CITES Convention on International Trade in Endangered Species [of Wild Fauna and Flora]

cito disp. *Latin* cito dispensetur (let it be dispensed quickly)

CIU computer interface unit; control interface unit

civ. civil; civilian

civie civilian

civvy civilian

civvies civilian clothes

CIWS close-in weapons system

C.J. chief justice

CJD Creutzfeldt-Jakob disease

CJE Council for Jewish Elderly

CJS *Corpus Juris Secundum* (Principles of American Law)

CK Calvin Klein; check (shortwave transmission); Christ the King; creatine kinase

ck. cask; check; cook; creek

.ck Cook Islands

CKT circuit (shortwave transmission)

ckt. circuit

ckw. clockwise

cl centiliter

Cl chlorine

CL call (shortwave transmission); civil law; common law; Sri Lanka (international vehicle ID)

cl. class; classification; clause; clearance; closet; cloth

.cl Chile

c.l. carload; common law

C/L cash letter

CLA Children's Liver Alliance

CLAS Clinical Ligand Assay Society

class classic; classical; classification; classified

CLASS cross-chain LORAN atmospheric sounding system

CLCW command link control word

cld. called; cleared; cooled

cldy cloudy

CLE Cleveland Browns; Cleveland Hopkins International Airport; Cleveland Indians

CLEK Collaborative Longitudinal Evaluation of Keratoconus Study

CLEP College Level Examination Program

CLF Conservation Law Foundation

clg. ceiling

Cl. Gk Classical Greek

CLI command line interface; cost of living index

CLIA Clinical Laboratory Improvement Act

CLIBCON Chiropractic Library Consortium

CLICOM climate computing

CLID caller identification

clin. clinical

CLIP corticotropin-like intermediate-lobe peptide

clk. clerk; clock

CLL chronic lymphocytic leukemia

Cl. L Classical Latin

cl liq clear liquid (diet)

CLM career-limiting maneuver

clm. column

CLMA Clinical Laboratory Management Association

cln. clean

CLO close (shortwave transmission)

clo. closet; clothing

clos. closet; closets

CLP Chile—peso; common law procedure

CLQ cognitive laterality quotient

CLR classical linear regression (model); clear (shortwave transmission)

clr. clear; color; cooler

CLS Chicago Linguistics Society; Commission on Life Sciences

CLSF Coffin-Lowry Syndrome Foundation

CLST closet

CLT Charlotte/Douglas International Airport

CLU chartered life underwriter

CLV constant linear velocity

cm centimeter

cM centimorgan

Cm curium

CM *Latin* Chirurgiae Magister (Master in Surgery); common market; countermeasure

.cm Cameroon

c.m. center of mass; circular mil; court-martial

c/m call of more

CMA Canis Major; certified medical assistant

C-MAN Coastal Marine Automated Network (National Weather Service)

CMAWS common missile approach warning system

CMB chemical mass balance; combine (shortwave transmission)

CMBR cosmic microwave background radiation

cmc critical micelle concentration

CMC certified management consultant; Commandant of the Marine Corps

cmd. command; commander

CMDF Children's Motility Disorder Foundation

cmdg. commanding

CMDL [National Oceanic and Atmospheric Administration] Climate Monitoring and Diagnostics Laboratory

Cmdr. commander

Cmdre. commodore

CME Chicago Mercantile Exchange; continuing medical education

CMEA Council for Mutual Economic Assistance

CMEIS Continuing Medical Education Information Services

CMF Christian Medical Fellowship; Compressed Mortality File

CMG Companion of the Order of St. Michael and St. George; cystometrogram

CMH Port Columbus International Airport (Columbus, OH)

CMHC Community Mental Health Center

CMHS Center for Mental Health Services

CMI Canis Minor; computer-managed instruction; Council for Media Integrity; University of Illinois/Willard Airport (Champaign-Urbana, IL)

CMIIW correct me if I'm wrong

CMIP Common Management Information Protocol

CMIS Computerized Medical Imaging Society

CMIST Configuration Management Integrated Support Tool

CML current mode logic

cml. commercial

CMLB ceramic multilayer board

CMM [United Nations] Commission for Marine Meteorology

CMMD VER command verification

CMN Mohammed V International Airport (Casablanca, Morocco)

CMO calculated mean organism; chief medical officer; collateralized mortgage obligation

CMOS complementary metal oxide semiconductor

CMP Coastal Management Programs; competitive medical plan; cytidine monophosphate

cmpd. compound

CMPE Certified Medical Practice Executive

CMPH Clinical Microbiology Procedures Handbook

cmpt compute

CMR common mode rejection

CMRS Clinical Magnetic Resonance Society

CMS *The Chicago Manual of Style*; command management system

CMSA Consolidated Metropolitan Statistical Area

CMSC Consortium of Multiple Sclerosis Centers

CMSE command management systems engineer

CMSgt chief master sergeant

CMSS Council of Medical Specialty Societies

CMT Certified Medical Transcriptionist

CMTA Charcot-Marie-Tooth Association

CMU Carnegie-Mellon University

CMV cytomegalovirus

CMWS common missile warning system

CM-XMP cloud model with explicit microphysics

CMY cyan-magenta-yellow

CMYK cyan-magenta-yellow-black

CN Certified Nutritionist; cranial nerve

.cn China

C/N circular note; credit note

CNA Center for Naval Analysis; certified nursing assistant

CNBC Consumer News and Business Channel

CNC Cancer (constellation); computer numerical control

CNCB Clinical Nutrition Certification Board

CNCS Corporation for National and Community Service

CND Commission on Narcotic Drugs

CNE Continuing Nursing Education

CNFN Cable News Financial Network

CNG compressed natural gas

CNI Community Nutrition Institute

CNM certified nurse midwife

CNN Cable News Network

CNO carbon-nitrogen-oxygen; chief nursing officer; chief of naval operations

CNR [United Nations] Committee on Natural Resources

CNS Catholic News Service; central nervous system; clinical nurse specialist

cnvt convert

CNVRTBL convertible

CNY China—yuan renminbi (currency)

co Corsican

Co cobalt; Corinthians

CO carbon monoxide; cardiac output; cash order; Colorado; Colombia (international vehicle ID); commanding officer; conscientious objector; cutoff; cut out

co. company; county

Co. company; county

.co Colombia

c.o. carried over

C.O. common orders

c/o care of; carry over; complains of

C/O cash order; certificate of origin

CoA coenzyme A

COA certificate of authenticity; certificate of authority

COADS Comprehensive Ocean—Atmosphere Data Set

coag coagulation

COAP [National Oceanic and Atmospheric Administration] Center for Ocean Analysis and Prediction; Clinical Outcomes Assessment Program

coax coaxial cable

COB chip on board; close of business; coordination of benefits

COBOL Common Business-Oriented Language

cobot cooperative robot

COBRA Consolidated Omnibus Budget Reconciliation Act

COBS central on board software

COC cathodal opening contraction; certificate of competency; certificate of coverage

coch. *Latin* cochleare (spoonful)

coch. amp. *Latin* cochleare amplum (tablespoonful)

coch. parv. *Latin* cochleare parvum (teaspoonful)

COCl cathodal opening clonus

COCO contractor-owned/contractor-operated

COCOM Coordinating Committee on Export Controls

COD cash on delivery; cause of death; chemical oxygen demand; collect on delivery; *Concise Oxford Dictionary*

cod. *Latin* codex (manuscript volume); codicil

CoDA Co-Dependents Anonymous

CODA Children of Deaf Adults

CODAR Coastal Ocean Dynamics Applications Radar

CODATA Committee on Data for Science and Technology

CoDE coherent digital exciter

CODE Confederation of Dental Employers

codec coder/decoder; compression/decompression

COE Corps of Engineers

COEA cost and operational effectiveness analysis

coef. coefficient

coeff. coefficient

COEs Centers of Excellence

C. of C. chamber of commerce

C. of E. Church of England

COFF Common Object File Format

COFI Committee on Fisheries

C. of S. chief of staff

cog. cognate

COGA Collaborative Study on the Genetics of Alcoholism

cogn. cognate

COGSA Carriage of Goods by Sea Act

COH carbohydrate

C.O.H. cash on hand

COHIS Community Outreach Health Information System

COI cone of influence

Co-I co-investigator

COIL chemical oxygen-iodine laser

COIN counterinsurgency

coin-op coin-operated

coke cocaine

Col colonial

COL Colorado Rockies; Columba (constellation); computer-oriented language; cost of living; Council on Ocean Law

col. collect; college; colony; colophon; color; column

Col. Colombia; Colombian; colonel; Colorado; Colossians

COLA cost-of-living adjustment; cost-of-living allowance

COLD chronic obstructive lung disease; computer output to laser disk

colet. *Latin* coletur (let it be strained)

coll. collateral; collect; collection; college; colloquial

collab. collaboration; collaborator

collat. collateral

collect. collective; collectively

colloq. colloquial; colloquialism; colloquially

collut. *Latin* collutorium (mouth wash)

collyr. *Latin* collyrium (eye wash)

Colo. Colorado

colog cologarithm

COM Coma Berenices (constellation); Comedy Central; computer-output microfilm; computer-output microfilmer

com. combining; combustion; comedy; comic; comma; commentary; commerce; commission; commissioner; committee; common; commune; communication; community

Com. commander; commissioner; commodore; commonwealth; communist

.com commercial organization

COMB Center of Marine Biotechnology

comb. combination; combining; combustion

comb. form combining form

comd. command; commander

Comdex Communications and Data Processing Exhibition

comdg. commanding

Comdr. commander

Comdt. commandant

COMECON Council for Mutual Economic Assistance

COMET Cooperative Program for Operational Meteorology, Education, and Training (National Center for Atmospheric Research)

COMEX [New York] Commodity Exchange

Comintern *Russian* Kommunisticheskij Internatsional (Communist International)

commie communist

coml. commercial

comm. commentary; commerce; commercial; commission; committee; communication

Comm. commander; commonwealth; community

commo commodore

comp complimentary; composition (academic course)

comp. comparative; compensation; compiled; complete; composer; compound; comprehensive

compander compressor-expander

compar. comparative

compd. compound

Comp. Gen. Comptroller General

compl. complement; complete

compo composition material

COM port communications port

compt. compartment; comptroller

Comr. commissioner

Comsat Communications Satellite Corporation

COMSS Council of Musculoskeletal Specialty Societies

con confidence game; convict

CON certificate of need

con. concerto; conclusion; *Latin* conjunx (wife); connection; consolidate; consul; continued; *Latin* contra (against); convention

Con. Congo

con A concanavalin A

CONAD Continental Air Defense Command

conc. concentrate; concentrated; concentration; concerning; concrete

concl. conclusion

concn. concentration

concr. concrete

cond. condenser; condition; conductivity; conductor

condo condominium

conf. conference; confidential

confab confabulation

confed. confederation

Confed. confederate

config. configuration

cong. *Latin* congius (gallon)

Cong. Congregational; Congress

con game confidence game

Cong. Rec. *Congressional Record*

conj. conjugation; conjunction; conjunctive

con man confidence man

conn. connected; connotation

Conn. Connecticut

CONQUEST Computerized Needs-Oriented Quality Measurement Evaluation System

CONRAD Contraceptive Research and Development Program

Conrail Consolidated Rail Corporation

cons. consigned; consignment; consonant; constable; constitution; construction; consul

Cons. Constitution; conservative; consul

consec. consecutive

consol. consolidated

const. constable; constant; constitution; construction

Const. Constitution

constr. construction

cont. contents; continent; continued; contract; contraction; control

contd. continued

contemp. contemporary

contempt. contemptuous; contemptuously

contg. containing

contn. continuation

contr. contract; contracted; contraction; contractor; contralto; contrary; control

Contr. controller

contrail condensation trail

cont. rem. *Latin* continuentur remedia (continue the medicines)

contrib. contributor; contributing; contribution

CONUS continental United States

conv. convention; conversation; convertible; convocation

Conv. Conventual

CONVINCE Consortium of North American Veterinary Interactive New Concept Education

COO chief operating officer

coon raccoon

coop cooperative

co-op cooperative

coord. coordinate

COP coefficient of performance; Colombia—peso

cop. copper; copula; copy; copyright

Cop. Coptic

COPD chronic obstructive pulmonary disease

copr. copyright

COPS Coastal Ocean Prediction Systems Program; [Office of] Community Oriented Policing Services
Copt. Coptic
CoQ coenzyme Q
COR Center for Orthopaedic Research; College of Radiographers
cor. corner; cornet; coroner; corpus; correction; correlative; correspondence; corrupt
Cor. Corinthians
CORBA common object request broker architecture
CORD Council of Emergency Medicine Residency Directors
CORE Congress of Racial Equality
CORF comprehensive outpatient rehabilitation facility
Corn. Cornish; Cornwall
corol. corollary
coroll. corollary
Corp. corporal; corporation
Corpl. corporal
corpocrat corporate bureaucrat
CORR *Clinical Orthopaedics and Related Research*
corr. correction; correspondent; correspondence; corrugated; corrupt
correl. correlative
corresp. correspondence; corresponding
corrupt. corruption
cos cosine
COS Colorado Springs Airport
cos. companies; consul; counties
C.O.S. cash on shipment
COSE Common Open Software Environment

cosec cosecant
cosh hyperbolic cosine
COSHH control of substances hazardous to health
Cosmo *Cosmopolitan*
COSNA Composite Observing System for the North Atlantic
COSPAR Committee on Space Research
COSTED Committee on Science and Technology in Developing Countries
COSTEP comprehensive supra thermal and energetic particle analyzer
COSTR Collaborative Solar-Terrestrial Research
cot cotangent
COTA certified occupational therapy assistant; Children's Organ Transplant Association
COTe cathodal opening tetanus
coth hyperbolic cotangent
COTH Council of Teaching Hospitals
COTR contracting officer's technical representative
COTS commercial off-the-shelf
COTT Committee of Ten Thousand
coun. council; counsel
covers versed cosine
COW cellsite on wheels
COWPS Council on Wage and Price Stability
COWRR Committee on Water Resources Research
coz cousin
cp candlepower
cP centipoise
CP cerebral palsy; chemically pure; chest pain; command post; Common Prayer; Com-

munist Party; copy protected; creatine phosphate; cultural practices

cp. compare; coupon

C.P. Cape Province

C/P custom of the port

CPA certified public accountant

CPAF cost-plus-award-fee

CPAP continuous positive airway pressure

CPB Corporation for Public Broadcasting

CPC cheap personal computer; Climate Prediction Center; condensation particle counter

CPCA Cigarette Pack Collectors Association

CPCU Chartered Property and Casualty Underwriter

cpd. compound

CPDB Clinical Pathway Database

CPDS Commerce Procurement Data System

CPF carcinogenic potency factor; Cleft Palate Foundation

CPFF cost plus fixed fee

CPFS computer program functional specification

cph Considered and Passed House

cpi characters per inch

CPI consumer price index

CPIF cost-plus-incentive-fee

CPIO copy in and out

CPK creatine phosphokinase

cpl complete; complin; compline

CPL corporal; current privilege level

Cpl. corporal

cpm cost per thousand; cycles per minute

CPM continuous particle monitor; continuous passive motion

CPO chief petty officer

CPOM master chief petty officer

CPOS senior chief petty officer

CPPB continuous positive pressure breathing

CPPD calcium pyrophosphate deposition disease

CPPV continuous positive pressure ventilation

CPR cardiopulmonary resuscitation; customary, prevailing and reasonable reimbursement

CPRI Computer-based Patient Record Institute

cps characters per second; Considered and Passed Senate; cycles per second

CPS certified professional secretary; Coalition for Positive Sexuality

CPSC Consumer Product Safety Commission

CPS I [American Cancer Society] Cancer Prevention Study I

CPS II [American Cancer Society] Cancer Prevention Study II

cpt carpet

CPT Cape Town International Airport; captain; chest physical therapy; current procedural terminology

cpt. carport; counterpoint

cptd. carpeted

CPU central processing unit

CPUE catch per unit of effort

CPV canine parvo virus

CQ call to quarters

CQI continuous quality improvement

Cr chromium

CR carriage return; complete remission; complete response; conditioned reflex; conditioned response; consciousness raising; *Consumer Reports*; Costa Rica (international vehicle ID); critical ratio

cr. credit; creditor; creek; crescendo; crown

.cr Costa Rica

c.r. *Latin* curia regis (the king's court); chancery reports

C.R. Costa Rica

CRA Civil Rights Act; Corona Australis

CRAFT can't remember a fucking thing

CRAHCA Center for Research in Ambulatory Health Care Administration

C ration canned ration

CRB Commodity Research Bureau; Corona Borealis

CRC camera-ready copy; Civil Rights Commission; Costa Rica—colon (currency); cyclic redundancy check

CRD chronic respiratory disease

CRDC Climate Research Data Center

CREBBI Center for Cell Regulation and Enhancement of Biology/Biomaterial Interfaces

CREEP Committee to Reelect the President

CREF College Retirement Equities Fund

CREN Corporation for Research and Educational Networking

crep crepitation

Cres. crescent

cresc. crescendo

CRF chronic renal failure; corticotropin releasing factor

CRFA Cancer Research Foundation of America

CRH corticotropin releasing hormone

CRI Carpet and Rug Institute

crim. criminal

crim. con. criminal conversation (adultery)

criminol. criminologist; criminology

CRIR Caitlin Raymond International Registry

CRISD computer resources integrated support document

CRISP Computer Retrieval of Information on Scientific Projects; Consortium Research on Indicators of System Performance

crit. critic; critical; criticism; criticized

CRL crown-rump length

cr/lf carriage return/line feed

CRM cross-reacting material; customer relationship management

cRNA complementary ribonucleic acid

CRNA Certified Registered Nurse Anesthetist

crnr. corner

CRO cathode ray oscilloscope

Croat. Croatia; Croatian

croc crocodile

CROP consolidated rules of practice

cross-refs. cross-references

CRP Corpus Christi International Airport; C-reactive protein; Crop Reserve Program

crpt. carpet; carport

CRQ Chronic Respiratory Questionnaire

CRRB Change Request Review Board

CRREL Cold Regions Research and Engineering Laboratory

CRRES combined release and radiation effects satellite

CRS can't remember shit; can't remember stuff; Community Relations Service; Congressional Research Service

crt court; crate

CRT cathode-ray tube; Crater (constellation)

CRTT certified respiratory therapy technician

CRU Crux (constellation)

CRUFAD Clinical Research Unit for Anxiety Disorders

CRV Corvus (constellation)

crypto. cryptographer; cryptographic; cryptography

cryst. crystalline; crystallized; crystallography

cs cesarean section; Czech

Cs cesium

CS capital stock; caught stealing; chief of staff; cervical spine; Christian Science; civil service; conditioned stimulus

cs. case

CSA Community Services Administration; Confederate States of America

CSAP Center for Substance Abuse Prevention

CSAR combat search and rescue

CSAT Center for Substance Abuse Treatment

CSA/USA Celiac Sprue Association/United States of America

csc cosecant

CSC Civil Service Commission

CSCA Cardiovascular/Thoracic Surgery and Cardiology Assembly

C-SCAT C-band scatterometer

CSCE Coffee, Sugar, and Cocoa Exchange; Conference on Security and Cooperation in Europe

csch hyperbolic cosecant

CSCI computer software configuration item

CSCS consolidated scientific computing system

CSE Center for Social Epidemiology

CSEEE Center for the Study of Environmental Endocrine Effects

CSES Center for the Study of Earth from Space

CSETI Center for the Study of Extraterrestial Intelligence

C-section cesarean section

CSF cerebrospinal fluid

CSG Council of State Governments

csg. casing

CSHCN children with special health care needs

CSHS Cancer and Steroid Hormonal Study

CSI calculus surface index; conditional symmetric instability; Crime Scene Investigation

CSICOP Committee for the Scientific Investigation of Claims of the Paranormal

CSIS Canadian Security Intelligence System

csk. cask; countersink

CSM climate system monitoring; command sergeant major

CSN Children's Safety Network

CSNY Crosby, Stills, Nash & Young

CSO Chicago Symphony Orchestra; chief security officer; combined sewer overflow; computer security officials

CSOM computer systems operators manual

CSP casual sex partner; C-SPAN

CSPAAD Coarse Sun Pointing Attitude Anomaly Detection

C-SPAN Cable Satellite Public Affairs Network

CSPI Center for Science in the Public Interest

C-spine cervical spine

CSR certified shorthand reporter; customer service representative

CSRA Civil Service Reform Act

CSREES Cooperative State Research, Education, and Extension Service

CSRS Civil Service Retirement System; Cooperative State Research Service

CSS can't stop smiling; cascading style sheets; clerical support staff; combined sewer system

CSSA [Stanford] Center for Space Science and Astrophysics

CST Central Standard Time; convulsive shock treatment

CSTA computer-supported telephony applications

CSTC Consolidated Satellite Test Center

CSTD [United Nations] Center for Science and Technology for Development

CSTE Council of State and Territorial Epidemiologists

CSU California State University; Chicago State University; Cleveland State University;

Colorado State University; computer software unit

CSW Certificate in Social Work

CT Central Time; computerized tomography; Connecticut

ct. cent; certificate

Ct. carat; Connecticut; count; county; court

CTA Chicago Transit Authority; controlled thrust assembly

c.t.a. *Latin* cum testamento annexo (with the will annexed)

CTBT Comprehensive Test Ban Treaty

CTC centralized traffic control; Citizens' Training Corps

CTD cheapest to deliver; cumulative trauma disorder

CTDMPLUS improved complex terrain dispersion model

CTEP Cancer Therapy Evaluation Program

CTF capture the flag

ctf. certificate; certified

ctg. cartage; cartridge

ctge. cartage

CTIA capacitive feedback trans-impedance amplifier; Cellular Telecommunications Industry Association

CTL cytotoxic T lymphocytes

ctl. cental

CTMBL cloud-topped marine boundary layer

ctmo. centesimo; centimo

ctn cotangent

CTN can't talk now

ctn. carton

cto. concerto

c. to c. center to center

CTO chief technical officer

CTOF charge time-of-flight

CTOL conventional takeoff and landing

CTP cytidine 5c-triphosphate

CTR cash transaction report; currency transaction report

ctr. center; counter

ctrl control

CTS carpal tunnel syndrome; clear to send

CTU centigrade thermal unit

ctvo. centavo

Ctx contractions

Cty. city; county

cu Church Slavic

Cu copper; cumulus

CU civil union; close-up; see you

cu. cubic

.cu Cuba

CUA commonly used acronym; common user access; cost-utility analysis

cube cubicle

CUC chronic ulcerative colitis

cu. cm. cubic centimeter

CUD could (shortwave transmission)

CUFOS [J. Allen Hynek] Center for UFO Studies

CUFT Center for the Utilization of Federal Technology

cu. ft. cubic foot

cu. in. cubic inch

cuke cucumber

CUL catch you later; see you later

cul. culinary

CU L8R see you later

cult. culture

cum. cumulative

cu. m. cubic meter

Cumb. Cumbria

cu. mm. cubic millimeter

cUMP cyclic uridine 3c,5c-monophosphate

CUN Cancun International Airport

CUNA Credit Union National Association

CUNY City University of New York

CUP Cambridge University Press; cancer of unknown primary; Cuba—peso

cur. currency; current

curr. currency

cust. custodian; custody; customer

cu. yd. cubic yard

CUZ because (shortwave transmission)

'cuz because

cv Chuvash; convertible (bonds)

CV cardiovascular; code violations; coefficient of variation; *Latin* curriculum vitae (resumé)

cv. cultivar

.cv Cape Verde

c.v. chief value

C.V. Cape Verde

CVA cardiovascular accident; cerebrovascular accident

CVD cardiovascular disease

CVE Cape Verde—escudo (currency)

CVF compressed volume file

CVG Cincinnati/Northern Kentucky International Airport

CVI cerebrovascular insufficiency

CVIC Center for Violence and Injury Control

CVM [Food and Drug Administration] Center for Veterinary Medicine

CVN Canes Venatici
CVNRT convertible
CVO Credentials Verification Organization
CVP central venous pressure
cvr cover
CVS cardiovascular system; chorionic villus sampling; computer vision syndrome
CVSA Cyclic Vomiting Syndrome Association
CVT continuously variable transmission
cvt. convertible
CW call waiting; chemical warfare; carrier wave; continuous wave
cw. clockwise
c/w consistent with
C/W country western
CW2HY can't wait to hold you
CWA Central Wisconsin Airport (Mosinee, WI); Civil Works Administration; Clean Water Act; Communications Workers of America
CWAS contractor weighted average share in cost risk
CWHC Community Wholistic Health Center
CWO cash with order; chief warrant officer
CWOT complete waste of time
CWRU Case Western Reserve University
CWS Chicago White Sox; compressed work schedule
CWSU [Federal Aviation Administration] Central Weather Service Unit
cwt hundredweight
CWT Consumers for World Trade

CWU Central Washington University
CWW clinic without walls
CWYL chat with you later
cx cervix
cx. convex
.cx Christmas Island
CXBR cosmic x-ray background radiation
CXR chest x-ray
cy Welsh
Cy cyanide
CY calendar year; copy (shortwave transmission); current year; Cyprus (international vehicle ID)
cy. capacity; currency; cycle
Cy. county
.cy Cyprus
CYA cover your ass
cyber cybernetic; cybernetics
cyborg cybernetic organism
cyc. cyclopedia
cycl. cyclopedia
CYG Cygnus
CYL see you later
cyl. cylinder; cylindrical
Cym. Cymric
CYO Catholic Youth Organization
CYP Cyprus—pound (currency)
cytol. cytological; cytology
CZ Canal Zone; colorized version; Czech Republic (international vehicle ID)
.cz Czech Republic
CZCS Coastal Zone Color Scanner
CZE capillary zone electrophoresis
Czech. (former) Czechoslovakia
CZK Czech Republic—koruna (currency)

CZM [National Oceanic and Atmospheric Administration] Coastal Zone Management; Cozumel Airport

CZMA Coastal Zone Management Act

D

d deuteron; diameter; differential; down quark

D dative; day; Democrat; determiner; deuterium; [suggestive] dialogue (television rating); diction; divorced; down; Dutch; 500; Germany (international vehicle ID)

d. date; daughter; died; dose; drachma; pence

D. department; Deus; diopter; Don; duchess; duke

D2B direct to buyer

D2D dusk to dawn

D2T2 dye diffusion thermal transfer

D2W direct to web

da Danish

DA delayed action; Department of the Army; deposit account; dining area; didn't answer; *Dissertation Abstracts*; district attorney; Doctor of Arts; doesn't answer; don't answer

Da. Danish

D.A. duck's ass (hair style)

D/A digital/analog

DAA data availability acknowledgment

DAAC Distributed Active Archive Center

DAAPPP Data Archive on Adolescent Pregnancy and Pregnancy Prevention

DAB *Dictionary of American Biography*

DACS Data Acquisition and Control Subsystems

DAD delayed after depolarization; Dogs Against Drugs

dAdo deoxyadenosine

DAE *Dictionary of American English*

DAF divorced Asian female

dag decagram

DAG diacylglycerol

DAGC delayed automatic gain control

DAH *Dictionary of American History*; disordered action of heart

DAI *Dissertation Abstracts International*

dal decaliter

DAL Dallas Cowboys

dam decameter

DAM diacetylmonoxime; divorced Asian male

dAMP deoxyadenylic acid

DAN Divers Alert Network

Dan. Daniel; Danish

DANA Drug and Alcohol Nursing Association

D & C dilation and curettage; drugs and cosmetics

D & D drug and disease free

D & E dilation and evacuation; dilation and extraction

D & F determination and findings

D & O directors and officers

D & S domination and submission

D & X dilation and extraction

Danl Daniel

DANS 1-dimethylaminonaphthalene-5-sulfonic acid

DAO departmental administrative order

DAP Data Access Protocol; Diagnostic Accreditation Program

DAPI 4c6-diamidino-2-phenylindole•2HCl

DAR damage assessment routine; Daughters of the American Revolution

DARC Device for Automatic Remote Data Collection

DARE *Dictionary of American Regional English*; Drug Abuse Resistance Education

DARFC ducking and running for cover

DARPA Defense Advanced Research Projects Agency

DART Developmental and Reproductive Toxicology

DAS days at sea; dual attachment station

DASA Defense Atomic Support Agency

DASD direct access storage device

DASH Dietary Approaches to Stop Hypertension

DAT digital audiotape

dat. dative

dATP deoxyadenosinetriphosphate

dau daughter

DAU decryption authentication unit; Defense Acquisition University

DAV digital audio-video; Disabled American Veterans

DAW dispense as written

DAWN Drug Abuse Warning Network

DAWS defense automated warning system

DAX *German* Deutsche Aktienindex (German stock index)

DAY James M. Cox Dayton [OH] International Airport

dB decibel

Db dubnium

DB damp basement; data base; daybook; defensive back

d.b. day book

D.B. *Domesday Book*

DBA Doctor of Business Administration

d.b.a. doing business as

d/b/a doing business as

DBCP Data Buoy Cooperation Council; dibromochloropropane

DBCS Double Byte Character Set

DBD DNA-bonding domain

DBDDD [National Center for Environmental Health] Division of Birth Defects and Developmental Disabilities

d.b.e. *Latin* de bene esse (to be decided later)

DBE Dame Commander of the British Empire

DBEYR don't believe everything you read

DBF divorced Black female

d.b.h. diameter at breast height

dBI decibels referenced to isotropic gain

D.Bib. Douay Bible

DBIR Directory of Biotechnology Resources

dbl. double

dble. double

dBm decibels per milliwatt; decibels referenced to one milliwatt

DBM database manager; divorced Black male

DBMS data base management system

d.b.n. *Latin* de bonis non [administratis] (of the goods not administered)

DBP vitamin D-binding protein

DBPs disinfection by-products

DBQ Dubuque Regional Airport

DBS direct broadcast satellite

dBW Decibels referenced to one watt

dc discontinue; discounted

DC developed country; direct command; direct current; district court; District of Columbia; Doctor of Chiropractic; dual choice

D.C. da capo

d/c discharge

DCA [IBM's] Document Content Architecture; Ronald Reagan Washington [DC] National Airport

DCAA Defense Contract Audit Agency

DCASR's Defense Contract Administration Services Regions

DCC data country code; Dependent Care Connection

DCCPS Division of Cancer Control and Population Sciences

DCE data communications equipment; distributed computing environment

DCEG Division of Cancer Epidemiology and Genetics

DCF data capture facility

DChE Doctor of Chemical Engineering

DCHP *Dictionary of Canadianisms on Historical Principles*

DCI duplicate coverage inquiry

DCIS ductal carcinoma in situ

DCL declare; Doctor of Canon Law; Doctor of Civil Law

DCM Distinguished Conduct Medal

dCMP deoxycytidylic acid

DCOM Distributed Component Object Model

DCN document change notice; document control number

DCP Division of Cancer Prevention

DCPC Division of Cancer Prevention and Control

DCS Defense Communications System; Direct Credits Society

DCS/2 Data Collection System/2

dCTP deoxycytidine triphosphate

DD days after date; demand draft; developmental disability; developmentally delayed; dishonorable discharge; *Latin* Divinitatis Doctor (Doctor of Divinity); double density; drydock; due date; E.I. DuPont de Nemours & Co.

dd. delivered

DDA data delivery acknowledgment; dideoxyadenosine

DDB double-declining-balance depreciation

DDBMS distributed database management system

D/DBP Disinfectant and Disinfection By-Product Rule (Environmental Protection Agency)

ddC dideoxycytidine

DDC Dewey Decimal Classification

DDD direct distance dialing

DDE Dwight David Eisenhower; dynamic data exchange

DDF data distribution facility; drug and disease free

D/DF drug and disease free

ddI dideoxyinosine

DDI device driver interface; dideoxyinosine

DDIM dry deposition inferential method

DDL Data Definition Language; Data Description Language

DDM distributed data management

DDN data delivery notice

DDNA Developmental Disabilities Nurses Association

DDS Doctor of Dental Science; Doctor of Dental Surgery

DDT dichlorodiphenyl-trichloroethane

DDTE design, development, test, and evaluation

DDVP dimethyl dichlor vinyl phosphate

DDW Digestive Disease Week

de German

DE defensive end; Delaware; Doctor of Engineering; donor eggs

.de Germany

DEA Drug Enforcement Administration

DEAL-MCH Data Enhancement for Accountability and Leadership in Maternal and Child Health

deb debutante

deb. debenture

DEBRA Dystrophic Epidermolysis Bullosa Research Association

dec decoration

dec. deceased; declaration; declension; declination; decorated; decorative; decrease; decrescendo

Dec. December

DEC decorated; Department of Environmental Conservation; Digital Equipment Corporation

decaf decaffeinated coffee

decal decalcomania

DecCen decadal-to-centennial

decd. deceased

decl. declension

decn. decision

decomp. decomposition

ded. dedication; deduct

DEd Doctor of Education

de d. in d. *Latin* de die in diem (from day to day)

DEECS digital electronic engine control system

DEERS Defense Enrollment Eligibility Reporting System

DEET diethyl toluamide; n-diethyltoluamide; N,N-diethyl-m-toluamine

def definite; definitely

def. defective; defendant; defense; deferred; definite; definition

DEFCON defense readiness condition

deg. degree

deglut. *Latin* deglutiatur (swallow)

DEGT don't even go there

DEI Dutch East Indies (now Indonesia)

DEIS draft environmental impact statement

Del delete

DEL data evaluation laboratory; Delphinus (constellation)

del. delegate; delegation;

delete; delivered; delivery

Del. Delaware

dele delete

deli delicatessen

delts deltoid muscles

dely delivery

dem demodulator

DEM Germany—deutsche mark

dem. demonstrative; demurrage

Dem. Democrat; Democratic

demo demonstration

demob demobilize

demon. demonstrative

demonstr. demonstrative

DEN Denver Broncos; Denver International Airport

den. denotation

Den. Denmark

DEng Doctor of Engineering

DENIX Defense Environmental Network and Information Exchange

denom. denomination

dens. density

dent. dental; dentist; dentistry

DEP dedicated experiment processor

dep. department; departure; dependency; deponent; deposed; deposit; depot; deputy

depr. depreciation; depression

dept. department; deputy

DEPT department

DEQ Department of Environmental Quality

der. derivation; derivative

d.e.r.i.c. *Latin* de ea re ita censuere (concerning that matter have so decreed)

deriv. derivation; derivative

derm. dermatitis; dermatology

derog. derogatory

DERWeb Dental Education Resources on the Web

DES data encryption standard; diethylstilbestrol

des. designation; dessert

Des. desert

desc. descendant; descending; describe

destn. destination

DET Detroit City Airport; Detroit Lions; Detroit Tigers; diethyltryptamine

det. detachment; detail

DETI don't even think it

DETLA double extended three-letter abbreviation

detn. determination

DEU dead-end user

Deut. Deuteronomy

DEV duck embryo origin vaccine

dev. developed by; development; deviation

devel. development

DEW directed energy weapon; distant early warning

DF direction finder; Doctor of Forestry

d.f. degrees of freedom

D.F. Defender of the Faith

DFA Doctor of Fine Arts

DFC Distinguished Flying Cross

DFCD data format control documents

DFD data flow diagram

dFdC difluorodeoxycytidine

DFI disease-free interval

DFK direct free kick (soccer)

DFM Distinguished Flying Medal

DFP diisopropyl fluorophosphate

dft. defendant; draft

DFW Dallas/Fort Worth International Airport

dg decigram

D.G. *Latin* Dei gratia (by the grace of God); *Latin* Deo gratias (thanks to God); Director General

DGA Directors Guild of America

dgl dangling construction

dGlc 2-deoxyglucose

dGMP deoxyguanylic acid

DGPS differential global positioning system

DGT don't go there

dgt digit

dGTP deoxguanosine triphosphate

DH Darling Husband; Dear Husband; designated hitter; Doctor of Humanities

DHA docosahexaenoic acid

DHAC dihydro-5-azacytidine; doesn't have a clue; don't have a clue

DHAP dihydroxyacetone phosphate

DHCP Dynamic Host Configuration Protocol

DHEA dihydroepiandrosterone

DHEAS dihydroepiandrosterone sulfate

DHF dihydrofolic acid; divorced Hispanic female

DHFR dihydrofolate reductase

DHHS [United States] Department of Health and Human Services

DHJ doing his job

DHL Doctor of Hebrew Letters; Doctor of Hebrew Literature

DHM divorced Hispanic male

DHP direct high power

DHS Demographic and Health Surveys; Department of Homeland Security; Division of HIV Services

DHSS data handling subsystem

DHT dihydrotestosterone

DHTML Dynamic Hypertext Markup Language

D.Hy. Doctor of Hygiene

Di didymium

DI diabetes insipidus; diagnostic imaging; donor insemination; drill instructor

DIA Defense Intelligence Agency; document interchange architecture

dia. diameter

diab diabetic

diag. diagonal; diagonally; diagram

DIAL differential absorption lidar

dial. dialect; dialectal; dialectally; dialogue

diam. diameter

DIARAD dual irradiance absolute radiometer

DIB device independent bitmap

DIC dissolved inorganic carbon; Drug Information Center

DICE data integration and collection environment

dict. dictation; dictionary

DID data item description; direct inward dial

DIEB Department of the Interior Energy Board

dieb. alt. *Latin* diebus alternis (every other day)

dies non. *Latin* dies non juridicus (not a court day)

diet. dietary

Diet. dietitian

di. et fi. *Latin* dilecto et fideli

(to one's beloved and faithful)

DIF data interchange format; device input format; Drug Information Fulltext

dif. difference

diff difference

diff. difference

dig. digest; digitalis

digiverse digital universe

DIIK damned if I know

dil. dilute

dim. dimension; diminished; diminuendo; diminutive

dimin. diminuendo; diminutive

DIMM dual in-line memory module

din dining room

Din dinar

DINFOS Defense Information School

DINK double income, no kids

dioc. diocese; diocesan

DIP desquamative interstitial pneumonia; digital imaging processing; distal interphalangeal joint; dual in-line package

dip. diploma

D.I. particle defective interfering particle

DIPEC Defense Industrial Plant

diph. diphtheria

DIPI direct intraperitoneal insemination

dipl. diploma; diplomat; diplomatic

dir. direct; direction; director

DIRCM directed infrared countermeasures

DIRLINE Directory of Information Resources Online

dir. prop. *Latin* directione propria (with proper direction)

dis disease; to be disrespectful toward

DIS Defense Investigative Service; Disney Channel; Walt Disney Co.

dis. discharge; discount; distance; distant

DISA Defense Information Services Activity; Defense Information Systems Agency

disab. disability

DISAM Defense Institute of Security Assistance Management

disc. discount; discovered

DISC domestic international sales corporation

disch. discharge

disco discotheque

DISH diffuse idiopathic skeletal hyperostosis

DISIDA diisopropyl iminodiacetic acid

disp. dispensary

displ. displacement

diss to be disrespectful toward

diss. dissertation

dissd. dissolved

dist. distance; distant; district

Dist. Atty. district attorney

Dist. Ct. district court

distn distillation

distr. distribution; distributor

distrib. distributive

DIT diiodotyrosine

DITD down in the dumps

div. divergence; divergency; diversion; divided; dividend; division; divorced

div. in p. aeq. *Latin* divide in partes aequales (divide into equal parts)

divvy divide

divx digital video express
DIY do-it-yourself
dj dust jacket
DJ disc jockey
.dj Djibouti
D.J. district judge; *Latin* Doctor Juris (Doctor of Law)
DJD degenerative joint disease
DJF December-January-February; Djibouti—franc
DJI Dow-Jones Index
DJIA Dow-Jones Industrial Average
DJS Doctor of Juridical Science
DK Denmark (international vehicle ID)
dk. dark; deck; dock
.dk Denmark
DKDC don't know, don't care
dkg dekagram
DKK Denmark—krone (currency)
dkl dekaliter
dkm dekameter
dkt. docket
dl deciliter
DL disturbance lines; Doctor of Law; download
d.l. quiet (from "down low")
D/L demand loan; downlink
DLA Defense Logistics Agency
DLC data link control
DLC/LLC data link control/logical link control
DLD delivered (shortwave transmission); Direct Link for the Disabled, Inc.
DLG devilish little grin
DLit *Latin* Doctor Litterarum (Doctor of Letters, Doctor of Literature)
DLitt *Latin* Doctor Litterarum

(Doctor of Letters, Doctor of Literature)
DLL dynamic-link library
DLM Dynamic Link Module
DLO dead letter office
dlr. dealer
DLS Doctor of Library Science
dls. dollars
DLSA Defense Legal Services Agency
DLT digital linear tape; dose-limiting toxicity
dlvy. delivery
dm decimeter
DM data management; deutsche mark; diabetes mellitus; diastolic murmur
.dm Dominica
DMA Defense Mapping Agency; Direct Marketing Association; direct memory access; Doctor of Musical Arts
DMAHTC Defense Mapping Agency Hydrographic/Topographic Center
D-mark deutsche mark
DMAT Disaster Medical Assistance Team
DMC p,p,c-dichlorodiphenyl methyl carbinol
DMCL dust metal concentration limit
DMD *Latin* Dentariae Medicinae Doctor (Doctor of Dental Medicine); digital micromirror device
DME distance-measuring equipment; durable medical equipment
DMF decayed, missing, and filled teeth
DMFO Defense Medical Facilities Office

DMFS decayed, missing, and filled surfaces

DMH [United States] Department of Mental Health

DML direct memory load; Doctor of Modern Languages

DMP dot matrix printer

DMPP dimethylphenylpiperazinium

DMR detailed mission requirements

DMRF Dystonia Medical Research Foundation

DMS Defense Mapping School; digital matrix switch; dimethylsulfide

DMSA Defense Medical Support Activity

DMSO dimethylsulfoxide

DMSP Defense Meteorological Satellite Program

DMSSC Defense Medical System Support Center

DMT N,N-dimethyltryptamine

DMV Department of Motor Vehicles

DMY day/month/year

DMZ demilitarized zone

Dn Daniel

DN dibucaine number

dn. down

DNA Defense Nuclear Agency; deoxyribonucleic acid; Dermatology Nurses Association

DNAase deoxyribonuclease

DNase deoxyribonuclease

DNB *Dictionary of National Biography*

DNC Democratic National Committee

DNF did not finish

DNFSB Defense Nuclear Facilities Safety Board

DNI Director of National Intelligence

DNR Department of Natural Resources; do not resuscitate

DNS Domain Name Service; Domain Name System

DNT dinitrotoluene

DO defense order; dissolved oxygen; Doctor of Optometry; Doctor of Osteopathy

do. ditto

.do Dominican Republic

D/O delivery order

DOA dead on arrival; Department of Agriculture

DOALOS [United Nations] Division for Ocean Affairs and the Law of the Sea

DOB date of birth

doc doctor

DOC Department of Commerce; dissolved organic carbon; Doctors Opposing Circumcision

doc. document

DOCSIS Data-Over-Cable Service Interface Specification

DOD Department of Defense

DODDS Department of Defense Dependent Schools

DODEA Department of Defense Education Activity

DoDIIS Department of Defense Intelligence Information System

DOE Department of Education; Department of Energy; dyspnea on exertion

DOF degree of freedom

DOI Department of the Interior; digital object identifier

DOJ Department of Justice

DOL Department of Labor

dol. dolce; dollar

DOM dirty old man; dissolved organic matter; 2,5-dimethoxy-4-methylamphetamine; Dominican Republic (international vehicle ID)

dom. domestic; dominant; dominion

Dom. Dominica; Dominican

D.O.M. *Latin* Deo Optimo Maximo (to God, the best and the greatest)

Dom. Proc. *Latin* Domus Procerum (House of Lords)

Dom. Rep. Dominican Republic

DOMSAT domestic communications satellite; domestic satellite

DON dissolved organic nitrogen

Don. Donegal

DOO departmental organization order

DOP Dominican—Republic peso

dopa dihydroxy-phenylalanine

DOPLIGHT Doppler-lighting

DOPLOON Doppler-balloon

DOR Dorado (constellation)

Dor. Doric

DORA Directory of Rare Analyses

DORIS Doppler orbitography and radiopositioning integrated by satellite

dorm dormitory

Dors. Dorset

DOS denial of service; Department of State; disk operating system

DOST direct oocyte-sperm transfer

DOT death on [the operating] table; Department of Transportation

doublexing double-crossing

doz. dozen

dozer bulldozer

dp dot pitch

DP data processing; demolition proceeding; development prototype; dew point; director of photography; disabled person; displaced person; Doctor of Podiatry; double penetration; double play

DPC Data Product Code; Domestic Policy Council

DPD Drug Product Database

DPDT double pole, double throw

DPE Data Processing Engineer; Doctor of Physical Education

DPF divorced professional female

DPh Doctor of Philosophy

DPH Department of Public Health; Doctor of Public Health

DPhil Doctor of Philosophy

dpi dots per inch

DPI Data Processing Installation

DPL diode-pumped laser

DPLX duplex

DPM divorced professional male; Doctor of Podiatric Medicine

DPMS display power-management signaling

DPN diphosphopyridine nucleotide

DPNH reduced diphosphopyridine nucleotide

DPO days post-ovulation

DPN+ oxidized diphosphopyridine nucleotide

DPP [National Center for Environmental Health] Disabilities

Prevention Program

DPSK differential phase shift keying

DPST double pole, single throw

DPT diphtheria, pertussis, tetanus

dpt. department; deponent

DPU data processing unit

DPW Department of Public Works

DQ disqualified; disqualify

DQDB distributed queue data bus

DQM data quality message

DQOTD dumb question of the day

DQT design qualification test

DQYDJ don't quit your day job

DR dead reckoning; dining room

dr. debtor; door; dram

Dr. Doctor; drive

DRA Deficit Reduction Act; Draco (constellation)

DRADA Depression and Related Affective Disorders Association

DRAM dynamic random access memory

dram. dramatic; dramatist

dram. pers. *Latin* dramatis personae (the cast of the play)

DR & A data reduction and analysis

dr. ap. apothecaries' dram

dr. avdp. avoirdupois dram

DRE digital rectal examination

DRFM digital radio frequency memory

DRG diagnosis-related group

DRH [Centers for Disease Control and Prevention] Division of Reproductive Health

DRI Diabetes Research Institute

DRK dark

DRL Department of Regulation and Licensing; [Bureau of] Democracy, Human Rights, and Labor

DRM digital rights management

drng drainage

DRO destructive readout; Durango-La Plata County [CO] Airport

DrPH Doctor of Public Health

DRR deployment readiness review

DRS data receiving system; data relay satellite; direct receiving station

drsg dressing

DRT dead right there

dr. t. troy dram

DRTC Diabetes Research and Training Center

DRU data recovery unit

ds double stranded

Ds darmstadtium

DS data set; double sided; double strength

d.s. dal segno; days after sight; document signed

DSA digital subtraction angiography; Direct Selling Association

DSAA Defense Security Assistance Agency

DSB Defense Science Board

DSc Doctor of Science

DSC Discovery Channel; Distinguished Service Cross; Doctor of Surgical Chiropody

DSCC Deep Space Communications Complex

DSCS defense satellite communication system

DSD direct stream digital

DSDD double sided/double density

DSDS data storage and distribution system

DSHD double sided/high density

DSL digital subscriber line; document style language

DSM Des Moines International Airport; *Diagnostic and Statistical Manual [of Mental Disorders]*; Distinguished Service Medal

DSN deep space network; defense switched network

DSNA Dictionary Society of North America

DSO Distinguished Service Order

DSP digital signal processing; digital signal processor

d.s.p. *Latin* decessit sine prole (died without issue)

DSPS delayed sleep phase syndrome

DSR delivery status report

DSRS Drug Services Research Survey

DSS digital satellite system

DSSSL Document Style Semantics and Specification Language

DST daylight-saving time

DSTN Double-layer Supertwisted Nematic

DSU data servicing unit

DSUM data summary

DSVD digital simultaneous voice and data

DSW Doctor of Social Welfare; Doctor of Social Work

dT diphtheria

Dt Deuteronomy

DT Daylight Time; defensive tackle; Doctor of Theology

d.t. double time

DTA disk transfer address

DT & E development test and evaluation

DTaP diphtheria, tetanus, and acellular pertussis

DTD document type definition

dTDP thymidine 5c-diphosphate

DTF diagnostic turbulent flux

DTH delayed-type hypersensitivity; direct-to-home

D.Th. Doctor of Theology

dThd thymidine

DTheol Doctor of Theology

DTIC dacarbazine; Defense Technical Information Center

DTM data transfer module

DTMF dual tone multifrequency

dTMP deoxythymidylic acid; thymidine 5c-monophosphate

DTP desktop publishing; diphtheria, tetanus, and pertussis

DTPA diethylenetriamine pentaacetic acid

DTPH diphtheria, tetanus, pertussis, and Hib

DTR data transfer rate; deep tendon reflex

DTRA Defense Threat Reduction Agency

DTRT do the right thing

DT's delirium tremens

DTSA Defense Technology Security Administration

dTTP thymidine 5c-triphosphate

DTV digital television

DTW Detroit Metropolitan Wayne County Airport

DU distribution uniformity;

Dobson unit (for measuring ozone concentration); duodenal ulcer

Du. duke; Dutch

DUB Collinstown Airport (Dublin, Ireland); dysfunctional uterine bleeding

Dub. Dublin

Dubl. Dublin

DUI driving under the influence [of alcohol or drugs]

DUMBO Down Under the Manhattan Bridge Overpass (Manhattan neighborhood)

dup. duplicate

DUR drug utilization review

dur. dolor. *Latin* durante dolare (while pain lasts)

DUT Unalaska Airport

dUTP deoxyuridine 5-triphosphate

DUX duplex (shortwave transmission)

DV digital video

D.V. *Latin* Deo volente (God willing); Douay Version

DVB digital video broadcasting

DVD digital versatile disc; digital videodisc

DVD-R digital versatile disk—recordable

DVD-RAM digital versatile disk—random-access memory

DVD-ROM digital versatile disk—read-only memory

DVRS Digital Voice Recording System

DVD-RW digital versatile disk—read-write

DVM Doctor of Veterinary Medicine

DVP delivery versus payment

DVT deep vein thrombosis

DW Darling Wife; dead weight; Dear Wife; distilled water

D/W dishwasher; dock warrant

DWA damaging winds algorithm

DWB Doctors Without Borders

DWBC deep western boundary current

DWD Dying with Dignity

DWEM dead White European male

DWF divorced White female

DWI died without issue; driving while intoxicated

DWM divorced White male

dwnstrs downstairs

DWR Doppler Weather Radar

DWSN Dandy-Walker Syndrome Network

DWT deadweight tonnage; deadweight tons

dwt. pennyweight

dx diagnosis

DX distance

DXF drawing interchange file

Dy dysprosium

DY Benin (international vehicle ID)

dy. delivery; duty

dyn dyne

DYNMX dynamic mixing model

DYOH do your own homework

DYSIM dynamic simulator

dz Dzongkha

DZ Algeria (international vehicle ID); drop zone

dz. dozen

.dz Algeria

DZA Algeria

DZD Algeria—Algerian dinar

E

e electron; error

e. eastern; engineering

e- electronic

E east; eastern; electronic; English; error; especial; etiology; excellent; extra; Spain (international vehicle ID)

E. earl; English

E2 estradiol

E2EG ear to ear grin

E3 Electronic Entertainment Expo

ea editor's alteration

ea. each

EA electronic attack; Endometriosis Association; environmental auditing

EAA earth attitude angle; equal areas/equal aspect

EAC external auditory canal

EAD early after depolarization

EADB East African Development Bank

EAE experimental allergic encephalitis

EAF effort adjustment factor; electric arc furnace; experimenter's analysis facility

eah Engrossed Amendment House

EAK Kenya (international vehicle ID)

EAM *Greek* Ethniko Apeleftherotiko Metopo (National Liberation Front)

E & OE errors and omissions excepted

EAP Edgar Allan Poe; Elvis Aron Presley; employee assistance program; environmental action plan; Extensible Authentication Protocol

eas Engrossed Amendment Senate

EAS equivalent airspeed; expert agent selection

EAT earnings after taxes; Tanzania (international vehicle ID)

EAU Uganda (international vehicle ID)

EB eastbound; elementary bodies; emissions balancing; Epstein-Barr [virus]; exabyte

EBCDIC extended binary coded decimal interchange code

EBE extraterrestrial biological entity

EBIT. earnings before interest and taxes

EBITDA earnings before interest, taxes, depreciation, and amortization

EBL external blood loss

EBM evidence-based medicine

EbN east by north

EBNF Extended Backus-Naur Form

EBOZ Ebola virus, Zaire strain

E-BPR enhanced bottom pressure recorder

EBRD European Bank for Reconstruction and Development

EBRT external-beam radiation therapy

EbS east by south

EBS emergency broadcast system

EBSA Employee Benefits Security Administration

EBT examination before trial

EBU European Broadcasting Union

e-business electronic business

EBV Epstein-Barr virus

ec emerging company

Ec Ecclesiastes

EC Ecuador (international vehicle ID); effective concentration; European Community

Ec. Ecuador

.ec Ecuador

ECA Economic Commission for Africa

ECAFE Economic Commission for Asia and the Far East

ECAL electronic calibration

ECAP Employee Counseling and Assistance Program

e-cash electronic cash

ECC error checking and correction; error correction code

ECB [acute] exacerbations of chronic bronchitis

Eccl Ecclesiastes

eccl. ecclesiastic; ecclesiastical

Eccles. Ecclesiastes

Eccl. Gk. Ecclesiastical Greek

Eccl. L Ecclesiastical Latin

Ecclus. Ecclesiasticus

ECCM electronic counter-countermeasures

ECCS emergency core cooling system

ECD electron capture detector

ECDIN Environmental Chemicals Data and Information Network

ECDIS Electronic Chart Display Information System

ECDSA Elliptic Curve Digital Signature Algorithm

ECF extended care facility; extracellular fluid

ECF-A eosinophil chemotactic factor of anaphylaxis

ECFMG Educational Commission for Foreign Medical Graduates

ECFV extracellular fluid volume

ECG electrocardiogram; electrocardiograph

EC-GC electron capture-gas chromatograph

ECHO Each Community Helps Others; Exchange Clearing House; Expo Collectors and Historians Organization

ECL emitter-coupled logic; executive control language

ECLA Economic Commission for Latin America

ECLAC Economic Commission for Latin America and the Caribbean

ECM electronic countermeasures; Emerging Company Marketplace; Error Correction Mode; European Common Market

ECMA European Computer Manufacturers Association

ECN electronic communications network

ECO Economic Cooperation Organization

ECoG electrocorticography

ECOG Eastern Cooperative Oncology Group

ecol. ecology

E. coli Escherichia coli

e-commerce electronic commerce

econ economics

econ. economics; economy

ECOR Engineering Committee on Oceanic Resources

ECOSOC Economic and Social Council

ECOWAS Economic Community of West African States

ECP extended capabilities port

ECRA Economic Cleanup Responsibility Act

ECRI Emergency Care Research Institute

ECS electrocerebral silence; environmental control system

ECSC European Coal and Steel Community

ECT electroconvulsive therapy

ECU emergency care unit; European currency unit; extreme close-up

Ecua. Ecuador

ECWA Economic Commission for Western Asia

ed education

ED$_{50}$ electrical damage; erectile dysfunction; extensive disease

ed. edited by; edition; editor; education

E.D. election district; emergency department

EDA Economic Development Administration; embedded document architecture

EDB ethylene dibromide

Ed.B. *Latin* Educationis Baccalaureus (Bachelor of Education)

EDC estimated date of confinement (pregnancy); ethylene dichloride

EdD *Latin* Educationis Doctor (Doctor of Education)

EDD *English Dialect Dictionary*; expected date of delivery

EDF Environmental Defense Fund

ED$_{50}$ median effective dose

EDI electronic data interchange

EDIFACT Electronic Data Interchange for Administration, Commerce, and Transport

EDIMS Environmental Data and Information Management Systems

EDIS [National Oceanic and Atmospheric Administration] Environmental Data and Information Service

edit. edition; editor

EDL Ethernet data link

EDLIN line editor program

EdM *Latin* Educationis Magister (Master of Education)

EDO extended duration orbiter

EDO RAM extended data out random access memory

EDP electronic data processing

EDR electrodialysis reversal; environmental data record

E-dress electronic address

EDRF endothelium-derived relaxing factor

EdS Specialist in Education

EDS enter day stop order; [National Oceanic and Atmospheric Administration] Environmental Data Service

EDSA Eating Disorders Shared Awareness

EDSP exchange delivery settlement price

EDT Eastern Daylight Time

EDTA ethylenediaminetetraacetic acid

.edu educational institution

educ. educated; education; educational

EE Early English

.ee Estonia

e.e. errors excepted

E.E. electrical engineer; electrical engineering

EEA energy and environmental analysis

EEC European Economic Community

EEE eastern equine encephalomyelitis

EEG electroencephalogram; electroencephalograph

EEK Estonia—kroon (currency)

EELV evolved expendable launch vehicle

EEMS enhanced expanded memory system

EENT eyes, ears, nose, and throat

EEO equal employment opportunity

EEOC Equal Employment Opportunity Commission

EEP exports enhancement program

EEPROM electrically erasable programmable read-only memory

EERU environmental emergency response unit

EE.UU. *Spanish* Estados Unidos (United States)

EEZ exclusive economic zone

EF efficiency (apartment); emission factor

EFA Epilepsy Foundation of America; essential fatty acids

EFCI Explicit Forward Congestion Indication

EFF Electronic Frontier Foundation; Experimental Forecast Facility

EFI electronic fuel injection [system]

eff. effective; efficiency

effic. efficiency

EFFNCY efficiency (apartment)

EFL English as a foreign language

EFM electronic fetal monitor

EFP exchange for physicals

EFris. East Frisian

EFS exchange of futures for swaps

EFT electronic funds transfer

EFTA European Free Trade Association

EFTPS Electronic Federal Tax Paying System

EFTS electronic funds transfer system

Eg. Egypt; Egyptian

.eg Egypt

e.g. *Latin* exempli gratia (for example)

EGA enhanced graphics adapter; enhanced graphics array; estimated gestational age

EGD electrogasdynamics

EGE Eagle County [CO] Regional Airport

EGF epidermal growth factor

EGmc East Germanic

EGP Egypt—pound (currency); exterior gateway protocol

EGSE electrical ground support equipment

EGTA ethyleneglycotetraacetic acid

Egypt. Egyptian

egyptol. egyptology

eh Engrossed in House

.eh Western Sahara

EHA Environmental Health Administration

eHEAL Electronic Health Economics Analysis Letters

EHEC enterohemorrhagic Escherichia coli

eHEL Electronic Health Economics Letters

EHF extremely high frequency

EHHE Environmental Hazards and Health Effects

EHIS Environmental Health Information Services

EHLS National Center for Environmental Health's Division of Environmental Health Laboratory Sciences

EHO emerging healthcare organization

EHP effective horsepower; electric horsepower

EHPC extended high priority command

ehr Engrossed in House—Reprint

EHR Environmental Health Review

EHS extremely hazardous substance

EHSA enhanced high system availability

EHV extra-high voltage

EHz exahertz

EI echo intensity

EIA Energy Information Administration; environmental impact assessment

EIB European Investment Bank

EIDE enhanced integrated drive electronics

EIEC enteroinvasive Escherichia coli

EIK eat-in kitchen

EIMWT Echo Integration-Mid-Water Trawl

EIN employer identification number

e-ink electronic ink

EIP engine intake pressure

EIRP Effective Isotropic Radiated Power

EIS electronic information standards; environmental impact statement

EISA extended industry standard architecture

EIT extreme-ultraviolet imaging telescope

EJ electronic announcer (patterned after DJ)

EJP excitatory junction potential

EK Eastman Kodak Co.

EKG electrocardiogram; electrocardiograph

EKY electrokymogram

el elevated railroad; Greek

EL electroluminescent; exposure level

el. elevation

E-LAM endothelial-leukocyte adhesion molecule

ELAP EtherTalk Link Access Protocol

ELCA Evangelical Lutheran Church of America

ELD electroluminescent display

ELEC electronics

elec. electric; electrical; electrician; electricity

elect. electronic

electr. electricity

elem. element; elementary

elev. elevator; elevation

ELF extremely low frequency

ELH early life history

el-hi elementary and high school

ELINT electronic intelligence

ELISA enzyme-linked immunoadsorbent assay

Eliz. Elizabethan

ellipt. elliptical; elliptically

ELM electronics module

ELMC electrical load management center

ELMI Enhanced Local Management Interface

ELN Environmental Librarian's Network

ELP El Paso International Airport

ELSI Ethical, Legal and Social Implications

ELSS extravehicular life support system

ELT emergency locator transmitters

ELV expendable launch vehicle

EM electromagnetic; electron microscope; enlisted man

E.M. Engineer of Mines

EMA Emergency Medicine Assembly

e-mail electronic mail

EMAP Environmental Monitoring and Assessment Program

EMB endometrial biopsy; eosin-methylene blue

EMBBS Emergency Medicine Bulletin Board System

EMC electromagnetic compatibility; electronic media claims

emcee master of ceremonies

EMEA Europe, Middle East, Asia

emer. emergency; *Latin* emerita (retired female); *Latin* emeritus (retired male)

EMF electromagnetic field; Emergency Medicine Foundation

e.m.f. electromotive force

EMFBI excuse me for butting in

EMFP Ethnic/Racial Minority Fellowship Programs

EMF RAPID Electric and Magnetic Fields Research and Public Information Dissemination Program

EMG electromyogram

EMGY emergency (shortwave transmission)

EMI educable mentally impaired; electromagnetic interference

EMIC Environmental Mutagen Information Center

EMIT enzyme-multiplied immunoassay technique

EMM expanded memory manager

e-money electronic money

emp emperor; empire

EMP electromagnetic pulse

emp. emperor; empire; empress

e.m.p. *Latin* ex modo praescripto (in the manner prescribed)

EMRA Emergency Medical Response Agency; Emergency Medicine Residents' Association

EMRS Electronic Medical Record System

EMS electrical muscle stimulation; Element Management System; Emergency Medical Service; European Monetary System; Event Management Service; expanded memory specification; expanded memory system

EMSC Emergency Medical Services for Children

EMT emergency medical technician

EMT-P emergency medical technician paramedic

EMTS environmental methods testing site

emu   electromagnetic unit

EMU   Eastern Mennonite University; Eastern Michigan University; European Monetary Union; extravehicular mobility unit

en   English

EN   end node; endocardium

ENA   Emergency Nurses Association

ENC   Encore

enc.   enclosed; enclosure

encl.   enclosed; enclosure

ency.   encyclopedia

encyc.   encyclopedia

encycl.   encyclopedia

Encycl. Brit.   *Encyclopaedia Britannica*

ENDEX   environmental index

endo   endocrine

ENDO   endometriosis

ENE   east-northeast; ethylnor-epinephrine

ENFJ   Extroversion iNtuition Feeling Judging (Myers-Briggs [personality] Type Indicator)

ENFP   Extroversion iNtuition Feeling Perception (Myers-Briggs [personality] Type Indicator)

ENG   electronystagmogram; electronystagmograph; electronystagmography

eng.   engine; engineer; engineering

Eng.   England; English

engg.   engineering

engin.   engineering

engr.   engineer; engrave; engraved; engraver; engraving

ENIAC   Electronic Numerical Integrator and Computer

enl.   enlarged; enlisted

ENMOC   El Niño Monitoring Center

ENS   ensign; ethylnorepinephrine

ENSO   El Niño/Southern Oscillation

ENT   ear, nose, and throat

ENTJ   Extroversion iNtuition Thinking Judging (Myers-Briggs [personality] Type Indicator)

entom.   entomology

enr   Enrolled bill

ENTP   Extroversion iNtuition Thinking Perception (Myers-Briggs [personality] Type Indicator)

entr.   entrance

env.   envelope

environ.   environment; environmental

ENW   Emergency Nursing World

eo   Esperanto

EO   ethylene oxide; executive order

e.o.   *Latin* ex officio (by virtue of office)

EOA   end of activity

EOB   end of block; executive office building; explanation of benefits

EOD   end of discussion

EOE   equal opportunity employer; errors and omissions excepted

EOF   end of file

EOG   electro-oculography; electro-olfactogram

EOGB   electro-optically guided bomb

EOH   Equal Opportunity Housing

EOI   evidence of insurability; expression of interest

EOJ end of job

EOL end of line

EOM end of message; end of month; extraocular motion; extraocular movement

EOMB explanation of Medicare benefits

EOMF extraocular motion full; extraocular movement full

EOMI extraocular muscles intact

EOS earth observation satellite; earth observing system; end of story; enter stop order

EOSAT Earth Observation Satellite Company

EOSDIS Earth Observing System Data and Information System

EOT end of thread; end of track; end of transmission

EOU end of user

EOUSA Executive Office for United States Attorneys

EOY end of year

Ep Ephesians

EP electro-photographic; European plan; extended play

EPA eicosapentanoic acid; Environmental Protection Agency

EPAct [National] Energy Policy Act

EPAD electrically powered actuation device

EP & R emergency preparedness and response

EPAT Early Psychosis Assessment Team

EPC Economic Policy Council; Evidence-based Practice Centers

EPCA Energy Policy and Conservation Act

EPCOT Experimental Prototype Community of Tomorrow

EPCRA Emergency Planning and Community Right-to-Know Act

EPD early packet discard

EPEC enteropathogenic Escherichia coli

EPG electronic program guide

Eph. Ephesians

EPHDP Electronic Public Health Development Project

EPHIN electron proton helium instrument

EPIC Electronic Privacy Information Center

EPIRB emergency position-indicating radio beacon

Epis. Episcopal; Episcopalian; Epistle

Episc. Episcopal; Episcopalian

Epist. Epistle

EPNL effective perceived noise level

EPO [Centers for Disease Control] Epidemiology Program Office; exclusive provider organization

EPP enhanced parallel port

EPR electron paramagnetic resonance; engine-pressure ratio

EPRI Electric Power Research Institute

E-print electronic [pre]print (that is, before publishing in a print journal)

EPROM erasable programmable read-only memory

EPS earnings per share; encapsulated PostScript

EPSF encapsulated PostScript files

EPSP excitatory postsynaptic potential

EPSS electrical power subsystem

EPT early pregnancy

EPU emergency power unit

e-publishing electronic publishing

e-purse electronic purse

EPV extended precision vector

EQ educational quotient; emotional quotient; equalize; equalizer; equip (shortwave transmission)

eq. equal; equation; equivalent

EQPT equipment (shortwave transmission)

eqq equations

EQU Equuleus (constellation)

equip. equipment

equiv. equivalence; equivalency; equivalent

Er erbium

ER emergency room; endoplasmic reticulum; Eritrea (international vehicle ID)

.er Eritrea

ERA earned run average; Economic Regulatory Administration; Equal Rights Amendment; exchange rate agreement

ERASER enhanced recognition and sensing radar

ERB Earth radiation budget

ERBE Earth Radiation Budget Experiment

ERBF effective renal blood flow

ERBS Earth Radiation Budget Satellite

ERC Easily Recognizable Code; emission reduction credit; Endometriosis Research Center

ERCP endoscopic retrograde cholangiopancreatography

ERDA Energy Research and Development Administration

ERF Engineering Research Facility

ERG electroretinogram

ERGO Euthanasia Research and Guidance Organization

ERI Eridanus (constellation)

ERIC Educational Resources Information Center

ERINT extended range interceptor

ERISA Employee Retirement Income Security Act

ERL [National Oceanic and Atmospheric Administration] Environmental Research Laboratories

ERM employee relationship management

ERN Eritrea—nakfa (currency)

ERO Energy Regulatory Office

EROS Earth Resources Observing Satellite

ERP early receptor potential

erron. erroneous; erroneously

ERS Economic Research Service

ert earth Relative Time

ERT estrogen replacement therapy

ERTS Earth Resources Technology Satellite

ERV expiratory reserve volume

es Engrossed in Senate; Spanish

Es einsteinium

ES El Salvador (international vehicle ID); end system; Extension Service

.es Spain

ESA Ecological Society of America; Economics and Statistics

Administration; Employment Standards Administration; Endangered Species Act; Environmentally Sensitive Area; European Space Agency

ESAD eat shit and die; electronic safe and arm device

ES & H environmental safety and health

ESB electrical stimulation of the brain

Esc escape

ESCA electron spectroscopy for chemical analysis

ESCAP Economic and Social Commission for Asia and the Pacific

ESCON Enterprise System Connection

ESCWA Economic and Social Commission for Western Asia

ESD electrostatic discharge

Esd. Esdras

ESDI enhanced small device interface

ESDIM [National Oceanic and Atmospheric Administration] Earth System Data and Information Management

Esdr. Esdras

ESDS electrostatic discharge sensitive

ESE east-southeast

ESF extended superframe

ESI end system identifier

ESFJ Extroversion Sensing Feeling Judging (Myers-Briggs [personality] Type Indicator)

ESFP Extroversion Sensing Feeling Perception (Myers-Briggs [personality] Type Indicator)

ESI enhanced serial interface

e-signature electronic signature

ES-IS End System-to-Intermediate System

e-site electronic site

Esk. Eskimo

ESL English as a second language

ESMC Eastern Space and Missile Center

ESMR electronic scanning microwave radiometer

ESMTP Extended Simple Mail Transfer Protocol

ESOL English for speakers of other languages

ESOP employee stock-ownership plan

ESP English for Specific Purposes; extrasensory perception; Spain—peseta (currency)

esp. especially

Esq. Esquire

esr Engrossed in Senate—Reprint

ESR electron spin resonance; erythrocyte sedimentation rate

ESRB Entertainment Software Ratings Board

Est Esther

EST Eastern Standard Time; electroshock therapy; Estonia (international vehicle ID)

est. established; estate; estimate; estimated

Est. Estonia; Estonian

estab. established

e-stamp electronic [postage] stamp

Esth. Esther

ESTJ Extroversion Sensing Thinking Judging (Myers-Briggs [personality] Type Indicator)

e-store   electronic store

ESTP   Extroversion Sensing Thinking Perception (Myers-Briggs [personality] Type Indicator)

esu   electrostatic unit

ESV   Earth satellite vehicle

ESWL   electrohydraulic shock wave lithotripsy; extracorporeal shock wave lithotripsy

ESWTR   [Environmental Protection Agency] Enhanced Surface Water Treatment Rule

et   Estonian

Et   ethyl

ET   Eastern Time; Egypt (international vehicle ID); elapsed time; embryo transfer; endotrachial; extraterrestrial

.et   Ethiopia

ETA   embryo toxicity assay; Employment and Training Administration; estimated time of arrival

e-tailing   electronic retailing

et al.   *Latin* et alia (and other things); *Latin* et alii (and other people)

ETAW   evapotranspiration of applied water

ETB   Ethiopia—birr (currency)

etc.   *Latin* et cetera (and so forth)

ETD   estimated time of departure

ETDP   Expert Tsunami Database for the Pacific

ETEC   enterotoxigenic Escherichia coli

ETF   embryo toxic factor

ETH   Ethiopia (international vehicle ID)

Eth.   Ethiopia; Ethiopian

ethnol.   ethnologist

ETIC   Environmental Teratology Information Center

e-ticket   electronic ticket

ETL   [National Oceanic and Atmospheric Administration] Environmental Technology Laboratory

ETLA   extended three-letter acronym (that is, four letters or more)

ETMS   enhanced traffic management system

ETO   European theater of operations; exchange traded option

ETOH   alcohol (ethanol)

ETP   early termination of pregnancy

ETR   equal transit rate

Etr.   Etruria

e-trader   electronic trader

ETS   Educational Testing Service; environmental tobacco smoke

et seq.   *Latin* et sequens (and the following one)

et. seqq.   *Latin* et sequentes (and the following ones)

ETSR   extraterrestrial solar spectral irradiance

ETT   endotrachial tube

et ux.   *Latin* et uxor (and wife)

ETV   educational television

ETX   end of text

etym.   etymological; etymology

eu   Basque

Eu   europium

EU   electronic unit; engineering units; European Union

EUA   examination under anesthesia

EUC   end-user computing; equatorial undercurrent

EUG Eugene Airport/Mahlon Sweet Field

EULA end-user license agreement

euphem. euphemistic; euphemistically

EUR European Economic and Monetary Union—euro

Eur. Europe; European

EURAILPASS European Railway Pass

EURATOM European Atomic Energy Community

EUROPOL European Police Office

EUS endoscopic ultrasonography; esophageal ultrasonography

Eutelsat European Telecommunications Satellite Organization

EUV extreme ultraviolet

eV electron volt

ev. evening; evenings

EVA extravehicular activity

eval. evaluation

evan. evangelical; evangelist

evang. evangelical; evangelist

evap. evaporate

EV-DO Evolution Data Only

eve. evening; evenings

evg. evening

EVV Evansville [IN] Regional Airport

EW emergency ward; enlisted woman

e-wallet electronic wallet

EWGA Executive Women's Golf Association

EWMP efficient water management practice

EWR Newark International Airport

EWRP [United States Department of Agriculture] Emergency Wetland Reserve Program

EWTN Eternal Word Television Network

EWU Eastern Washington University

Ex Exodus

ex. examination; example; except; exception; exchange; executive; exercise; express; extra

exam examination

exc. excellent; except; exception; excision

Exc. Excellency

excel. Excellent

exch. exchange; exchequer

excl. exclamation; excluding; exclusive

exclam. exclamation

exec executive

exec. executor

exerhead someone addicted to physical exercise

exh. exhibit

Ex-Im Export-Import Bank of the United States

Eximbank Export-Import Bank of the United States

EXLITE extended life tire

Exod. Exodus

exor. executor

exp exploratory; exponent; exponential

exp. expenses; experiment; experimental; expiration; export; express

expat expatriate

expd experienced

expo exposition

expr. expressing; expressive

expt. experiment

exptl. experimental

expwy expressway

expy expressway

exr. executor

exrx. executrix

ext. extension; exterior; external; externally; extinct; extra; extract; extremity

exx. examples

EY edition year

EYW Key West International Airport

Ez Ezekiel

EZ easy

EZE Ezeiza International Airport (Buenos Aires, Argentina)

Ezek. Ezekiel

e-zine electronic fan magazine

Ezk Ezekiel

F

f feminine; focal length; forte; function

F Fahrenheit; fail; false; farad; female; filial generation; fine; fluorine; fog; foul; franc; France (international vehicle ID); Friday

f. farthing; fine; folio; following; guilder

F. French

f/ f stop (relative aperture of a lens)

F2F face-to-face

fa Persian

FA fair; field artillery; fielding average; fire alarm; fluorescent antibody; football association

FAA Federal Aviation Administration; free of all average

f.a.a. free of all average

FAACTS Free AIDS Advice Counseling Treatment Support for People with or Affected by AIDS

FAAGL Foundation of the American Association of Gynecologic Laparoscopists

FAALC Federal Aviation Administration Logistics Center

FAAN Fellow of the American Academy of Nursing

FAATC Federal Aviation Administration Technical Center

fab fabulous

FAC freestanding ambulatory care

fac. facility; facilities; facsimile; faculty

FACCP Fellow of the American College of Chest Physicians

FACD Fellow of the American College of Dentists

FACHE Fellow of the American College of Healthcare Executives

FACM friable asbestos-containing material

FACMPE Fellow of the American College of Medical Practice Executives

FACNM Fellow of the American College of Nuclear Medicine

FACNP Fellow of the American College of Nuclear Physicians

FACOG Fellow of the American College of Obstetricians and Gynecologists

FACP Fellow of the American College of Physicians

FACR Fellow of the American College of Radiology

FACS Fellow of the American College of Surgeons

FACSM Fellow of the American College of Sports Medicine

FAD fish aggregating device; flavin adenine dinucleotide

FADM fleet admiral

FAF financial aid form

fah Failed Amendment House

Fah. Fahrenheit

FAHCT Foundation for the Accreditation of Hematopoietic Cell Therapy

Fahr. Fahrenheit

FAHS Federation of American Health Systems

FAI Fairbanks International Airport

FAIA Fellow of the American Institute of Architects

FAIM Foundation for the Advancement of Innovative Medicine

FALN *Spanish* Fuerzas Armadas de Liberación Nacional (Armed Forces of National Liberation)

fam. family; familiar

FAM Family Channel; Free and Accepted Masons

FAMC Federal Agricultural Mortgage Corporation

FAMOUS French-American Mid-Ocean Undersea Study

FAN Fetal Alcohol Network; Food Allergy Network

f and a fore and aft

fanzine fan magazine

FAO [United Nations] Food and Agriculture Organization

FAP Familial Adenomatous Polyposis

FAQ frequently asked questions

FAR Federal Acquisition Regulations

Far. faraday

FARB Federal Assistance Review Board

FARC *Spanish* Fuerzas Armadas Revolucionarias de Colombia (Revolutionary Armed Forces of Colombia)

Farmer Mac Federal Agricultural Mortgage Corporation

FARNET Federation of American Research Networks

FARS Fatal Accident Reporting System; Financial Accounting and Reporting System

FAS Federation of American Scientists; fetal alcohol syndrome; Foreign Agricultural Service

f.a.s. free alongside ship

FASA Federated Ambulatory Surgery Association

FASAB Federal Accounting Standards Advisory Board

FASB Financial Accounting Standards Board

fasc. fascicle

FASC freestanding ambulatory surgery center

FASEB Federation of American Societies for Experimental Biology

FAST flow actuated sediment trap; Food Allergy Survivors Together; fore-aft scanning technique

FAT file allocation table; Fresno Yosemite International Airport

fath fathom

FAU Florida Atlantic University

fax facsimile

FB foreign body; freight bill; fullback

FBA flexible benefit account

FBB Federal Bulletin Board

FBFM flood boundary floodway map

FBI Federal Bureau of Investigation

FBL fly by light

FBOC Figural Bottle Opener Collectors

FBS fasting blood sugar

FBW fly by wire

fc foot-candle

FC fire control

f.c. follow copy

FCA Farm Credit Administration

FCAP Fellow of the College of American Pathologists

fcap. foolscap

FCC Federal Communications Commission; fluid catalytic converter

f/cc fibers per cubic centimeter [of air]

FCCP Fellow of the College of Chest Physicians

FCCSET Federal Coordinating Council for Science, Engineering, and Technology

FCFS First Come First Served (scheduling method)

FCI Family Care International

FCIA Foreign Credit Insurance Association

FCIC Federal Crop insurance Corporation

FCIM Federated Council for Internal Medicine

FCIP fiber channel over IP

FCL Foldback Current Limiter

FCLB Federation of Chiropractic Licensing Boards

FCN function

FCO Leonardo da Vinci/Fiumicino Airport (Rome, Italy)

FCOJ frozen concentrated orange juice

FCOL for crying out loud

fcp. foolscap

FCRDC [National Cancer Institute] Frederick Cancer Research and Development Center

FCS Fellow of the Chemical Society; frame check sequence

FCST Federal Council for Science and Technology

FCV flow control valve

fcy. fancy

FCZ fishery conservation zone

Fd ferredoxin

FD fatal dose; fire department; focal distance; foundation damage

F.D. *Latin* Fidei Defensor (Defender of the Faith)

FDA Food and Drug Administration

FDC fully distributed cost

FD & C food, drugs, and cosmetics

FDD floppy disk drive

FDDI fiber distributed data interface

FDE Failure Detection Electronics; Flight Dynamics Engineers

FDF flight dynamics facility; fundamentally different factors

FDG 18F-fluorodeoxyglucose

FDHD floppy drive high density

FDI foreign direct investment

FDIC Federal Deposit Insurance Corporation

FDISK fixed disk [command]

FDLI facility data link

FDLI Food and Drug Law Institute

FDLP Federal Depository Library Program

FDM frequency-division multiplexing

FDMD Foundation for Depression and Manic Depression

FDNB fluoro-2,4-dinitrobenzene

FDP fibrin/fibrinogen degradation products

FDQN fully qualified domain name

FDR flight data recorder; formal dining room; Franklin Delano Roosevelt

FDROTFL falling down rolling on the floor laughing

Fe iron

FE field evaluation

FEA Federal Energy Administration; finite element analysis

Feb. February

FEB Federal Executive Board

fec. *Latin* fecit (he or she made or did it)

FEC Federal Election Commission; forward error correction

FECA Federal Employees' Compensation Act

FECN forward explicit congestion notification

fed federal agent

Fed Federal Reserve System

FED field emission device; field-emitting diode

fed. federal; federated; federation

FEDLINK Federal Library and Information Network

fedn. federation

FEDRIP Federal Research in Progress (database)

FEDS federal energy data system

FEF forced expiratory flow

FEHEM front-end hardware emulator

FEI Federal Executive Institute

FEIP Fast Ethernet Interface Processor

FEIS final environmental impact statement

FELA Federal Employer's Liability Act

FeLV feline leukemia virus

fem. female; feminine

FEMA Federal Emergency Management Agency

FEOM full extraocular motion; full extraocular movement

FEP front-end processor

FEPA Fair Employment Practices Act

FEPC Fair Employment Practices Commission

FEPCA Federal Environmental Pesticides Control Act

FERA Federal Emergency Relief Administration

FERC Federal Energy Regulatory Commission

FERS Federal Employees Retirement System

fess confess

FET federal estate tax; federal excise tax; field-effect transistor; frozen embryo transfer

FETLA further extended three-letter acronym (that is, five letters)

feud. feudal; feudalism

FEV forced expiratory volume

ff fortissimo

FF fast forward

ff. folios; following

FFA free for all; free from alongside; Future Farmers of America

FFALP free for all links page

FFB Federal Financing Bank; Foundation Fighting Blindness

FFDCA Federal Food, Drug and Cosmetic Act

fff fortississimo

FFFSG Fossil Fuel Fired Steam Generator

FFP firm-fixed price; fresh frozen plasma

FFR Fellow of the Faculty of Radiologists

FFRDC federally funded research and development center

FFS fee-for-service; for further study

FFT fast Fourier transform

FFV First Families of Virginia

FG field goal; fine grain

FGA foreign general average

FGAR N-formylglycinamide ribotide

FGF fibroblast growth factor

FGIS Federal Grain Inspection Service

FGM female genital mutilation

FH family history; Food for the Hungry; future husband

FHA Farmers Home Administration; Federal Highway Administration; Federal Housing Administration; forced hot air (furnace); Future Homemakers of America

FHBC Federation of Historical Bottle Clubs

FHBM floodway hazard boundary map

FHC Friends' Health Connection

FHCQ Foundation for Health Care Quality

FHF International Federation of Health Funds

FHFB Federal Housing Finance Board

FH$_4$ tetrahydrofolic acid

FHI Family Health International; Food for the Hungry International

FHLB Federal Home Loan Banks

FHLBB Federal Home Loan Bank Board

FHLMC Federal Home Loan Mortgage Corporation

fhp friction horsepower

FHR fetal heart rate; fetal heart rhythm

FHSA Federal Hazardous Substances Act

FHT fetal heart tone

FHWA Federal Highway Administration

FHx family history

fi Finnish

FI fiscal intermediary

.fi Finland

FIA Federal Insurance Administration; feline infectious anemia

FIAT *Italian* Fabbrica Italiana Automobili Torino (Italian Automobile Factory of Turin)

fib fibrillation

FIBS field by information blending and smoothing

FIC Federal Information Centers

FICA Federal Insurance Contributions Act

FICO Financing Corporation

FICON fiber connectivity

fict. fiction; fictitious

FID free induction decay

fid. fidelity

FIDI Fishery Information, Data, and Statistics Service

FIFA Federation of International Football (that is, soccer) Associations

fi.fa. *Latin* fieri facias (cause [it] to be done)

FIFO first in, first out

FIFRA Federal Insecticide, Fungicide, and Rodenticide Act

FIG fishing industry grants

fig. figurative; figuratively; figure

FIGLU formiminoglutamic acid

FIGS fully integrated groups

FIIK fucked if I know

FIL father-in-law

FIM Finland—markka (currency); friable insulation material

FIMA financial management system

FIMIS Fishery Management Information System

FIN Finland (international vehicle ID)

fin. finance; financial; finish; finished

Fin. Finland; Finnish

fin indep financially independent

Finn. Finnish

fin sec financially secure

FIO free in and out

FIO2 fraction of inspired oxygen

FIOS free in and out stowage

FIR far infrared

fireplc fireplace

FIRM flood insurance rate map

FIRS Federal Information Relay Service

FIRST Foundation for Ichthyosis and Related Skin Types

FIS Flood Insurance Study; Foundation for Infinite Survival

FISH first in, still here

FISU fill-in signal unit

FIT frequent international traveler

FITB fill in the blank

FITC fluorescein isothiocyanate

FITS flexible image transport system

FIV feline immunodeficiency virus

5-HTP 5-hydroxytryptamine

FIX Federal Internet Exchange

fj Fijian

FJ found (shortwave transmission)

.fj Fiji

FJD Fiji—dollar

FJI Fiji (international vehicle ID)

.fk Falkland Islands

fka formerly known as

F key function key

FKNMS Florida Keys National Marine Sanctuary

FKP Falkland Islands—pound (currency)

fL foot-lambert

FL finished lower level; flanker (football); floor; Florida; focal length; Liechtenstein (international vehicle ID)

fl. flanker; floor; *Latin* floruit (flourished); flourished; fluid

FLA Florida Marlins; foreign language acquisition

Fla. Florida

FLAME Family Life and Maternity Education

FLASER forward looking infrared laser radar

fld. field

fl. dr. fluid dram
Flem. Flemish
FLETC Federal Law Enforcement Training Center
Flint. Flintshire
FLIR forward-looking infrared
FLK funny-looking kid
FLL Fort Lauderdale/Hollywood International Airport
F/LMR first and last month's rent
FLO Florence [SC] Regional Airport
flop floating-point operation
flops floating-point operations per second
Flor. Florida
FLOTUS First Lady of the United States
fl. oz. fluid ounce
flr. floor
FLRA Federal Labor Relations Authority
FLS Front Line States
FLSA Fair Labor Standards Act
flu influenza
Fm fermium
FM field manual; field marshal; frequency modulation; friable material
fm. fathom; from
.fm Micronesia
FMA Federal Marriage Amendment
FMB Federal Maritime Board
FMC Federal Maritime Commission
FMCS Federal Mediation and Conciliation Service
FMD foot-and-mouth disease
fMet formylmethionine
fMet-tRNA formylmethionyl tRNA

FMHA Farmers Home Administration
FMI for more information
FMIS Field Management Information System; Financial Management Information System
FMLA Family Medical Leave Act
fml dr formal dining room
FMN flavin mononucleotide
FMO Flatland Meteorological Observatory
FMP Fisheries Management Plan
FMPOV from my point of view
FMS financial management service; flight management system
FMT flexible metallic tubing
FMTY from me to you
FMU Francis Marion University
FMV fair market value
FN foreign national
fn. footnote
FNA fine needle aspiration [biopsy]
FNASR first North American serial rights
FNC Federal Networking Council
FNIC Food and Nutrition Information Center
FNLM Friends of the National Library of Medicine
FNMA Federal National Mortgage Association
FNS Food and Nutrition Service
FNT Bishop International Airport (Flint, MI)
FNU first name unknown
fo Faroese
FO field-grade officer; field order; finance officer; flight officer; foreign office; fuck off

fo. folio

.fo Faeroe Islands

FOA full operational assessment

FOAD fall over and die; fuck off and die

FOAF friend of a friend

foamcrete concrete foam

FOB father of the bride; foreign body

f.o.b. free on board

FOBT fecal occult blood testing

FOC Faint Object Camera; freedom of choice

f.o.c. free of charge

FOCI [National Oceanic and Atmospheric Administration] Fisheries-Oceanography Coordinated Investigations

FOCUS Fisheries Oceanography Cooperative Users System

FOD foreign object damage

FOE Fraternal Order of Eagles; Friends of the Earth

FOG fiber optic gyro; father of the groom

FOI freedom of information

FOIA Freedom of Information Act

FOIRL fiber-optic inter-repeater link

FOK fill or kill order

fol. folio; following

FOLAN Flight Operations Local Area Network

foll. folios; followed

FOM field operations manual

FOMC Federal Open Market Committee

FONSI finding of no significant impact

FOP flight operations plan

FOR Fornax (constellation)

for. foreign; forest; forestry

f.o.r. free on rail

FORRUM Foundation for Objective Research and Reporting on the Unexplained Mysterious

fort. fortification; fortified

fortif. fortification

FORTRAN formula translator (programming language)

FOS free on steamer

FOSA Federation of Spine Associations

FOSE Federal Office Systems Exposition

FOT free on truck

FOTCL falling off the chair laughing

4-H head, heart, hands, and health (program)

4WD four-wheel drive

FoV field of view

f.o.w. first open water

fp fireplace; freezing point

FP family practice; fireplace; flight plan

fp. foolscap

FPA Fair Practices Act; Federal Pesticide Act; focal plane array; Foreign Press Association; Franklin P. Adams; free of particular average

FPC family practice clinic; Federal Power Commission; fish protein concentrate; Friends Peace Committee

FPCA Family Planning Councils of America

FPD flame photometric detector; flat panel display

FPGA field programmable gated array

FPI fixed price incentive

FPIA Family Planning International Assistance

fpl fireplace

FPLC fast protein liquid chromatography

fpm feet per minute

FPO federal protective officer; fleet post office

FPR Federal Procurement Regulations; fixed price redeterminable

FPRA forward pricing rate agreement

FPRS Federal Property Resources Service

fps Failed Passage Senate; feet per second; foot-pound-second; frames per second

FPS first person shooter

FPSS fine pointing sun sensor

FPSSE fine pointing sun sensor electronics

FPU family protection unit; floating point unit

FQDN fully qualified domain name

FQHN fully qualified host name

fr fraction; French

Fr francium

FR family room; *Federal Register*; fire damage; full rate

fr. frame; franc; from

Fr. Father; France; Frau; French; Friar; Friday

.fr France

f.r. *Latin* folio recto (right-hand page *or* obverse of page)

FRA Federal Railroad Administration; Rhein-Main Airport (Frankfurt, Germany)

FRACP Fellow of the Royal Australasian College of Physicians

FRAD Frame Relay access device

frag fragment

FRAME Fund for the Replacement of Animals in Medical Experiments

Frank. Frankish

FRAP Federal Rules of Appellate Procedure

frat fraternity

FRAXA Fragile X Syndrome Research Foundation

FRB Federal Reserve Board

FRC Federal Records Center; functional redundancy checking; functional residual capacity

FRCD Family Resource Center on Disabilities

FRCP Federal Rules of Civil Procedure; Fellow of the Royal College of Physicians

FRCP(C) Fellow of the Royal College of Physicians (Canada)

FRCP(E) Fellow of the Royal College of Physicians (Edinburgh)

FRCP(I) Fellow of the Royal College of Physicians (Ireland)

FRCS Fellow of the Royal College of Surgeons

FRCS(C) Fellow of the Royal College of Surgeons (Canada)

FRCS(E) Fellow of the Royal College of Surgeons (Edinburgh)

FRCS(I) Fellow of the Royal College of Surgeons (Ireland)

FRD Federal Rules Decisions; functional requirements document

FREIDA Fellowship and Residency Electronic Interactive Database Access System

freq. frequency; frequent; frequentative; frequently

frex for example

FRF follicle-stimulating hormone-releasing factor; France—franc

FRG Federal Republic of Germany

FRGS Fellow of the Royal Geographical Society

FRH follitropin-releasing hormone

Fri. Friday

Fris. Frisian

Frisco San Francisco

Frl. Fräulein

FRM fixed rate mortgage

FRMAC Federal Radiological Management Assessment Center

FRN floating rate note

FRNT front

FROM full range of motion; full range of movement

front. frontispiece

frosh freshman

FRP fiberglass reinforced plastic

FRPG fantasy role playing game

frplc. fireplace

FRS Federal Reserve System; Fellow of the Royal Society

Frs. Frisian

FRSC Fellow of the Royal Society (Canada)

FRSI Flexible Reusable Surface Insulation

frt. freight

FRTM functional requirements traceability matrix

frwy. freeway

FS File Separator; Foreign Service; Forest Service

FSA flexible spending account; Food Security Act

FSAA full scene anti-aliasing

FSC Food Safety Consortium

FSD full scale development; Sioux Falls Airport/Joe Foss Field

FSE fetal scalp electrode; file server Ethernet

FSH follicle stimulating hormone

FSH-RF follicle stimulating hormone-releasing factor

FSH-RH follicle stimulating hormone-releasing hormone

FSI Forensic Science International

FSIS Food Safety and Inspection Service

FSL [National Oceanic and Atmospheric Administration] Forecast Systems Laboratory

FSLIC Federal Savings and Loan Insurance Corporation

FSM flight synchronizer module; Fort Smith [AR] Regional Airport

FSMB Federation of State Medical Boards of the United States

FSO Foreign Service Office

FSS Federal Supply Service; Forensic Science Society

FSSP forward-scattering spectrometer probe

FSSRP Fast Simple Server Redundancy Protocol

FST Fast Sequenced Transport

FSTS Federal Secure Telephone Service

FSU Florida State University; former Soviet Union

FSW flight software

FT Fourier transform; free throw

ft. foot; fort; fortification

F/T full time

FTA fun, travel, and adventure; Future Teachers of America

FTA-ABS fluorescent treponemal antibody absorption

FTAM File Transfer, Access, and Management; file transfer and access method

FTASB faster than a speeding bullet

FTC Federal Trade Commission

ft-c foot-candle

FTCM Foundation for Traditional Chinese Medicine

FTE full-time equivalent

FTF face-to-face

fth. fathom

FTI free thyroxine index

FTIR Fourier transform infrared radiometer

FTL faster than light

ft-lb foot-pound

FTN finger to nose (neurological test)

FTO field training officer

FTP File Transfer Protocol

FTRS National Library of Medicine's Full-Text Retrieval System

FTS Federal Telecommunications System; Fourier transform spectrometer

FTSG full thickness skin graft

FTT failure to thrive

FTTC fiber to the curb

FTTH fiber to the home

FTU Formazin Turbidity Unit

FTZ free trade zone

FU fouled up; fucked up

F/U follow-up

fubar fouled (or fucked) up beyond all reality (or recognition or repair)

FUBB fucked up beyond belief

fuc fucose

fuck The claim that *fuck* is an

acronym is demonstrably false. It is an old word of Germanic origin.

fud fuddy-duddy

FUD fear, uncertainty, and disinformation; fear, uncertainty, and doubt

FUDR fluorodeoxyuridine

FUDT Newsletter *Forensic Urine Drug Testing Newsletter*

FUF Facing the Uncertain Future (study)

FUNI frame user network interface

FUO fever of unknown origin

fur. furlong

furn furnished

fut. future; futures

FUTA Federal Unemployment Tax Act

FV fantasy violence

f.v. *Latin* folio verso (on the back of the page)

FVC forced vital capacity

FW filter wheel; future wife

FWA Fixed Wireless Access; Fort Wayne International Airport

FWB friend with benefits; four-wheel brake

FWCA Fish and Wildlife Coordination Act

fwd forward

FWD four-wheel drive; front-wheel drive

FWHM full width at half maximum

FWIW for what it's worth

F-word fuck

FWPCA Federal Water Pollution Control Act

FWS Fish and Wildlife Service

FWV fixed-wing vehicle

fwy freeway

fx fracture

FX foreign exchange; Fox cable TV channel

FXA foreign exchange agreement

FXN function

FXO Foreign Exchange Office

FXS Foreign Exchange Station

fy Frisian

FY fiscal year

FYA for your advice; for your amusement; for your attention

FYC for your consideration

FYEO for your eyes only

FYF for your file

FYI for your information

FYROM The Former Yugoslav Republic of Macedonia

FYV Drake Field/Fayetteville [AR] Municipal Airport

FZS Fellow of the Zoological Society

G

g acceleration of gravity; gram; -ing (shortwave transmission)

G conductance; games played; gauss; gay (as in personal ads); general admission; genitive; German; gigabyte; good; grand (that is, $1000); gravitational constant; guanine

g. gender; gourde; guilder; guinea

G. gulf

<G> grin

G2G got to go

G2H go to hell

G2LKB got to leave keyboard

G2R got to run

G7 Group of 7 (Canada, France, Germany, Italy, Japan, United Kingdom, United States)

G8 Group of 8 (Canada, France, Germany, Italy, Japan, Russia, United Kingdom, United States)

ga go ahead; Irish

Ga Galatians; gallium

GA general agent; general anesthesia; General Assembly; general average; Georgia; go ahead (shortwave transmission); good afternoon (shortwave transmission)

ga. gauge

.ga Gabon

GAA Gastroenterolgy Administration Assembly; goals against average

GAAP generally accepted accounting principles

GAAS generally accepted auditing standards

GABA gamma-aminobutyric acid

GAC get a clue; global area coverage; granular activated carbon

GACT granular activated carbon treatment

GAD glutamate decarboxylase

Gael. Gaelic

GAF gay Asian female; geographic adjustment factor; global assessment of functioning

GAG Graphic Artists Guild

GAGAS generally accepted government auditing standards

GAL get a life

gal. gallon

Gal. Galatians

gal/cycle gallons per cycle

GALEN Generalized Architecture for Languages, Encyclopaedias, and Nomenclatures [in Medicine]

GALT gut-associated lymphoid tissue

galv. galvanized

GAM gay Asian male

G & A general and administrative [cost]

G & S Gilbert and Sullivan

GAO General Accounting Office

GAP Group for the Advancement of Psychiatry

GAPA ground-to-air pilotless aircraft

gar garden

GAR Grand Army of the Republic

GAS group A streptococci

GASNET Global Anesthesiology Server Network

GASP Group Against Smoking in Public

GATT General Agreement on Tariffs and Trade

GAW Global Atmospheric Watch; guaranteed annual wage

GAWH Global Alliance for Women's Health

gaz. gazette; gazetteer

Gb gigabit

GB gallbladder; gigabyte; government and binding; Great Britain; Great Britain (international vehicle ID); Green Bay Packers

.gb United Kingdom (United Kingdom of Great Britain and Northern Ireland)

GBA Alderney [Channel Islands] (international vehicle ID); give better address (short-

wave transmission)

GBC general business conditions

GBF gay Black female; Great Books Foundation

GBFN goodbye for now

GBG gonadal steroid-binding globulin; Guernsey [Channel Islands] (international vehicle ID)

GBH gamma benzene hexachloride; great big hug

GBJ Jersey [Channel Islands] (international vehicle ID)

GBL ground-based laser

GBM gay Black male; Isle of Man (international vehicle ID)

GBP Great Britain—pound sterling

Gbps gigabits per second

GBps gigabytes per second

GBRS generic block recording system

GBS George Bernard Shaw

GBTM get back to me

GBTW get back to work

GByte gigabyte

GBZ Gibraltar (international vehicle ID)

Gc gigacycle

GC gas chromatograph; gas chromatography; guanine and cytosine (base pair in polynucleic acids)

GCA ground-controlled approach; Guatemala (international vehicle ID)

GCAC generic connection admission control

GCB Knight of the Grand Cross, Order of the Bath

GCC global climatic change; Gulf Cooperation Council

g.c.d. greatest common divisor

GCDIS Global Change Data and Information System

GCF ground communications facility

g.c.f. greatest common factor

GCMD Global Change Master Directory

GC/MS gas chromatography/mass spectrometry

GCPS Global Climate Perspectives System

G-CSF granulocyte colony-stimulating factor

GCT Greenwich civil time

GCW gross combination weight

gd Scots Gaelic

Gd gadolinium

GD geologic division; goddamn; good (shortwave transmission); good for the day order

gd. good

.gd Grenada

G.D. grand duchy

GD & R grinning, ducking, and running

GD & T geometric dimensioning and tolerancing

GDB Genome Data Base

GDC General Dental Council

GDI graphic device interface

G.D.I. one who is not a member of a fraternity or sorority (from "god-damned independent")

GDIP General Defense Intelligence Program

GDL Miguel Hidalgo y Costilla Airport (Guadalajara, Mexico)

gd lkg good-looking

GDP gross domestic product; ground into double plays (baseball)

GDPS global data-processing system

GDR German Democratic Republic

GDS great dark spot; ground data system

GDSIDB Global Digital Sea Ice Data Bank

GDT global descriptor table

Ge germanium

GE gastroesophageal; General Electric Co.; Georgia (international vehicle ID); good evening (shortwave transmission)

.ge Georgia (Republic of)

GEBA Global Energy Balance Archive

GEBCO General Bathymetric Chart of the Oceans

GEC global environmental change

GED general equivalency diploma; general educational development

GEENET Global Environmental Epidemiology Network

GEG Spokane International Airport

G-8 Group of 8 (Australia, Canada, EU, Japan, Spain, Sweden, Switzerland, United States)

GEK geomagnetic electrokinetograph

gel gelatin

GEL Georgia—lari (currency)

GELNET Global Health and Environment Library Network

GEM Gemini; ground-effect machine

GEMS Global Environment Monitoring System

gen. gender; general; generally; generator; generic; genitive; genus

Gen. general; Genesis

GENE-TOX Genetic Toxicology

genit. genitive

genl. general

Gen-X Generation X

Gen-Y Generation Y

GEO genetically engineered organism; geosynchronous earth orbit

GEODAS Geophysical Data System

geog. geographic; geography

geogr. geographic; geography

geol. geologic; geological; geology

geom. geometric; geometry

GEOS Geodynamics Experimental Ocean Satellite

GEOSAT Geodetic Satellite

GEOTAIL Geomagnetic Tail Laboratory

G=F grips equal and firm

GER gastroesophageal reflux

ger. gerund

Ger. German; Germany

GERD gastroesophageal reflux disease

Germ. German; Germany

GESS Graphics Executive Support System

GEU gyroscope electronics unit

GeV giga-electron volts

GF girlfriend

.gf French Guiana

GFCI ground fault circuit interrupter

GFDL [National Oceanic and Atmospheric Administration]

Geophysical Fluid Dynamics Laboratory

GFE government-furnished equipment

GFF glass fiber filter

GFI government-furnished information

GFP government-furnished property

GFR glomerular filtration rate

GFWC General Federation of Women's Clubs

GG going (shortwave transmission)

GGN gotta go now

GGP Gateway-to-Gateway Protocol

GGPA graduate grade-point average

GGS global geospace science

GH Ghana (international vehicle ID); growth hormone

.gh Ghana

GHA Greenwich hour angle

GHAA Group Health Association of America

GHB gamma y-hydroxybutyrate

GHC Ghana—cedi (currency)

GHCN Global Historical Climate Network

GHDNet Global Health Disaster Network

GHF gay Hispanic female

GHG greenhouse gas

GHM gay Hispanic male

GHNet Global Health Network

GHQ general headquarters

GHRF growth hormone-releasing factor

GHRH growth hormone-releasing hormone

GHz gigahertz

gi gill

GI galvanized iron; gastrointestinal; general issue; glycemic index; Government Issue

.gi Gibraltar

Gib. Gibraltar

Gibr. Gibraltar

GID general improvement district

GIF graphics interchange format

GIFA Governing International Fisheries Agreement

GIFT gamete intrafallopian tube transfer

gig gigabyte

GIG Galeão International Airport (Rio de Janeiro, Brazil)

GIGO garbage in, garbage out

GIH growth hormone inhibiting hormone

GILS Government Information Locator Service

GIN Greenland-Iceland-Norway

GINC Global Information Network on Chemicals

GIP gastric inhibitory polypeptide; gastric inhibitory peptide; Gibraltar—pound (currency)

GIPME Global Investigation of Pollution in the Marine Environment

GIS Geographic Information System

GISS Goddard Institute for Space Studies

GIT Group Inclusive Tour

GIWIST gee I wish I'd said that

GIX Global Internet Exchange

GJ gigajoule

GJF gay Jewish female

GJM gay Jewish male

GJT Walker Field Airport (Grand Junction, CO)

Gk. Greek

GKA government key access

gl Galician

GL guidelines

gl. gloss

.gl Greenland

Gla 4-carboxyglutamic acid

GLA gamma-linoleic acid; Glasgow International (Abbotsinch) Airport

GLAAD Gay and Lesbian Alliance Against Defamation

GLAMIS Grants and Loans Accounting and Management Information System

GLAS Goddard Laboratory of Atmospheric Sciences

GLBT gay/lesbian/bisexual/transgender

GLBTQ gay/lesbian/bisexual/transgender/queer; gay/lesbian/bisexual/transgender/questioning

GLC gas-liquid chromatography

GLCFS Great Lakes Coastal Forecasting System

gld. guilder

GLERL Great Lakes Environmental Research Laboratory

GLFC Great Lakes Fisheries Commission

GLFS Great Lakes Forecasting System

GLG goofy little grin

GLGH good luck and good hunting

GLIN Great Lakes Information Network

gliss. glissando

GLMA Gay and Lesbian Medical Association; Great Lakes Maritime Academy

GLO General Land Office

GLOBE Global Learning and Observations to Benefit the Environment

G-LOC G[ravity]-induced loss of consciousness

Glos. Gloucestershire

GLOSS Global Sea Level Observing System

gloss. glossary

GLOW gross lift-off weight

GLPF Great Lakes Protection Fund

gls glass

glu glucose

glutes gluteus muscles

GLWQA Great Lakes Water Quality Agreement

GM general manager; General Motors Corp.; good morning (shortwave transmission); grand master

gm. gram

.gm Gambia

GMAC General Motors Acceptance Corporation

GMAN general maneuver

G-man [United States] Government man (FBI agent)

GMAT Graduate Management Admissions Test; Greenwich mean astronomical time

Gmc Germanic

GMC General Motors Corporation; giant molecular cloud

GMCC Geophysical Monitoring for Climatic Change

GMCSF granulocyte-macrophage colony-stimulating factor

GMD Gambia—dalasi (currency)

GMDSS Global Maritime Distress and Safety System

GME graduate medical education

GMENAC Graduate Medical Education National Advisory Committee

GMF general mailing facility

G/Mi grams per mile

GMIS Grants Management Information System

GMO genetically modified organism

GMP guanosine monophosphate

GMS Gomori's methenamine-silver stain

gmt gourmet

GMT Greenwich mean time

GMTA great minds think alike

GMU gyro mechanical unit

GMW gram-molecular weight

gn general; green; Guarani; guinea

Gn Genesis

GN good night (shortwave transmission); ground network

.gn Guinea

GND ground (shortwave transmission)

gnd. ground

GNF Guinea—franc

GNI gross national income

GNMA Government National Mortgage Association

GNP geriatric nurse practitioner; gross national product

GnRH gonadotropin-releasing hormone

GNS get nearest server

GO general order; ground out

GOCO government-owned/contractor-operated

GOES Geostationary Orbiting Environmental Satellite

GOGO government-owned/government-operated

GOK God only knows

GOLDFISH Generation of Little Descriptions for Improving and Sustaining Health

GOLF global oscillations at low frequency

golf crs golf course

GOMER get out of my emergency room

GOMOS Global Ozone Monitoring by Occultation of Stars

GOMS Geostationary Operational Meteorological Satellite

GOOS Global Ozone Observing System

GOP Grand Old Party (the Republican Party)

GO PRI send private mail (that is, don't send e-mail)

GOPO government-owned/privately-operated

GOsC General Osteopathic Council

GOT glutamic-oxaloacetic transaminase; Landvetter Airport (Göteborg, Sweden)

GOTFIA groaning on the floor in agony

Goth. Gothic

gour gourmet

gov. government

Gov. governor

GOV government owned vehicle

.gov government agency

govt. government

GOWON Gulf Offshore Weather Observing Network

GP games played; general practitioner; general purpose

gp. group

.gp Guadeloupe

GPA grade point average

GPAD gallons per acre per day

GPB glossopharyngeal breathing

GPC general purpose computer; gallons per capita

GPCC Global Precipitation Climatology Center

GPCD gallons per capita per day

GPCI geographic practice cost index

gpd gallons per day

gpf gallons per flush

gpg grams per gallon

GPF gay professional female; general protection fault

gph gallons per hour

GPI Gingival-Periodontal Index; Graphics Programming Interface

GPIB general purpose interface bus

GPIEM International Marine Environment Award

GPIN Group Practice Improvement Network

gpm gallons per minute

GPM gay professional male

GPN graduate practical nurse

GPO general post office; Government Printing Office

GPPM graphics pages per minute

GPR ground penetrating radar

GPRA Government Performance and Results Act

GPRS general packet radio service

gps gallons per second

GPS global positioning satellite; global positioning system

GPSG generalized phrase structure grammar

GPT glutamic-pyruvic transaminase

GPWW group practice without walls

GQ general quarters; *Gentlemen's Quarterly*

.gq Equatorial Guinea

GR general relativity; Greece (international vehicle ID)

gr. grade; grain; gram; gravity; great; gross; group

Gr. Greece; Greek

.gr Greece

GR8 great

GRA Geriatric Resource Assembly

grad graduate

grad. gradient

gram. grammar

GR & D grinning, running, and ducking

GRAS generally recognized as safe

GRASS Geographic Resources Analysis Support System

GRB Austin Straubel International Airport (Green Bay, WI); gamma-ray burst

Gr. Brit. Great Britain

GRC Government Relations Committee

GRD Greece—drachma

grdn garden

GRE Graduate Record Examination

GRE-A Graduate Record Exam-Analytical

GRE-Q Graduate Record Exam-Quantitative

GRE-V Graduate Record Exam-Verbal

GRH gonadotropin-releasing hormone

GRIB gridded binary (data format)

GRID Global Resource Information Database

GRM Geophysical Research Mission

grn green

grnd ground

gro. gross

GRP glass-reinforced plastic

grp. group

GRR Gerald R. Ford International Airport (Grand Rapids, MI)

GRS great red spot

GRT gross register ton

grt. great

GRU *Russian* Glavnoe razvedyvatel'noe upravlenie (Chief Intelligence Directorate); Grus (constellation); Guarulhos International Airport (São Paulo, Brazil)

gr. wt. gross weight

GS games started; general staff; ground speed

GSA Gay-Straight Alliance; General Services Administration; Genetics Society of America; Geological Society of America; Gerontological Society of America; Girl Scouts of America; Great Salinity Anomaly

GSC general staff corps

GSCR group-specific community rating

GSDB Genome Sequence Data Base

GSE geocentric solar ecliptic; ground support electronics; ground support equipment

gse down goose down

GSFC [National Aeronautics and

Space Administration] Goddard Space Flight Center

GSH glutathione; grand slam home runs

GSL Guaranteed Student Loan

GSM global system for mobile communications

GSO general staff officer; Piedmont Triad International Airport (Greensboro, NC)

GSP Greenville/Spartanburg International Airport

GSR galvanic skin response

GSRIF Goldenhar Syndrome Research and Information Fund

GSSG glutathione disulfide

GST Greenwich sidereal time

GSTT generation-skipping transfer tax

G-suit gravity suit

GSUSA Girl Scouts of the United States of America

GSW gunshot wound

GT Grand Touring; Gran Turismo; gross ton

gt. gilt; great; *Latin* gutta (a drop, as of liquid medicine)

.gt Guatemala

GTAS Generic Testing and Analysis System

Gt. Brit. Great Britain

GTC good 'til canceled

gtd. guaranteed

GTG getting (shortwave transmission)

GTFOOH get the fuck out of here

GTN Global Trends Network

GTOS Global Terrestrial Observing System

GTP guanosine triphosphate

GTQ Guatemala—quetzal (currency)

gtr. guitar

GTS gas turbine ship; Global Telecommunications Service

GTT Global Title Translation; glucose tolerance test

gtt. *Latin* guttae (drops, as of liquid medicine)

gu Gujarati

GU genitourinary; Guam

.gu Guam

Gua guanine

GUA La Aurora International Airport (Guatemala City, Guatemala)

Guad. Guadelupe

guar. guarantee; guaranteed

Guat. Guatemala

GUC Gunnison County [CO] Airport

GUD good (shortwave transmission)

GUI graphical user interface

Guin. Guinea

GUT grand unified theory

guttat. *Latin* guttatim (drop by drop)

GUY Guyana (international vehicle ID)

Guy. Guyana

gv Manx

GV give (shortwave transmission)

g.v. gravimetric volume

GVA Geneva International Airport

GVH graft versus host

GVHR graft versus host reaction

GVM gross vehicle mass

GVP gasoline vapor pressure

GVW gross vehicle weight

GW gigawatt; groundwater

.gw Guinea-Bissau

GWB George Washington Bridge

GWF gay White female

GWH gigawatt-hour

GWI Greenhouse Warming Index

GWM gay White male

GWOT global war on terror

GWP global warming potential; gross world product

GWTW *Gone with the Wind*

GWU George Washington University

GWVI Gulf War veteran's illnesses

Gy gray

.gy Guyana

GYD Guyana—dollar

gym gymnasium

gym. gymnastics

gyn. gynecology

gyro gyrocompass; gyroscope

GySgt gunnery sergeant

H

h height; hour; Planck's constant

H enthalpy; Hamiltonian; handicapped accessible; haze; henry; heroin; Hispanic; hit; humidity; Hungary (international vehicle ID); hydrogen

h. harbor; hard; hardness; high; horn; hundred; husband

ha Hausa; hectare; hour angle

HA headache; Hydrocephalus Association; hyperalimentation

Ha. Hawaii

h.a. *Latin* hoc anno (this year)

HAA hepatitis-associated antigen

Hab. Habakkuk

hab. corp. *Latin* habeas corpus (a writ to determine whether a prisoner ought to be released)

HACCP hazard analysis critical control point

HACU Hispanic Association of Colleges and Universities

HAF hCG associated factor

Hag. Haggai

HAGD have a good day

HAGN have a good night

HAGO have a good one

HAIN Health Action Information Network

HAK hugs and kisses

HAL hardware abstraction layer

HAM Hamburg (Fuhlsbuttel) Airport

HAMSTeRS Haemophilia: A Mutation, Structure, Test, and Resource Site

HAN home area network

HAND have a nice day

H & E hemorrhage and exudate

H & P history and physical

HANP Homeopathic Academy of Naturopathic Physicians

HANS Health Action Network Society

HAO Health Action Overseas; high altitude observatory

HAP hazardous air pollutant

HAPA Haitian-American Psychiatric Association

HAPFACT Hazardous Air Pollutant Health Effects Fact Sheets

HaPI Health and Psychosocial Instruments

HAPI high altitude plasma instrument

HARM high-speed antiradiation missile

HARP Health Administration Responsibility Project

HAV hepatitis A virus

Haw. Hawaiian

HazDat Hazardous Substance Release/Health Effects Database

HAZMAT hazardous material

hb halfback

Hb Habakkuk; hemoglobin

H.B. [United States] House [of Representatives] bill

HB$_c$Ab antibody to the hepatitis B core antigen

HB$_c$Ag hepatitis B core antigen

HbCO carboxyhemoglobin

HBCU historically Black colleges and universities

HBCU/MI historically Black colleges and universities and minority institutions

HBD has been drinking

HBe hepatitis B e antigen

HBE His-bundle electrogram

HB$_e$Ab antibody to the hepatitis B e antigen

HBM Her (or His) Britannic Majesty

HBO Home Box Office

H-bomb hydrogen bomb

HBP high blood pressure; hit by pitch

HBR high bit rate

Hb S sickle cell hemoglobin

HB$_s$Ab antibody to the hepatitis B surface antigen

HB$_s$Ag hepatitis B surface antigen

HBT heterojunction bipolar transistor

HBV hepatitis B virus

HC hard cover [book]; hazardous constituents

h.c. *Latin* honoris causa (for the sake of honor)

H.C. Holy Communion; House of Commons

HCA heterocyclic amines

HCAA National CPA Health Care Advisors Association

HCBP hexachlorobiphenyl

HCC Hubcap Collectors Club; [25-]hydroxycholecalciferol

HCCPD hexachlorocyclopentadiene

HCF Hepatitis C Foundation; high-cycle fatigue; Hispanic Christian female

h.c.f. highest common factor

HCFA Health Care Financing Administration

HCFC hydrochlorofluorocarbon

hCG human chorionic gonadotropin

HCH National Health Care for the Homeless Council

HCIS Health Care Information System

HCL high cost of living

HCLA Health Care Liability Alliance

HCM Hispanic Christian male

HCMA Hypertrophic Cardiomyopathy Association

HCN Health Communication Network

H.Con.Res. House Concurrent Resolution

HCP health care practitioner; [Environmental Protection Agency] Habitat Conservation Plan

HCQIP Health Care Quality Improvement Program

HCRES [United States] House [of Representatives] concurrent resolution

HCRMS Health Care Resource Management Society

HCRP Hardcopy Cable Replacement Profile

HCS host computer system; human chorionic somatomammotropic hormone; human chorionic somatomammotropin

HCSA Hospital Consultants and Specialists Association

Hct hematocrit

HCUP-3 Healthcare Cost and Utilization Project

HCV hepatitis C virus

HCVD hypertensive cardiovascular disease

HCVR High Capacity Voice Recorder

Hcy homocysteine

HD hard disk; hardwood; heating system damage; heart disease; heavy duty; high density; Hodgkin's disease; Home Depot, Inc.

hd. head

h.d. *Latin* hora decubitus (at bedtime)

HDA hail detection algorithm; Holistic Dental Association

hdbk. handbook

HDCV human diploid cell vaccine; human diploid cell rabies vaccine

HDDV heavy-duty diesel vehicle

HDF Hereditary Disease Foundation; hierarchical data format

hdg. heading

HDGECP Human Dimensions of Global Environmental Change

hdh Held at Desk House

hdkf. handkerchief

HDL high-density lipoprotein

H. Doc. House Document

HDPE high-density polyethylene

hdqrs. headquarters

hds Held at Desk Senate

HDR high dose rate

HD-ROM high-density [CD]ROM

HDS Office of Human Development Services

HDSA Huntington's Disease Society of America

HDT heavy-duty truck

HDTV high-definition television

HDV heavy-duty vehicle; hepatitis D virus

hdwe. hardware

he Hebrew

He helium

HE Her (or His) Excellency; high explosive; His (or Her) Eminence

HealthSTAR Health Services, Technology, Administration, and Research

HEAO high energy astronomy observatory

HEAPS Health Education and Promotion System

HEAST Health Effects Assessment Summary Tables

Heb. Hebrew; Hebrews

Hebr. Hebrew

HEC header error control

HED High Energy Detector

HEDIS Health Plan Employer Data and Information Set

HEDM high energy density matter

HEENT head, eyes, ears, nose, and throat

HEL Helsinki-Vantaa Airport; high energy laser; history of the English language

HELM Health and Environment Library Modules

helo helicopter

HELP Health Education Library for People

HEMPAS hereditary erythroblastic multinuclearity associated with positive acidified serum

HEMT high electron mobility transistor

Hep hepatitis

HEPA hamster egg penetration assay; high-efficiency particulate accumulator; high-efficiency particulate air; high-efficiency particulate arresting

HEPI higher education price index

HepNet Hepatitis Information Network

her. heraldry

HER Hercules (constellation)

HEV hepatitis E virus

HEW Department of Health, Education, and Welfare

hex. hexagon; hexagonal

Hf hafnium

HF high frequency; Hispanic female

hf. half

HFC hybrid fiber coaxial; hydrofluorocarbon

HFI Hepatitis Foundation International

HFMA Healthcare Financial Management Association

HFO heavy fuel oil

hfs hyperfine structure

hg hectogram; hemoglobin

Hg Haggai; mercury

HG High German; Holy Grail

HGA high gain antenna

hgb. hemoglobin

HGED high gain emissive display

HGF hyperglycemic-glycogenolytic factor

hGH human growth hormone

HGH human growth hormone

HGHF/SF hepatocyte growth factor/scatter factor

HGL hydraulic grade line

HGMD Human Gene Mutation Database

HGMIS Human Genome Management Information System

HGPRT hypoxanthine guanine phosphoribosyltransferase

hgt. height

hgwy. highway

HH Her (or His) Highness; His Holiness

HHA home health agency; home health aide

HHC highly hazardous chemical

HHANES Hispanic Health and Nutrition Examination Survey

hhd hogshead

HHD *Latin* Humanitatum Doctor (Doctor of Humanities)

HHE Health Hazard Evaluation Program

HHFA Housing and Home Finance Agency

HHIS hanging head in shame

HHMI Howard Hughes Medical Institute

HHNA Home Healthcare Nurses Association

HHOJ ha-ha, only joking

HHOK ha-ha, only kidding

HHS [Department of] Health and Human Services

HHT Hereditary Hemorrhagic Telangiectasia Foundation International

HHTYAY happy holidays to you and yours
HHV higher heating value; human herpes virus
HHW household hazardous waste
hi high; Hindi
HI Hawaii; high intensity; humidity index
H.I. Hawaiian Islands
HIA Hearing Industries Association
HIAA Health Insurance Association of America
Hib Haemophilus influenza type b conjugate (meningitis)
HIB health insurance benefits
HIBCC Health Industry Business Communications Council
HIBR Huxley Institute for Biosocial Research
HIC Health Information Center; Health Insurance Commission
HICPAC Hospital Infection Control Practices Advisory Committee
HID host interface device
HIDA dimethyl iminodiacetic acid; Health Industry Distributors Association
hi-fi high fidelity
HIFO highest in, first out
HIH Her (or His) Imperial Highness
HII health information infrastructure
HIM Her (or His) Imperial Majesty
HIMA Health Industry Manufacturers Association
HiMaTE high mach turbine engine

HIMSS Healthcare Information and Management Systems Society
HIN Health Information Network
Hind. Hindi; Hindustani
HIO health insuring organization
HIP Help for Incontinent People (now **NAFC**: National Association for Continence)
HIPAA Health Insurance Portability and Accountability Act
HIPC health insurance purchasing cooperative
hippo hippopotamus
HIPRA high speed digital processor architecture
HIRA Health Industry Representatives Association
hi-res high resolution
HIRF high intensity radiation field
HIRIS high resolution imaging spectrometer
HIRS Heath Information Resources and Services; high resolution infrared sounder
HIRU Health Information Research Unit
HIS high resolution interferometer spectrometer
hist. historian; historical; history
HISTLINE History of Medicine Online
histol. histology
hi-tech high technology
HITH Hospital in the Home
Hitt. Hittite
HIV human immunodeficiency virus

HIVATIS HIV/AIDS Treatment Information Service

HIVD herniated intervertebral disc

HIV- HIV negative

HIV+ HIV positive

HIV-1 human immunodeficiency virus-1

HIV-2 human immunodeficiency virus-2

HJ *Latin* hic jacet (here lies)

HJR House [of Representatives] joint resolution

H.J.Res. House [of Representatives] Joint Resolution

HK Hong Kong (international vehicle ID); housekeeping

.hk Hong Kong

HKD Hong Kong—dollar

HKG Hong Kong Chek Lap Kok International Airport

HKJ Jordan (international vehicle ID)

hl hectoliter

H.L. House of Lords

HLA human leukocyte antigen; human lymphocyte antigens

HLC heavy lift capability

hld. hold

HLI Human Life International

HLL high level [computer] language

HLMS high latitude monitoring station

HLN Helena Regional Airport

HLPS hot liquid process simulator

hlqn harlequin

HLS *Latin* hoc loco situs (laid in this place); holograph letter signed

HLV heavy lift vehicle

hm hectometer

HM Her (or His) Majesty; him (shortwave transmission); Hispanic male

hm. home

.hm Heard and McDonald Islands

HMA high memory area

HMAS Her (or His) Majesty's Australian Ship

HMBS Her (or His) Majesty's British Ship

HMC Her (or His) Majesty's Customs

HMCS Her (or His) Majesty's Canadian Ship

HMD History of Medicine Division; hyaline membrane disease

HMF Her (or His) Majesty's Forces

HMG human menopausal gonadotropin

HMG-CoA *-hydroxy-*-methylglutaryl-CoA

HMMWV high mobility multipurpose wheeled vehicle

HMO health maintenance organization

HMPAO hexametazimepropyleneamine oxime; hexamethylpropyleneamine oxime

HMRI Hospital Medical Records Institute

HMS Her (or His) Majesty's Ship

HMSO Her (or His) Majesty's Stationery Office

HMT Hazardous Materials Table

HMTA Hazardous Materials Transportation Act

HMX high melting point explosive

HN head nurse; Honduras (international vehicle ID)

.hn Honduras

HNA Hospice Nurses Association

HNGR hangar

HNL Honduras—lempira (currency); Honolulu International Airport

HNP herniated nucleus pulposus

HNPCC hereditary non-polyposis colon cancer

hnRNA heterogeneous nuclear RNA

hny honey

Ho holmium; Hosea

h/o history of

ho. house

HOAS hold on a second

HOC hydrophobic organic compound

HOCA high osmolar contrast agent

HOCM high osmolar contrast medium

HOH hard of hearing

HOI Health Outcomes Institute

hol holiday

hom. homily; homonym

HOMES Huron, Ontario, Michigan, Erie, Superior (mnemonic device for remembering the Great Lakes)

homie homeboy

hon honey

HON Health on the Net Foundation; Honeywell International Inc.

hon. honor; honorable; honorary

Hon. Honduras; honorable; honorary

Hond. Honduras

hood neighborhood

HOP high oxygen pressure

HOPE Health Opportunity for People Everywhere

HOR Horologium (constellation)

hor. horizontal

hor. decub. *Latin* hora decubitus (at bedtime)

horol. horology

horr. horticulture

hor. som. *Latin* hora somni (at the hour of sleep—that is, at bedtime)

hort. horticultural; horticulture

Hos. Hosea

hosp. hospital

HOST Healthcare Open Systems and Trials

HOTO health of the oceans

HOU Houston Astros; Houston Texans; William P. Hobby Airport (Houston, TX)

HOV high-occupancy vehicle

HOW home owners warranty

hp horsepower

HP high pressure; Hewlett-Packard Company

HPA high power amplifier

HPBW half-power band width

HPC handheld personal computer; high pressure compressor

HPCS High Performance Computing and Communications

HPCS High Performance Computing Systems

HPD hourly precipitation data

HPE holoprosencephaly

HPF highest possible frequency; Hispanic professional female

HPFS high performance file system

hPG human pituitary gonadotrophin

HPGL Hewlett-Packard Graphics Language

HPI history of present illness

HPIB Hewlett-Packard Interface Bus

HPL human placental lactogen

HPLC high pressure liquid chromatography; high performance liquid chromatography

HPM high power microwave; Hispanic professional male

HP-MSOGS high performance-molecular sieve oxygen generation system

HPN Westchester County [NY] Airport

HPO healthcare purchasing organization; hospital provider organization

HPPA Hospital Purchaser-Provider Agreement

HPPC health plan purchasing cooperatives

HPPS high performance file system

HPS Hanta virus Pulmonary Syndrome; Heath Physics Society

HPSA health professional shortage area

HPSG head-driven phrase structure grammar

HPSLT high power semiconductor laser technology

HPT high pressure turbine; home pregnancy test

HPV human papillomavirus

H. pylori Helicobacter pylori

HQ headquarters

hr Croatian

HR Croatia (international vehicle ID); heart rate; home rule; home run; human relations; human resources

hr. hour

Hr. Herr

.hr Croatia

h.r. home run

H.R. House of Representatives

HRA Health Resources Administration; health risk assessment

HRCT high resolution computed tomography

HRD human resources director

HRE Holy Roman Empire

H. Rept. House [of Representatives] Report

H. Res. House [of Representatives] Resolution

HREX Human Radiation Experiments Information Management System

HRG Health Research Group

HRH Her (or His) Royal Highness

HRIR high resolution infrared radiometer

hrly. hourly

HRPT high resolution picture transmission

HRQL health-related quality of life

HRS [Environmental Protection Agency] Hazardous Ranking System; high resolution spectrometer; House Resolution; Human Resources Society

hrs. hours

HRSA [United States] Health Resources and Services Administration

HRt hard-return

HRT hormone replacement therapy

hrzn horizon

Hs hassium

HS high school; his (shortwave transmission)

h.s. *Latin* hora somni (at the hour of sleep—that is, at bedtime)

HSA health service agreement

HSAL high speed algebraic logic

HSB hue, saturation, and brightness

HSCT high speed civil transport

HSDB Hazardous Substances Data Bank

hse. house

HSG hysterosalpingogram

HSGT high speed ground transit

HSH Her (or His) Serene Highness

HSI Health Services International; Hispanic-serving institution; hyperspectral imaging

HSIK how should I know

HSIO high speed input/output

HSLC Health Sciences Libraries Consortium

HSMHA Health Services and Mental Health Administration

hsp heat shock proteins

HSPC Health and Science Policy Committee

HSQB Health Standard and Quality Bureau

HSRPROJ Health Services Research Projects [in Progress]

HSS Hospital Shared Services

HSSTD Historical Sea Surface Temperature Dataset

HST Harry S. Truman; Hawaii-Aleutian Standard Time; Hubble Space Telescope; hypersonic transport

HST&M History of Science, Technology, and Medicine

HSTAR Health Services/Technol-ogy Assessment Research

HSTAT Health Services/Technol-ogy Assessment Texts

HSV herpes simplex virus; Huntsville International Airport/Carl T. Jones Field

ht height

Ht hypertension

HT halftime; halftone; high tension; high tide; hydrother-mally treated

.ht Haiti

h.t. *Latin* hoc titulo (this title, under this title)

HTA health technology assess-ment

HTF hard to find

HTG Haiti—gourde (currency)

HTH hope this helps

HTHL horizontal takeoff, hori-zontal landing

HTLV human T-cell lym-photropic virus

HTLV-I T-cell lymphotrophic virus type I; human lym-photropic virus, type 1

HTLV-II T-cell lymphotrophic virus type II; human lym-photropic virus, type 2

HTLV-III human T-cell lym-photropic virus type III

HTM hypertext markup

HTML Hypertext Markup Lan-guage

HTN hypertension

HTP high temperature and pres-sure

hTRT human telomerase reverse transcriptase

HTS high throughput screening

Hts. heights

http Hypertext Transfer Proto-col

HTVL horizontal takeoff; vertical landing

HTWS Hawaii Tsunami Warning System

hu Hungarian

hU dihydrouridine

.hu Hungary

HUAC House Un-American Activities Committee

HUD Department of Housing and Urban Development

HUF Hungary—forint (currency)

HUGO Human Genome Organization

humies humanists

Hung. Hungarian; Hungary

HUS hemolytic uremic syndrome

HV half-value; have (shortwave transmission); high velocity; high voltage

h.v. *Latin* hoc verbo (this word)

HVA homovanillic acid

HVAC heating, ventilating, and air-conditioning

HVD high voltage differential; hypertensive vascular disease

HVL half-value layer

HVN Tweed-New Haven Airport

HVO Health Volunteers Overseas

HVPS high voltage power supply

hvy. heavy

HW hardware; hardwood; hazardous waste; high water; hot water; how (shortwave transmission)

H/W hot water

HWC Hurricane Warning Center

HWCI hardware configuration item

HWD height x width x depth

HWM high-water mark

HWO Hurricane Warning Office (National Weather Service)

HWP height/weight proportional; Hewlett-Packard Co.

hwy. highway

hx [medical] history

hy Armenian

HYA Hydra (constellation)

hyd. hydraulics; hydrostatics

hydro. hydroelectric

HYI Hydrus (constellation)

Hyp hypoxanthine; hydroxyproline

hyp. hypotenuse; hypothesis; hypothetical

hyperbol. hyperbolically

hyph. hyphenated

hypo hypodermic [injection]; sodium hyposulfite; sodium thiosulfate

hypoth. hypothesis

HyTech hypersonic technology

Hz hertz

I

i imaginary unit

I current; ice; incomplete; institute; intelligence; interstate; iodine; isospin; Italy (international vehicle ID); 1

i. interest; intransitive

I. island; isle

i12n implementation (begins with *i*, ends with *n*, 12 letters in between)

i18n internationalization (begins with *i*, ends with *n*, 18 letters in between)

IA intra-arterial; Iowa

Ia. Iowa

i.a. *Latin* in absentia (in absence)

IAA indoleacetic acid

IAACN International and American Associations of Clinical Nutritionists

IAAF International Amateur Athletic Federation

IAB Internet Architecture Board

IABO International Association of Biological Oceanography

IABP International Arctic Buoy Program

IAC in any case

IACI International Association for Craniofacial Identification

IACP International Academy of Compounding Pharmacists

IACPO Inter-American Council of Psychiatric Organizations

IACS International Association of Chemical Societies

IAD internal audit division; Washington [DC] Dulles International Airport

IADB Inter-American Defense Board; Inter-American Development Bank

IADR International and American Associations for Dental Research

IAE in any event

IAEA International Atomic Energy Agency

IAER International Association of Electronics Recyclers

IAF Inter-American Foundation

IAFP International Association for Financial Planning

IAG International Association of Geodesy

IAGA International Association of Geomagnetism and Aeronomy

IAGD Illinois Academy of General Dentistry

IAGLR International Association for Great Lakes Research

IAH George Bush Intercontinental Airport (Houston, TX)

IAHC Internet International Ad Hoc Committee

IAHE International Alliance of Healthcare Educators

IAHS International Association of Hydrological Sciences

IAI Inter-American Institute for Global Change Research

IAIMS Integrated Advanced Information Management System

IALMH International Academy of Law and Mental Health

IAM International Association of Machinists

IAMA International Arts Medicine Association

IAMAP International Association of Meteorology and Atmospheric Physics

IAMAW International Association of Machinists and Aerospace Workers

IAMSLIC International Association of Aquatic and Marine Science Libraries and Information Centers

IANA Internet Assigned Numbers Authority

IANAL I am not a lawyer

IANC International Anatomical Nomenclature Committee

I & D incision and drainage

I & M inspection and maintenance

I & O intake and output

I & T integration and test

IAP indoor air pollution; international airport; International Association of Pancreatology

IAPA International Association of Physicians in Audiology

IAPAC International Association of Physicians in AIDS Care

IAPM International Association of Medical Prosthesis Manufacturers

IAPSO International Association for the Physical Sciences of the Ocean

IARC International Agency for Research on Cancer

IARCC Interagency Arctic Research Coordination Committee

IARCH Institute of Action Research for Community Health

IARU International Amateur Radio Union

IAS indicated air speed

IASC Inter-American Society for Chemotherapy

IASD interatrial septal defect

IASIA Institute for Advanced Studies in Immunology and Aging

IASO International Association for the Study of Obesity

IASOSFRGDOH International Amalgamated Society of Searchers for Rare, Greasy, Dirty Old Hubcaps

IASP International Association for Suicide Prevention; International Association for the Study of Pain

IASPEI International Association of Seismology and Physics of the Earth's Interior

IASSMD International Association for the Scientific Study of Mental Deficiency

IATA International Air Transport Association

IATTC Inter-American Tropical Tuna Commission

IAU International Association of Universities; International Astronomical Union

IAVCEI International Association of Volcanology and Chemistry of the Earth's Interior

IAVH International Association of Veterinary Homeopathy

IB in bond; incendiary bomb

ib. *Latin* ibidem (in the same place)

IBA Industrial Biotechnology Association; International Bar Association

I-bahn infobahn (that is, information superhighway)

I band isotropic band

IBB intentional base on balls

IBC International Bathymetric Chart; iron-binding capacity

IBD inflammatory bowel disease

IBEC International Bank for Economic Cooperation

IBF International Boxing Federation

IBG interblock gap

ibid. *Latin* ibidem (in the same place)

IBIS Interactive BodyMind Information System

IBM International Business Machines [Corporation]

IBMTR International Bone Marrow Transplant Registry

IBNR incurred but not reported

I-Bond inflation-indexed [United States government savings] bond

IBR infectious bovine rhinotracheitis

IBRD International Bank for Reconstruction and Development

IBS Irritable Bowel Syndrome

IBT immunobead binding test

IBV infectious bronchitis virus

IBY International Biological Year

IC immediate constituent; integrated circuit; I see

ICA International Cancer Alliance; International Chiropractors Association; International Cooperative Alliance; Interstitial Cystitis Association

ICAAC Interscience Conference on Antimicrobial Agents and Chemotherapy

ICACGP International Commission on Atmospheric Chemistry and Global Pollution

ICAEL Intersocietal Commission for the Accreditation of Echocardiography Laboratories

ICAF Industrial College of the Armed Forces

ICAM-1 intercellular adhesion molecule-1

ICAMI International Committee Against Mental Illness

ICAN International Children's Anophthalmia Network

ICANN Internet Corporation for Assigned Names and Numbers

ICAO International Civil Aeronautics Organization

ICAP inductively coupled argon plasma

ICARE International Cancer Alliance for Research and Education

ICAS integrated circuit applications specifications

ICAVL Intersocietal Commission for the Accreditation of Vascular Laboratories

ICBEN International Commission on the Biological Effects of Noise

ICBM intercontinental ballistic missile

ICBW I could be wrong; it could be worse

ICC Indian Claims Commission; Interface Controller Card; International Chamber of Commerce; Interstate Commerce Commission

ICCH International Commodities Clearing House

ICCHHH International Club for Collectors of Hatpins and Hatpin Holders

ICCS International Classification of Clinical Services

ICD interface control document; International Classification of Diseases

ICDA *International Classification of Diseases,* Adapted for Use in the United States

ICDO International Classification of Diseases for Oncology

ICE in case of emergency; Institute for Christian Economics; internal-combustion engine; International Cultural Exchange

Ice. Iceland; Icelandic

ICEA International Childbirth Education Association

ICEDOC International Committee for Establishment and Development of Oncology Centers

Icel. Iceland; Icelandic

ICEM Intergovernmental Committee for European Migration; International Conference on Emergency Medicine

ICES International Council for the Exploration of the Seas

ICF intracellular fluid

ICFTU International Confederation of Free Trade Unions

ICGA International Carnival Glass Association

ICHNA International Child Health Nursing Alliance

ICHP Institute for Child Health Policy

ICHPPC International Classification of Health Problems in Primary Care

ICHSRI International Clearinghouse of Health System Reform Initiatives

ichth. ichthyology

ICI intracervical insemination

ICIC International Cancer Information Center

ICIDH International Classification of Impairments, Disabilities, and Handicaps

ICIDH-2 International Classification of Impairments, Activities, and Participation

ICIRN International Council on Information Resources for Nursing

ICJ International Court of Justice

ICLARM International Center for Living Aquatic Resources Management

ICLEI International Council for Local Environmental Initiatives

ICLRN Interagency Council on Library Resources for Nursing

ICM Intelligent Call Management; Intergovernmental Committee for Migration

ICMJE International Committee of Medical Journal Editors

ICML International Congress on Medical Librarianship

ICMP Internet Control Message Protocol

ICMS InterNational Center for Medical Specialties

ICNAF International Convention of the Northwest Atlantic Fisheries

ICNIRP International Commission on Non-Ionizing Radiation Protection

ICO International Coffee Organization

I/CO installation and check-out

ICOCBW I could, of course, be wrong

ICOI International Congress of Oral Implantologists

ICP inductively coupled plasma; intracranial pressure

ICPA International Chiropractic Pediatric Association

ICPC International Classification of Primary Care

ICPD International Conference on Population and Development

ICPO International Criminal Police Organization

ICQ I seek you

ICRA Industrial Chemical Research Association

ICRC International Committee of the Red Cross

ICRDB International Cancer Research Databank Branch

ICRIN Injury Control Resource Information Network

ICRM International Red Cross and Red Crescent Movement

ICRP International Commission on Radiological Protection

ICRSDT International Committee on Remote Sensing and Data Transmission

ICRU International Commission on Radiation Units and Measurements

ICRW International Center for Research on Women

ICS Institute for Chemical Studies; intercostal space; International Cloning Society

ICSC International Chemical Safety Cards

ICSEAF International Commission for the South-East Atlantic Fisheries

ICSEM International Commission for the Scientific Exploration of the Mediterranean Sea

ICSH interstitial cell-stimulating hormone

ICSI International Commission on Snow and Ice; intracytoplasmic sperm injection

ICSPRO [United Nations] Inter-Secretariat Committee on Scientific Programs Relating to Oceanography

ICSU International Council of Scientific Unions

ICSW International Council on Social Welfare

ICT internal cold target; Wichita Mid-Continent Airport

ICTP International Center for Theoretical Physics

I-ctus. *Latin* jurisconsultus

(one learned in the law)

ICU intensive care unit

ICV interdecadal climate variability

ICW in connection with (shortwave transmission); Intracoastal Waterway

ICWM Institute for Chemical Waste Management

ICWP Interstate Conference on Water Problems

ICZM integrated coastal zone management

id Indonesian

ID Idaho; identification; infecting dose; infectious disease; insect damage; Intelligence Department; intradermal

id. *Latin* idem (the same)

Id. Idaho

.id Indonesia

i.d. inner diameter; inside diameter; internal diameter

IDA International Development Association; Institute for Defense Analyses

Ida. Idaho

IDAA International Diabetic Athletes Association

IDAPI Integrated Database Application Programming Interface

IDB Inter-American Development Bank; interface description block; intermediary dealer broker

IDC International Data Company; International Diabetes Center

IDCA United States International Development Cooperation Agency

IDD interface design document

IDDD international direct distance dialing

IDDM insulin-dependent diabetes mellitus

IDE integrated disk electronics; integrated drive electronics; interface design enhancement

IDEA Individuals with Disabilities Education Act; International Data Encryption Algorithm

IDEAS Information on Disability—Equipment Access Service

IDF Immune Deficiency Foundation; International Diabetes Federation

IDG International Data Group

IDHS Intelligence Data Handling System

IDIC infinite diversity in infinite combinations

IDIDAS Interactive Digital Image Display and Analysis System

IDIQ indefinite delivery, indefinite quantity

IDK I don't know

IDL instrument detection limit; interactive data language; intermediate density lipoprotein

IDLH immediately dangerous to life and health

IDM intelligent dance music

IDN International Data Number

IDP integrated data processing; international driving permit

IDPR Interdomain Policy Routing

IDR incremental design review; Indonesia—rupiah (currency)

IDS integrated delivery system

IDSA Infectious Disease Society of America; Interactive Digital Software Association

IDTS I don't think so

IDU injection drug user

IE Indo-European

I E inspiratory expiratory

.ie Ireland

I.E. industrial engineer; industrial engineering

i.e. *Latin* id est (that is)

IEA International Energy Agency

IEC International Electrotechnical Commission

IED improvised explosive device

IEEE Institute of Electrical and Electronics Engineers

IEF International Eye Foundation

IEH Institute for Environment and Health

IEP initial enrollment period; Ireland—punt (currency); isoelectric point

IEPA International Early Psychosis Association

IEPC Individual Education Planning Committee; Interagency Emergency Planning Commission

IEPG Internet Engineering Planning Group

IERC International Enuresis Research Center

IESG Internet Engineering Steering Group

IESS Integrated Electromagnetic System Simulator

IETF Internet Engineering Task Force

IETM Interactive Electronic Technical Manual

IEVS Income Eligibility Verification Systems

IF infertility; interferon; intermediate frequency

I/F interface

IFA International Federation on Aging

IFAD International Fund for Agricultural Development

IFAP Industrial Foundation for Accident Prevention

IFB invitation for bids

IFBD International Foundation for Bowel Dysfunction (now **IFFGD:** International Foundation for Functional Gastrointestinal Disorders)

IFC International Finance Corporation

IFCC International Federation of Clinical Chemistry

IFCTU International Federation of Christian Trade Unions

IFEH International Federation of Environmental Health

iff if and only if

IFF identification, friend or foe

IFFGD International Foundation for Functional Gastrointestinal Disorders

IFFS International Federation of Fertility Societies

IFGE International Federation of Gynecologic Endoscopists

IFGR International Foundation for Genetic Research

IFIAS International Federation of Institutes for Advanced Study

IFIC International Food Information Council

IFIP International Federation for Information Processing

IFJ International Federation of Journalists

IFK indirect free kick (soccer)

IFLA International Federation of Library Associations

IFMP International Federation for Medical Psychotherapy

IFMS Integrated Financial Management System

IFMSA International Federation of Medical Students' Associations

IFMSS International Federation of Multiple Sclerosis Societies

IFN interferon

IFN-α interferon alpha

IFN-β interferon beta

IFN-γ interferon gamma

IFO identified flying object

IFOV instantaneous field of view

IFPOS International Federation of Pediatric Orthopaedic Societies

IFPRI International Food Policy Research Institute

IFPS International Federation of Psychoanalytic Societies

IFR instrument flight rules

IFRCS International Federation of Red Cross and Red Crescent Societies

IFRRO International Federation of Reproduction Rights Organizations

IFS Information Fatigue Syndrome; International Foundation for Science

IFST Institute of Food Science and Technology

IFUFOCS Institute for UFO Contactee Studies

Ig immunoglobulin

IG inspector general

IgA immunoglobulin A

IGA integrated graphics array

IGADD Inter-Governmental Authority on Drought and Development

IGBP International Geosphere-Biosphere Program

IGBT Insulated Gate Bipolar Transistor

IGC International Geological Congress

IgD immunoglobulin D

IGDOD Inspector General, Department of Defense

IgE immunoglobulin E

IGF insulin-like growth factor

IgG immunoglobulin G

IgM immunoglobulin M

IGM intergalactic medium

IGMP Internet Group Management Protocol

ign. ignition

IGOM integrated global ocean monitoring

IGOSS Integrated Global Ocean Services System

IGP igneous and geothermal processes; Interior Gateway Protocol

IGS inner Gulf shelf

IGY International Geophysical Year

ih Introduced in House [of Representatives]

IH infectious hepatitis; inguinal hernia

IHA Indian Housing Authority; Integrated Healthcare Association

IHAS ideopathic hypertrophic aortic stenosis

IHC Internet Healthcare Coalition

IHCF Inherited High Cholesterol Foundation; International Healthy Cities Foundation

IHD ischemic heart disease

IHDS Integrated Health Delivery System

IHEA International Health Economics Association

IHGP International Human Genome Project

IHGT Institute for Human Gene Therapy

IHHRR International Health Human Resources Registry

IHI Index to Health Information; Institute for Healthcare Improvement

IHM [National Library of Medicine] Images from the History of Medicine

IHO integrated healthcare organization

IHOC International Healthcare Opportunities Clearinghouse

IHOP International House of Pancakes

ihp indicated horsepower

IHPO International Health Program Office

IHPP Intergovernmental Health Policy Project

IHPR Institute of Health Promotion Research

IHPS Integrated Healthcare Practice Society

ihr Introduced in House [of Representatives]—Reprint

IHR Institute of Historical Review; Internet Health Resources

IHS Indian Health Service; Institute of Health Sciences; Jesus

IHW Internet Health Watch

II illegal immigrants

IIA Institute of Internal Auditors

IIASA International Institute

for Applied Systems Analysis

IIB International Investment Bank

IIE Institute of Industrial Engineers

IIFS International Institute of Forensic Science

III Insurance Information Institute

IIP International Institute of Parasitology

IIR Imaging Infrared

IIRC if I recall correctly

IIRCAID if I recall correctly and I do

IIRV improved interrange vector

IIS inflationary impact statement

IISP Interim-Interswitch Signaling Protocol

IITA Information Infrastructure Technology Applications; International Institute for Tropical Agriculture

IITF Information Infrastructure Task Force

IIWM if it were me

IJP inhibitory junction potential

ik Inupiaq

IKE Internet Key Exchange

IL Illinois; interlanguage; Israel (international vehicle ID)

.il Israel

IL-1 interleukin-1

IL-1ra interleukin 1 receptor antagonist

IL-2 interleukin-2

ILA International Longshoremen's Association

ILAR Institute for Laboratory Animal Research

ILBRT endoluminal brachytherapy

ILC International Law Commission

ILEC incumbent local exchange carrier

ILGA International Lesbian and Gay Association

ILGWU International Ladies' Garment Workers' Union

ill. illustrated; illustration

Ill. Illinois

illus. illustrated; illustrated by; illustration; illustrator

ILM Industrial Light and Magic; information lifecycle management; Wilmington [NC] International Airport

ILO International Labor Organization

ILS instrument landing system; Israel—shekel (currency)

ILYA incompletely launched young adult

IM immediately (shortwave transmission); immunoassay; instant message; intermediate modeling; Internal Medicine; intramedullary; intramural; intramuscular

IMA International Monovision Association

IMAGE Integrated Molecular Analysis of Genomes and their Expression

IMAO in my arrogant opinion

IMAP Internet Message Access Protocol

IMAP4 Internet Messaging Access Protocol [version] 4

IMC instrument meteorological conditions

IMCDO in my conceited dogmatic opinion

IMCO in my considered opinion; Intergovernmental Maritime Consultative

IMD intermodulation distortion

IME in my experience

IMF International Monetary Fund

IMGT immunogenetics database

IMHO in my honest opinion; in my humble opinion

IMI International Market Index

IMIA International Medical Informatics Association

imit. imitation; imitative; imitatively

IML Ring International Medical Libraries Ring

IMM interactive multimedia

immed. immediately

IMMI Index of Medieval Medical Images in North America

immun. immunity; immunization

immunol. immunology

IMNERHO in my never even remotely humble opinion

IMNSHO in my not so humble opinion

IMO in my opinion; International Maritime Organization; International Meteor Organization

imp impression

IMP instrument mounting platform

imp. imperative; imperfect; imperial; import; imported; importer; imprimatur

imper. imperative; imperatively

imperf. imperfect; imperforate

impers. impersonal; impersonally

improv improvisation

IMS Information Management Society; information management system; Institute of Museum Services

IMSL International Mathematics and Statistics Library

IMT interactive media training

IMU inertial measurement unit

IMV in my view; intermittent mandatory ventilation

in inch

In indium

IN Indiana

.in India

inc. including; income; incomplete; increase

Inc. Incorporated

INCB International Narcotics Control Board

INCE Institute of Noise Control Engineers

incho. inchoative

INCIID InterNational Council on Infertility Information Dissemination

incl. including; inclusive

incog. incognita; incognito

incr. increase

IND India (international vehicle ID); Indianapolis Colts; Indianapolis International Airport; Indus (constellation); investigational new drug

ind. independence; independent; index; indigo; industrial; industry

in d. *Latin* in dies (daily)

Ind. India; Indian; Indiana; Indies

Ind.E. industrial engineer; industrial engineering

indef. indefinite; indefinitely

indic. indicative; indicator

indie independent

indiv. individual

individ. individual

indn. indication

Indon. Indonesia; Indonesian

indus. industrial; industry

INF intermediate-range nuclear forces

inf. infantry; inferior; infinitive; infinity; information; *Latin* infra (below)

infin. infinitive

INFJ Introversion iNtuition Feeling Judging (Myers-Briggs [personality] Type Indicator)

infl. inflected; influenced

info information

INFO International Fortean Organization

INFOCLIMA World Climate Data Information Referral Service

info-dense informationally dense

infomercial information commercial

INFOSEC Information Security

INFP Introversion iNtuition Feeling Perception (Myers-Briggs [personality] Type Indicator)

infra dig *Latin* infra dignitatem (beneath [one's] dignity)

ing inguinal

INH isonicotinic acid hydrazide

INI International Nursing Index

INIA International Institute on Aging

INIT initialization

init. initial

Inmarsat International Maritime Satellite Organization

INO Institute for Naval Oceanography

inorg. inorganic

INP International News Photo

INPFC International North Pacific Fisheries Commission

INPHO Information Network for Public Health Officials

INPO in no particular order

in pr. *Latin* in principio (in the beginning)

inq. inquiry

INQUA International Union for Quaternary Research

INR India—rupee; International Normalized Ratio

INRI *Latin* Iesus Nazarenus Rex Iudaeorum (Jesus of Nazareth, King of the Jews)

Ins insert key

INS Immigration and Naturalization Service; inertial navigation system; International News Service

ins. inches; inspector; insulation; insurance

INSAT Indian Geostationary Satellite

INSCOM [United States Army] Intelligence and Security Command

insol. insoluble

insp. inspected; inspector

inst. current month; instant; institute; institution; institutional

instr. instruction; instructor; instrument; instrumental

int. intelligence; intercept; interest; interim; interior; interjection; intermediate; internal; international; interval; interview; intransitive

INTC Intel Corp.

int. cib. *Latin* inter cibos (between meals)

intel intelligent

INTELSAT International Telecommunications Satellite

intens. intensive

inter. interjection; intermediate

interj. interjection

InterNIC Internet Network Information Center

interp. interpreter

INTERPOL International Criminal Police Organization

interrog. interrogative

INTJ Introversion iNtuition Thinking Judging (Myers-Briggs [personality] Type Indicator)

intl. international

intnl international

INTP Introversion iNtuition Thinking Perception (Myers-Briggs [personality] Type Indicator)

intr interested; interested in

intr. intransitive

INTRAH International Training in Health

intrans. intransitive; intransitively

intro introduction

intro. introduction; introductory

introd. introduction

INV in vitro fertilization

inv. invented; invention; inventor; investment; invoice

INVG investigate (shortwave transmission)

IO intraocular

.io British Indian Ocean Territory

I/O input/output

IOA International Ostomy Association

IOC International Olympic Committee

IOF International Oceanographic Foundation

IOL intraocular lens

IOLTA interest on lawyers' trust accounts

IOM Index and Options Market; International Organization for Migration

IOMP International Organization for Medical Physics

ION Institute of Nutrition

Ion. Ionic

IOOF Independent Order of Odd Fellows

IOP input output processor; intraocular pressure

IOR immature oocyte retrieval

IORT intraoperative ratio

IOSG International Oncology Study Group

IOSH Institution of Occupational Safety and Health

IOTP Internet Open Trading Protocol

IOU a note of debt (from "I owe you")

IOVS *Investigative Ophthalmology and Visual Science*

IOW in other words

IP image processor; inhalable particulate; innings pitched; intellectual property; Internet Protocol; International Paper Co.

i.p. isoelectric point

IPA International Phonetic Alphabet; International Phonetic Association; isopropyl alcohol

IPAA International Patient Advocacy Association

IPCC [United Nations] Intergovernmental Panel on Climate Change

IPCS International Program on Chemical Safety

IPD information processing division

IPEH International Physicians for Equitable Healthcare

IPEMB Institution of Physics and Engineering in Medicine and Biology

IPF idiopathic pulmonary fibrosis; interstitial pulmonary fibrosis

IPFSC International Pacific Salmon Fisheries Commission

iph Indefinitely Postponed in House [of Representatives]

IPHC International Pacific Halibut Commission

IPHIR interplanetary helioseismology with irradiance observations

I-phone Internet telephony

ipm inches per minute; inhalable particulate matter; integrated pest management; interprogram messaging

IPN integrated provider network

IPng Internet Protocol, next generation

IPO initial public offering

IPOD International Program of Ocean Drilling

IPOS International Psycho-Oncology Society

IPPB intermittent positive pressure breathing

IPPD integrated product and process development

IPPF International Planned Parenthood Federation

IPPNW International Physicians for the Prevention of Nuclear War

IPPV intermittent positive pressure ventilation

IPR intellectual property rights

IPRAF International Plastic, Reconstructive, and Aesthetic Foundation

IPRAS International Confederation for Plastic, Reconstructive, and Aesthetic Surgery

iPrSGal isopropylthiogalactoside

ips inches per second; Indefinitely Postponed in Senate

IPS inertial pointing system; innings per start; interplanetary scintillation

IPSA Institute for Psychological Study of the Arts

IPSP inhibitory postsynaptic potential

IPTG isopropylthiogalactoside

IP$_3$ inositol 1,4,5-trisphosphate

IPTS International Practical Temperature Scale

IPU Integrated Power Unit

IPV injectable poliovirus vaccine

IPWSO International Prader-Willi Syndrome Organization

IPX Internet packet exchange

IPX/SPX Internet packet exchange/sequenced packet exchange

IQ intelligence quotient; intelligent equalizer

.iq Iraq

i.q. *Latin* idem quod (the same as)

Ir iridium

IR information retrieval; infrared; Iran (international vehicle ID)

Ir. Irish

.ir Iran

IRA individual retirement account; Irish Republican Army

IRAC infrared array camera

IRAN individual retirement annuity

IR&D independent research and development

IRB Institutional Review Board

IRBM intermediate-range ballistic missile

IRC Internet Relay Chat; Internal Revenue Code

IRCM Infrared Countermeasures

IRD interface requirements document; international radiation detector

I.R.D. income in respect of decedent

IrDA infrared data association

Ire. Ireland

IRECA International Rescue and Emergency Care Association

IRG interrecord gap

IRH Institute for Reproductive Health

IRI immunoreactive insulin; ionospheric research instrument

IRICP International Research Institute for Climate Prediction

irid. iridescent

IRIS Integrated Risk Information System

IRL in real life; Ireland (international vehicle ID)

IRM Information Resources Management

IRMC Information Resources Management College

IRMFI I reply merely for information

IRMO Information Resources Management Office

IRMS Information Resources Management Service

IRMVS Institute for Reparative Medicine and Vascular Surgery

IRO International Refugee Organization

IROC International Rose O'Neill Club

iron. ironic; ironical; ironically

IRP Integrated Resource Planning

IRPA International Radiation Protection Association; International Retinitis Pigmentosa Association

IRPTC International Register of Potentially Toxic Chemicals

IRQ interrupt request; Iraq (international vehicle ID)

irreg. irregular; irregularly

IRR Iran—rial (currency); inter-range ratio

IRS infrared spectrograph; Internal Revenue Service

IRSA International Rett Syndrome Association

IRSC Internet Resources for Special Children

IRST infrared search and track

IRU inertial reference unit

IRV inspiratory reserve volume; interrange vector

is Icelandic; Introduced in Senate

Is Isaiah

Is. island; isle; Israel

IS Iceland (international vehicle ID); information services

.is Iceland

I/S information systems

ISA Industry Standard Architecture; Instrument Society of America; International Standards Association

Isa. Isaiah

ISAC International Society for Analytical Cytology

ISACCD International Society for Adult Congenital Cardiac Disease

ISAD International Society of Abortion Doctors

ISAKOS International Society of Arthroscopy, Knee Surgery, and Orthopaedic Sports Medicine

ISAM indexed sequential access method

ISAP Internet Self-Assessment in Pharmacology

ISAS Institute of Space and Astronautical Science

ISBN International Standard Book Number

ISC International Seismological Center; International Society of Chemotherapy

ISCAIC International Symposium on Computing in Anesthesia and Intensive Care

ISCAIP International Society for Child and Adolescent Injury Prevention

ISCB International Society for Clinical Biostatistics

ISCD International Society for Computerized Dentistry

ISD International Society of Differentiation

ISDA International Swaps and Derivatives Association

ISDN integrated services digital network

ISE ion-specific electrode

ISEA International Society of Exposure Analysis

ISEE International Society for Environmental Epidemiology; International Society for the Enhancement of Eyesight

ISFJ Introversion Sensing Feeling Judging (Myers-Briggs [personality] Type Indicator)

ISFP Introversion Sensing Feeling Perception (Myers-Briggs [personality] Type Indicator)

ISH isolated systolic hypertension

ISHBR International Society of Hepato-Biliary Radiology

ISHN Industrial Safety and Hygiene News

ISHTAR Inner Shelf Transfer and Recycling

ISI Instrument/Spacecraft Interface

ISICR International Society for Interferon and Cytokine Research

ISK Iceland—krona (currency)

ISKO International Society for Knowledge Organization

isl. island

ISLCBS International Seal Label and Cigar Band Society

ISM interstellar medium

ISMA International Securities Market Association

ISMAP indirect source model for air pollution

ISMC International Symposium on Medicinal Chemistry

ISMP Institute for Safe Medication Practices

ISN integrated service network; International Society of Nephrology

ISNA Intersex Society of North America

ISNCC International Society of Nurses in Cancer Care

ISNG International Society of Nurses in Genetics

ISO in search of; International Organization for Standardization (technically not an initialism—term is based on the prefix *iso*—, from the Greek *isos*, meaning 'equal'); intraseasonal atmospheric oscillation

ISOM International Society for Orthomolecular Medicine

ISONG International Society of Nurses in Genetics

ISOO Information Security Oversight Office; International Society of Online Ophthalmologists

ISP Internet service provider; Long Island MacArthur Airport

ISPD International Society for Peritoneal Dialysis

ISPE International Society for Pharmacoepidemiology

ISPO International Society for Preventive Oncology

ISQua International Society for Quality in Health Care

isr Introduced in Senate—Reprint

ISR interrupt service routine

Isr. Israel; Israeli

ISRS International Society of Refractive Surgery

iss. issue

ISS information security spe-

cialist; integrated sensor system

ISSC International Social Science Council

ISSN International Standard Serial Number

ISSSEEM International Society for the Study of Subtle Energies and Energy Medicine

IST Ataturk/Yesilkov International Airport (Istanbul, Turkey); insulin shock therapy

ISTAHC International Society of Technology Assessment in Health Care

isth. isthmus

ISTJ Introversion Sensing Thinking Judging (Myers-Briggs [personality] Type Indicator)

ISTM International Society of Travel Medicine

ISTP Index to Scientific and Technical Proceedings; Introversion Sensing Thinking Perception (Myers-Briggs [personality] Type Indicator)

ISTR I seem to recall

ISTSS International Society for Traumatic Stress Studies

ISU Idaho State University; Illinois State University; Indiana State University; Iowa State University

ISV International Scientific Vocabulary

ISWYM I see what you mean

ISY International Space Year

it Italian

IT information technology

It. Italian; Italy

.it Italy

ITA initial teaching alphabet; International Trade Administration

ITAA International Transaction-
al Analysis Association

ital. italic; italicize; italics

Ital. Italian; Italic

ITAR International Traffic in
Arms Regulations

ITC International Touring Car;
International Trade Commission

ITCZ Intertropical Convergence
Zone

ITEP Institute for Theoretical
and Experimental Physics

ITER International Thermonuclear Experimental Reactor; International Toxicity Estimates
for Risk

ITH Tompkins County [NY] Airport

ITI intratubal insemination

ITIC International Tsunami Information Center

itin. itinerary

ITL Italy—lira

ITM in the money

ITO International Trade Organization

ITOOTR in the opinion of the
referee

ITOS Improved TIROS Operational Satellite

ITP idiopathic thrombocytopenic purpura; inosine 5c-
triphosphate; Interactive
Testing in Psychiatry

ITPR infra-red temperature profile radiometer

ITQ individual transferable
quota

ITS intelligent tutoring system

ITSFWI if the shoe fits, wear it

ITT International Telephone
and Telegraph

ITU International Telecommu-
nication Union

ITU-T International Telecommunications Union—Telecom-
munication

ITV instructional television

ITWS Integrated Terminal
Weather System

iu Inuktitut

IU international unit

IUB International Union of
Biochemistry

IUBMB International Union of
Biochemistry and Molecular Biology

IUBS International Union of
Biological Sciences

IUCD intrauterine contraceptive
device

IUCN International Union for
Conservation of Nature and
Natural Resources

I/UCRC Industry/University Cooperative Research Center

IUD intrauterine device

IUE International Ultraviolet
Explorer

IUGG International Union of
Geodesy and Geophysics

IUGR intrauterine growth retardation

IUGS International Union of
Geological Sciences

IUI intrauterine insemination

IUP intrauterine pregnancy

IUPAC International Union of
Pure and Applied Chemistry

IUPAP International Union of
Pure and Applied Physics

IUPHAR International Union of
Pharmacology

IUSS International Union of
Soil Sciences

IV intravenous; intravenously
I-V intraventricular
IVAS International Veterinary Acupuncture Society
IVB intraventricular block
IVC inferior vena cava; intravaginal culture
IVCF InterVarsity Christian Fellowship
IVD intervertebral disc
IVF intravenous fluids; in vitro fertilization
IVF-ET in vitro fertilization and in vivo transfer of the embryo
IVHS Intelligent Vehicle Highway System
IVIg intravenous immunoglobulin
IVP intravenous pyelography; intravenous pyelogram
IVU intravenous urogram
IW index word; isotopic weight
i.w. inside width
I-way information superhighway
IWBNI it would be nice if
IWC International Whaling Commission
IWHC International Women's Health Coalition
IWRA International Water Resources Association
IWS instrument work station; ionizing wet scrubber
IWT internal warm target
IWW Industrial Workers of the World
IX it is (shortwave transmission)
IXC interexchange carrier
IYFEG insert your favorite ethnic group
IYSWIM if you see what I mean

J

j current density; joule
J jack; Japan (international vehicle ID); Jewish (as in personal ads)
J. Japanese; Journal; judge; justice
ja Japanese
JA Jamaica (international vehicle ID); joint account; judge advocate; Junior Achievement
Ja. January
JAC Jackson Hole [WY] Airport; Jacksonville Jaguars
Jac. *Latin* Jacobus (James)
JAG judge advocate general
JAL Japan Airlines
Jam. Jamaica
JAMA *Journal of the American Medical Association*
JAN Jackson [MS] International Airport
Jan. January
Jap. Japan; Japanese
JAP *derogatory* Jewish American Princess
Jas. James
jato jet-assisted takeoff
JATS job application tracking system
Jav. Javanese
JAWF Joint Agriculture-Weather Facility
JAX Jacksonville International Airport
JAYCEES Junior Chamber of Commerce
Jb Job
JBF just been fucked (that is, disheveled)
JBS John Birch Society
JC Jesus Christ; Julius Caeser; Junior College; juvenile court;

member of Junior Chamber of Commerce

JCAHO Joint Commission on Accreditation of Health Organizations

JCAHPO Joint Commission on Allied Health in Ophthalmology

JCB *Latin* Juris Canonici Baccalaureus (Bachelor of Canon Law)

JCC Jewish Community Center

JCD *Latin* Juris Canonici Doctor (Doctor of Canon Law)

JCEWS Joint Command, Control, and Electronic Warfare School

JCL Job Control Language; *Latin* Juris Canonici Licentiatus (Licentiate in Canon Law)

JCMHC Joint Commission on Mental Health of Children

JCMIH Joint Commission on Mental Illness and Health

JCOG Japanese Clinical Oncology Group

JCS Joint Chiefs of Staff

JCSOS Joint and Combined Staff Officer School

Jct. junction

Jd Jude

JD Jack Daniel's [bourbon whiskey]; *Latin* Juris Doctor (Doctor of Jurisprudence); Justice Department; juvenile delinquent

JdFR Juan de Fuca Ridge

JDI just do it!

JDL Jewish Defense League

Jdt. Judith

Je Jeremiah

Je. June

JEDA Joint Environmental Data Analysis Center

Jer. Jeremiah

jerry geriatric

JFK John Fitzgerald Kennedy; John F. Kennedy International Airport (New York, NY)

JFYI just for your information

jg junior grade

Jg Judges

JGB Japanese Government bonds

Jgs Judges

JHU Johns Hopkins University

JHVH Jehovah

JHWH Jehovah

JIC just in case

JICST Japan International Center of Science and Technology

jiff jiffy (that is, a very brief period of time)

JIFSAN Joint Institute for Food Safety and Applied Nutrition

JIT just in time

JITMT United States—Japan Industry and Technology Management Training

JJ judges; justices

JJA June-July-August

j/k just kidding

Jl Joel

Jl. July

JLC justification for limited competition

J-list journalist

Jm James

.jm Jamaica

JMD Jamaica—dollar

Jn John

JNB Johannesburg International Airport

JNCP justification for noncompetitive procurement

JND just noticeable difference

JNJ Johnson & Johnson

Jno. John

JNOV *Latin* judicium non obstante veredicto (judgment notwithstanding verdict)

jnr. junior

jnt. joint

Jo. Joel

.jo Jordan

J/O jack off

joc. jocular; jocularly

jockumentary jock documentary film

JOD Jordan—dinar

JOOC just out of curiosity

JOOTT just one of those things

Jos Joshua

Jos. Joseph

Josh. Joshua

jour. journal; journalist; journeyman

JOVIAL Jules' own version of the international algorithmic language

JP Jamaica Plain (Massachusetts); jet propulsion; justice of the peace

Jp. Japanese

.jp Japan

JPEG Joint Photographic Experts Group

JPL Jet Propulsion Laboratory

JPM J.P. Morgan Chase & Co.

Jpn. Japan

JPY Japan—yen

Jr Jeremiah

jr. junior

Jr. journal; Junior

JRA juvenile rheumatoid arthritis

JRC Junior Red Cross

Js. James

JSC Johnson Space Center

J-school journalism school

JSD *Latin* Juris Scientiae Doctor (Doctor of Juristic Science)

JSTARS Joint Surveillance and Target Attack Reconnaissance System

JT joint tenants, joint tenancy

jt. joint

JTC3A Joint Tactical Command, Control, and Communications Agency

JTLYK just to let you know

JTR Joint Travel Regulation

JTS jump the shark

JTU Jackson Turbidity Unit

Ju. June

JUCO junior college

JUD *Latin* Juris Utriusque Doctor (Doctor of Common and Canon Laws)

Jud. Judith

Judg. Judges

Jul. July

jun. junior

Jun. June

Junc. junction

juv. juvenile

juvie juvenile

jv Javanese

JV junior varsity

JVM Java Virtual Machine

JWARS Joint Warfare Simulation

jwlr. jeweler

Jy. July

K

k karat; 1000

K Cambodia (international vehicle ID); kaon; Kelvin; kicker; kilobyte; kindergarten; king; Kings; knight; 1,000; 1,024 (the closest number to 1,000 that is a power of 2—used for certain measurements, such as bytes); potassium; strikeout

k. kopek; krona; krone

K2K KEK to Kamioka [physics experiment]

K-12 kindergarten through twelfth grade

ka cathode; Georgian (language)

Ka kilo amperes

KAMT Keeping Abreast of Medical Transcription

Kan. Kansas

Kans. Kansas

K:A ratio ketogenic-antiketogenic ratio

Karmen Karlsruhe-Rutherford Medium Energy Neutrino Experiment

kat katal

KAZ Kazakhstan

kb kilobar

Kb kilobit

KB kilobyte; king's bishop; knowledge base

K.B. King's Bench

kbar kilobar

KBD keyboard

KBE Knight Commander of the Order of the British Empire

KBP Kiev-Borispol Airport

Kbps kilobits per second

KBps kilobytes per second

KByte kilobyte

kc kilocurie; kilocycle

KC Kansas City; Kansas City Chiefs; Kansas City Royals; King's Counsel; Knight of Columbus

kcal kilocalorie

KCB Knight Commander of the Order of the Bath

KCBT Kansas City Board of Trade

kcl kilocalorie

KCRT keyboard CRT

kc/s kilocycles per second

KD kiln-dried; knocked down

KDP key decision point

.ke Kenya

KEAS knots equivalent airspeed

KEF Keflavik [Iceland] Airport

KEGG Kyoto Encyclopedia of Genes and Genomes

KEK key-encrypting key; *Japanese* Koh-Ene-Ken (an abbreviation for a Japanese name of the National Laboratory for High Energy Physics)

KEN [National Mental Health Services] Knowledge Exchange Network

Ken. Kentucky

Ker. Kerry

KES Kenya—shilling

keV kiloelectron unit

KEW kinetic energy weapon

keypal Internet penpal

KFC Kentucky Fried Chicken

kg kilogram

kG kilogauss

KG Knight of the Order of the Garter

.kg Kyrgyzstan

KGAL kilogallon(s)

KGB *Russian* Komitet Gosudarstvennoj Bezopasnosti (Committee for State Security)

kgf kilogram force

kgm. kilogram

kg-m kilogram-meter

KGRA known geothermal resource area

KGS Kyrgyzstan—som (currency)

Kgs. Kings

KH Kelvin-Helmholtz

.kh Cambodia

KHN Knoop hardness number

KHR Cambodia—riel (currency)

KHYF know how you feel

kHz kilohertz

ki Kikuyu

.ki Kiribati

KIA killed in action

KIF Knowledge Interchange Format

kilo kilogram

KISS Keep it simple, stupid!

kit kitchen

kitch kitchen

KIX Kansai International Airport (Osaka, Japan)

kJ kilojoule

KJ knee jerk (reflex)

KJV *King James Version*

kk Kazakh

KKK Ku Klux Klan

KKt king's knight

kl Greenlandic (Kalaallisut); kiloliter

KLA Kosovo Liberation Army

km Cambodian (Kmher); kilometer

.km Comoros

KMF Comoros—franc

km/h kilometers per hour

kmph kilometers per hour

kmps kilometers per second

kn Kannada

KN king's knight

kn. knot

.kn Saint Kitts and Nevis

KNF model Koshland-Némethy-Filmer model

knowbot knowledge robot

Knt. knight

ko Korean

KO Coca-Cola Co.; knockout

K of C Knights of Columbus

K of P Knights of Pythias

KOOKS Keep Our Own Kids Safe

Kor. Korea; Korean

kosh kosher (that is, acceptable or up-to-date)

KOTC kiss on the cheek

KOTL kiss on the cheek

KP king's pawn; kitchen police

.kp Korea (Democratic People's Republic of)

kPa kilopascal

kpc kiloparsec

kph kilometers per hour

KPNO Kitt Peak National Observatory

kpps kilo pulses per second

KPW North Korea—won (currency)

Kr krypton

KR king's rook

kr. krona; krone

.kr Korea (Republic of)

K ration [Ancel Benjamin] Keys ration

KRW South Korea—won (currency)

ks Kashmiri

KS Kansas; Kaposi's sarcoma; Knee Society; Kyrgyzstan (international vehicle ID)

KSC Kennedy Space Center

KSU Kansas State University; Kent State University

kt or kT kiloton

Kt knight

kt. karat; knight; knot

K/T Cretaceous-Tertiary event (that is, comet or meteorite that hit earth 65 million years ago)

ktch kitchen

ku Kurdish

KUB kidneys, ureter, bladder

Kuw. Kuwait

kV kilovolt

kVA kilovoltampere

KVO keep vein open

kVp kilovolts peak

kw Cornish

kW kilowatt

KW know (shortwave transmission)

.kw Kuwait

KWBC National Weather Service Telecommunications Gateway

kWh kilowatt-hour

kW-hr kilowatt-hour

KWD Kuwait—dinar (currency)

KWIC keyword in context

KWIM [you] know what I mean?

KWT Kuwait (international vehicle ID)

ky Kirghiz

KY Kentucky

Ky. Kentucky

.ky Cayman Islands

KYD Cayman Islands—dollar

KYPO keep your pants on

KZ Kazakhstan (international vehicle ID)

.kz Kazakhstan

KZT Kazakstan—tenge (currency)

L

l length; liter

L 50; lambert; [coarse/ suggestive] language (television rat-

ing); large; Latino (as in personal ads); left; lesbian (as in personal ads); Luxembourg (international vehicle ID)

l. lake; land; late; line; lira

L. Lake; Latin; Licentiate; Linnaean; Lodge

L1 language one (that is, first or native language)

l10n localization (begins with *l*, ends with *n*, 10 letters in between)

L2 language two (that is, second or nonnative language)

L8R later

la Latin

La lanthanum

LA Latin America; Legislative Assembly; linoleic acid; Local Agent; Los Angeles; Los Angeles Dodgers; Louisiana

La. Louisiana

.la Laos

LAA Longest Available Agent

lab laboratory

Lab Labrador retriever

lab. label; labor; laboratory

Lab. Labrador

LAC Lacerta (constellation); LaCrosse encephalitis; large area coverage; local area coverage

LACI lipoprotein-associated coagulation inhibitor

lacq. lacquered

LAD leukocyte adhesion deficiency; leukocyte antibody detection assay

LADAR light amplification for detection and ranging

laddr local address

LAER lowest achievable emission rate

LAES Latin American Economic System

LaF Louisiana French

LAIA Latin American Integration Association

LAK Laos—kip (currency); lymphokine activated killer cells

LAM lymphagioleiomyomatosis

lam. laminated

Lam. Lamentations

LAN Capital City Airport (Lansing, MI); local area network

Lancs. Lancashire

LANDSAT land satellite

lang. language

LANL Los Alamos National Laboratory

LANTIRN low altitude navigation and targeting infrared for night

LAO Laos (international vehicle ID); left anterior oblique [projection]; limited attack options; local area office; local area operations

lap laparotomy

LAP leukocyte alkaline phosphatase

LAPD link access procedure on the D channel

LAPM link access procedure for modems

LAR Libya (international vehicle ID)

LaRC Langley Research Center

LARP live-action role playing

LAS League of Arab States; McCarran International Airport (Las Vegas, NV)

LASCO large angle spectrometric coronagraph; [white] light and spectrometric coronagraph

laser light amplification by stimulated emission of radiation

LASIK laser assisted in-situ keratomileusis

lat. lateral; latitude

Lat. Latin; Latvia; Latvian

LAT local-area transport

l.a.t. local apparent time

LATA local access and transport and area

LATS long-acting thyroid stimulator

LAV lymphadenopathy-associated virus

lav. lavatory

LAVH laparoscopic-assisted vaginal hysteroscopy

LAWN local area wireless network

LAWS laser atmospheric wind sounder

LAX Los Angeles International Airport

laun laundry room

LAUP laser-assisted uvulo-palatoplasty

lb luxemburgeois

LB Labrador; large bowel; Liberia (international vehicle ID); linebacker

lb. *Latin* libra (pound)

.lb Lebanon

LBB Lubbock International Airport

LBBB left bundle branch block

LBD laser beam detector

LBF Lactobacillus bulgaricus factor

LBI limited background investigation

LBJ Lyndon Baines Johnson

LBNL Lawrence Berkeley National Laboratory

LBO leveraged buyout

LBP Lebanon—pound (currency); low back pain

LBS land-based sources [of marine pollution]

lbs. *Latin librae* (pounds)

LBW low birthweight

lc lowercase

LC landing craft; leading cases; lethal concentration; Library of Congress; living children; liquid chromatography; Lord Chancellor; low consumption; Lower Canada

.lc Saint Lucia

l.c. lowercase

L/C letter of credit

LCA left coronary artery; life cycle assessment

LCAT lecithin-cholesterol acyltransferase

LCC life cycle cost

LCCG Lung Cancer Cooperative Group

LCCN Library of Congress Control Number

LCD liquid crystal display; local climatological data; loss of cell delineation

l.c.d. least common denominator

LCDR lieutenant commander

LCH Lake Charles [LA] Regional Airport

LCL lateral collateral ligament; less-than-carload lot; lower control limit

LCI landing craft, infantry; logical channel identifier

l.c.m. least common multiple

LCM landing craft, mechanized

LCMS Lutheran Church Missouri Synod

LCN logical channel number

LCP Link Control Protocol

LCpl lance corporal

LCS landing craft, support; liquid crystal shutter

LCSG Lung Cancer Study Group

LCT land conservation trust; landing craft, tank; local civil time

LCV Line Code Violation

L/cycle liters per cycle

LD laser disk; learning disability; learning disabled; lethal dose; light drinker; limited disease

ld. lead; load

Ld. limited; limited company; lord

LDA logical device address

LDAP Lightweight Directory Access Protocol

LDB liquidity data bank; [Genetic] Location Database

LDC less developed country

LDD light-duty diesel

ldg. landing; loading

LDH lactate dehydrogenase; lactic dehydrogenase

LDL low-density lipoprotein

L-dopa levodopa

LDPE low-density polyethylene

LDP label distribution protocol

LDR long-distance relationship; low-dose rate

ldr. leader

LDRR Laboratory of Diagnostic Radiology Research

LDS Latter-Day Saints

LDT light-duty truck; local descriptor table

LDu. Low Dutch

LDV light-duty vehicle

LE left end; lower extremity; lupus erythematosus
lea. league
Leaps long-term equity anticipation securities
Leb. Lebanon
LEC local exchange carrier
lect. lecture
lectr. lecturer
LED light-emitting diode; low energy detector; St. Petersburg [Russia] Pulkovo Airport
LEEP loop electrocautery excision procedure
LEF Life Extension Foundation
leg. legal; legate; legato; legislation; legislative; legislature
legis legislation; legislative; legislature
legit legitimate
Leics. Leicestershire
LEL lower explosive limit
LEM lunar excursion module
LEO Leo; low earth orbit
LEP Lepus; limited English proficiency
LES leave and earning statement; lower esophageal sphincter
LET linear energy transfer
LEV low-emission vehicle
Lev. Leviticus
Levit. Leviticus
LEX Blue Grass Airport (Lexington, KY)
lex. lexicon
lf line feed; lightface
LF Law French; ledger folio
L-F low frequency
LFA left frontoanterior (position); Lupus Foundation of America
LFD linear finite difference

LFG lexical functional grammar
LFIB label forwarding information base
LFL lower flammability limit
LFN long file name
LFP left frontoposterior (position); low frequency prediction
L.Fr. Law French
LFSR linear feedback shift register
LFT Lafayette [LA] Regional Airport; liver function test
LFU least frequently used
LGA La Guardia Airport (New York, NY); large for gestational age; low gain antenna
LG left guard; Low German
lg. language; large; long
LGB laser-guided bomb; Long Beach Airport/Daugherty Field
lge. large
LGk Late Greek
LGM last glacial maximum; little green men
LGN logical group node
L>R left greater than right
lgstcs linguistics
LGW London Gatwick Airport
LH left hand; liquid hydrogen; luteinizing hormone
LH2 liquid hydrogen
LHA Lincoln Highway Association
LHD *Latin* Litterarum Humanorum Doctor (Doctor of Humane Letters, Doctor of Humanities)
LHE limit hold 'em
LHeb Late Hebrew
LH/FSH-RF luteinizing hormone/follicle stimulating hormone-releasing factor
LHNCBC Lister Hill National

Center for Biomedical Communications

LHR London Heathrow Airport

LHRF luteinizing hormone releasing factor

LHRH luteinizing hormone releasing hormone

LHWCA Longshore and Harbor Workers' Compensation Act

LHX liquid hydrogen

li link

Li lithium

.li Liechtenstein

L.I. Long Island

lib liberation

LIB label information base; Libra; library

lib. liberal; liberalism; librarian; library

Lib. Liberia

libr library

lic license

LID poor operator (shortwave transmission)

lidar light detecting and ranging (laser radar)

Liech. Liechtenstein

Lieut. Lieutenant

LIF Laser Induced Fluorescence; Lifetime (cable channel)

LIFO last in, first out

lig ligation

Li-Ion lithium-ion [battery]

LIJ left internal jugular

LIH Lihue [HI] Airport

lim limit

LIM Jorge Chávez International Airport (Lima, Peru); Lotus Intel Microsoft [expanded memory specification]

Lim. Limerick

LIME laser induced microwave emissions

limo limousine

lin. lineal; linear

LINAC linear accelerator

Lincs. Lincolnshire

LINES long interspersed elements

ling. linguistics

lino linoleum

LION low energy ion and electron instrument

lipo liposuction

LIPS linear inferences per second

liq. liquid; liquor

LIS Portela de Sacavem Airport (Lisbon, Portugal)

LISA Laser Interferometer Space Antenna

LISP List Processing computer language

LISW Licensed Independent Social Worker

lit literature (academic course)

LIT leukocyte immunization therapy; Little Rock National Airport/Adams Field

lit. liter; literal; literally; literary; literature

LitB *Latin* Litterarum Baccalaureus (Bachelor of Letters, Bachelor of Literature)

lit crit literary criticism

LitD *Latin* Litterarum Doctor (Doctor of Letters, Doctor of Literature)

lith. lithograph; lithography

Lith. Lithuania; Lithuanian

litho lithograph

litho. lithograph; lithography

lithog. lithograph; lithography

LitM *Latin* Litterarum Magister (Master of Letters, Master of Literature)

LittB *Latin* Litterarum Baccalaureus (Bachelor of Letters, Bachelor of Literature)

LittD *Latin* Litterarum Doctor (Doctor of Letters, Doctor of Literature)

Litt.M. *Latin* Litterarum Magister (Master of Letters, Master of Literature)

liv. living [room]

L.J. law journal; law judge

Lk Luke

lk. like

Lk. lake

.lk Sri Lanka

LKR Sri Lanka—rupee

LKS liver, kidneys, and spleen

LL Late Latin; Law Latin; limited liability; lower left

ll. laws; leaves; lines

LLAP live long and prosper; LocalTalk Link Access Protocol

LLAT lysolecithin-lecithin acyltransferase

L.Lat. Law Latin

LL.B. *Latin* Legum Baccalaureus (Bachelor of Laws)

LLBA *Linguistics and Language Behavior Abstracts*

LLC limited liability company; logical link control

LL.D. *Latin* Legum Doctor (Doctor of Laws)

LLDC least developed country

LLE left lower extremity

LLETZ large loop excision of transformation zone (of the cervix of the uterus)

LLJ low level jet

LLL La Leche League; left lower lobe

LLLI La Leche League International

LLLTV low light level television

LL.M. *Latin* Legum Magister (Master of Laws)

LLNL Lawrence-Livermore National Laboratory

LLQ left lower quadrant

LLRW low-level radioactive waste

LLWAS Low Level Windshear Alert System

lm lumen

Lm Lamentations

LM Legion of Merit; lunar module

LMA local management association

LMDS local multipoint distribution service

LME large marine ecosystem; Late Middle English

LMFBR liquid metal fast breeder reactor

LMG light machine gun

LMI Leo Minor; Local Management Interface

L/min liters per minute

LMP last menstrual period

LMR living marine resource

LMT licensed massage therapist; local mean time

ln Lingala; natural logarithm

Ln. lane

LN lymph node

LN2 liquid nitrogen

LNA alpha-linoleic acid

LNAPL light non-aqueous phase liquid

LNB low noise block

lndg. landing

lndry laundry

LNEP low noise emission product

LNG liquefied natural gas

LNK Lincoln [NE] Municipal Airport

LNPF lymph node permeability factor

LNU last name unknown

lo Lao; low

LO love olympics (that is, sex with the intent to procreate)

LOA left occipitoanterior (position); letter of agreement; limited operational assessment

l.o.a. length overall

LOAFL lowest observed adverse effect level

LOBT local on-board time

LOC laxatives of choice; level of care; level of consciousness; Library of Congress; loss of consciousness

loc. location; locative

LOCA low osmolar contrast agent

LOCD loss of cell delineation

LOCIS Library of Congress Information System

loc. cit. *Latin* loco citato (in the place cited)

LOCM low osmolar contrast medium

LOCS Land-Ocean-Climate Satellite

LOE Late Old English; level of effort

LOEL lowest observed effect level

LOF loss of frame; lube, oil, and filter [change]

log. logic

logo logotype

LOL laughing out loud; little old lady; lots of love; lots of luck

Lond. London

long. longitude

Long. Longford

LONI Library of Neuropsychological Information

LOOM Loyal Order of Moose

LOP left occipitoposterior (position); loss of pointer

LOQ level of quantification

loq. *Latin* loquitur (speaks)

loran long range radio aid to navigation

LORCS League of Red Cross and Red Crescent Societies

lo-res low resolution

LOROPS long range oblique optical system

LOS law of the sea; length of stay; line of scrimmage; line of sight; loss of sight; loss of signal

LOT left occipitotransverse (position)

LOWR lower

LOX liquid oxygen

LP limited partnership; liquid petroleum; liquid propane; long-playing record; Lower Peninsula [of Michigan] lumbar puncture

LPBT Ladies Professional Bowlers Tour

LPC Licensed Professional Counselor; low pressure chamber

LPD line printer daemon; low probability of detection; luteal phase defect

Lpf liters per flush

LPG liquefied petroleum gas

LPGA Ladies Professional Golf Association

LPH lipotropic hormone

lpi lines per inch

lpm lines per minute

LPN licensed practical nurse

LPO left posterior oblique (position)

LPS lipopolysaccharide

LPV long period variable

LQ letter quality

Lr lawrencium

LR law reports; living room; long reach; lower right; low rate

.lr Liberia

L/R left/right

LRA *Law Reports Annotated*

LRB liquid rocket booster

LRC longitude rotation convention

LRCP Licentiate of the Royal College of Physicians

LRCP(E) Licentiate of the Royal College of Physicians (Edinburgh)

LRCP(I) Licentiate of the Royal College of Physicians (Ireland)

LRCS Licentiate of the Royal College of Surgeons

LRCS(E) Licentiate of the Royal College of Surgeons (Edinburgh)

LRCS(I) Licentiate of the Royal College of Surgeons (Ireland)

LRD Liberia—dollar

LRF Leukemia Research Foundation; luteinizing hormone-releasing factor

LRFA Lymphoma Research Foundation of America

LRFPS Licentiate of the Royal Faculty of Physicians and Surgeon

lrg. large

LRH luteinizing hormone-releasing hormone

LRMS low resolution mass spectroscopy

LRO labor relations officer

LRP live role playing

LRT light-rail transit

LRTI lower respiratory tract infection

LRU least recently used

LRV light-rail vehicle

LS Lesotho (international vehicle ID); level sensor; lumbosacral

.ls Lesotho

L.S. *Latin* locus sigilli (the place of the seal)

LSA left sacroanterior (position); Leukemia Society of America; Linguistic Society of America; link-state advertisement

LSAT Law School Admissions Test

LSB least significant bit

LSC label switch controller; least significant character; link state control

LSD least significant digit; lysergic acid diethylamide

L.S.D. pounds, shillings, and pence

LSF line spread function

LSG large-scale geostrophic

LSI large-scale integration

LSL Lesotho—loti (currency)

LSO landing signal officer; London Symphony Orchestra

LSOA Longitudinal Study of Aging

LSP least significant portion; left sacroposterior (position)

LSR label switch router

L/S ratio lecithin/sphingomyelin ratio

LSS lifesaving service; life-support system
LSSU link status signal unit
LST landing ship, tank; left sacrotransverse (position); local sidereal time; local solar time; low-solvent technology
LSU Louisiana State University
lt left; Lithuanian
LT left tackle; leukotriene; lieutenant; Lithuania (international vehicle ID); local time; long ton
lt. light
Lt. lieutenant
.lt Lithuania
LTC lieutenant colonel; long-term care; long-term concentration
Lt. Col. lieutenant colonel
Lt. Comdr. lieutenant commander
Ltd. limited; limited company
LTE line-terminating equipment
LTG lieutenant general
Lt. Gen. lieutenant general
Lt. Gov. lieutenant governor
lth Laid on Table in House [of Representatives]
LtH left-handed
LTh Licentiate in Theology
LTH luteotropic hormone
lthr leather
LTJG lieutenant junior grade
LTL less than truckload; Lithuania—lita (currency)
LTM long-term memory
LTMSH laughing 'til my sides hurt
LTNS long time no see
LTOP lease-to-ownership plan
LTOT long-term oxygen therapy

LTR long-term relationship
ltr. letter; lighter
lts Laid on Table in Senate
LTS launch telemetry station; launch tracking system
Lu lutetium
LU logical unit
.lu Luxembourg
lub. lubricant; lubricating
lube lubricant; lubricate
LUE left upper extremity
LUF luteinized unruptured follicle; Luxembourg—franc
LUL left upper lobe
LUP Lupus (constellation)
LUQ left upper quadrant
LURC Land Use Regulation Commission
LUST leaking underground storage tanks
LUT local user terminal; lookup table
Luth. Lutheran
luv love
LUWAMH love you with all my heart
lux luxurious
Lux. Luxembourg
Lv Latvian; Leviticus
LV Latvia (international vehicle ID); leave (shortwave transmission); left ventricle
lv. leave; livre
.lv Latvia
LVEDP left ventricle end diastolic pressure
LVET left ventricular ejection time
LVF left ventricular function
LVH left ventricular hypertrophy
lvl level
LVL Latvia—lat (currency)

LVN licensed vocational nurse

LVPS low voltage power supply

LVRS lung volume reduction surgery

LVT landing vehicle tracked

LW longwave; low water

LWCF Land and Water Conservation Fund

LWD low-water data

LWIR long wavelength infrared

LWL length at water line; load water line

LWM low-water mark

LWOP lease with option to purchase; leave without pay

LWR light water reactor

lwr. lower

LWV League of Women Voters

lx lux

.ly Libya

LYD Libya—dinar (currency)

lymph. lymphocyte

LYN Lynx (constellation); Lyon-Bron Airport

LYR Lyra (constellation)

lyr. lyric

lytes electrolytes

lytic osteolytic

LZ landing zone

LZW Lempel-Ziv-Welch [algorithm]

M

m masculine; mass; meter; minute; modulus

M em; Maccabees; Mach number; male; Malta (international vehicle ID); married (as in personal ads); medium; megabyte; mellow; metal; middle term; million; mint; molar; molarity; moment; Monday; month; more (shortwave transmission); [heart] murmur; mutual inductance; 1000

m. manual; married; *Latin* meridies (noon); meridian; mile; morning

M. majesty; mark; master; medieval; mill; minim; Monsieur

M16 model 16 [rifle]

mA milliampere

MA *Latin* Magister Artium (Master of Arts); Marijuana Anonymous; Maritime Administration; Massachusetts; mature audience; medical assistant; mental age; Morocco (international vehicle ID)

.ma Morocco

MAA macroaggregated albumin; master-at-arms; Medical Artists' Association

MAAC maximum allowable actual charge

MAB marine amphibious brigade; monoclonal antibody

MABE Master of Agricultural Business and Economics

MAC maximum allowable cost; media access control; membrane attack complex; military airlift command; minimal alveolar concentration; minimal anesthetic concentration

Mac. Maccabees; Macedonia; Macedonian

MACAP Major Appliance Consumer Action Program

Macc. Maccabees

Maced. Macedonia; Macedonian

mach. machine; machinery; machinist

MACHO massive astrophysical compact halo object

macro macroinstruction

MACTIS Marine and Coastal Technology Information Service

MAD Barajas Airport (Madrid, Spain); Morocco—dirham (currency); mutually assured destruction

Mad. Madagascar; madam

MADD Mothers Against Drunk Driving

MADER Management of Atmospheric Data for Evaluation and Research

MADI multichannel audio digital interface

MAE Master of Aeronautical Engineering; Master of Art Education; Master of Arts in Education; Metropolitan Area Ethernet; moves all extremities

MAEd Master of Arts in Education

MAER maximum allowable emission rate

MAESA Measurements for Assessing the Effects of Stratospheric Aircraft

MAEW moves all extremities well

MAF macrophage-activating factor; Midland [TX] International Airport; million acre-feet

mag magazine

mag. magnet; magnetism; magneto; magnitude

maglrv magnetic levitation [train]

MAgr Master of Agriculture

mahog. mahogany

MAI Mycobacterium avium-intracellulare; [World Trade Organization] Multilateral Investment Agreement

maint. maintenance

MAJ major

Maj. major

Maj. Gen. major general

MAL Malaysia (international vehicle ID)

Mal. Malachi; Malawi; Malawian; Malay; Malaysia; Malaysian

MALS Master of Arts in Liberal Studies; Master of Arts in Library Science

MAN Metropolitan Area Network; Ringway International Airport (Manchester, England)

man. manual

Man. Manitoba

M & A mergers and acquisitions

M & I municipal and industrial

M & IE meals and incidental expenses

M & S modeling and simulation

man. pr. *Latin* mane primo (early morning, first thing in the morning)

MANS Microcosm Autonomous Navigation System

MANTIS Manual, Alternative, and Natural Therapy Index System

manuf. manufacture; manufacturer

manufac. manufacture

MAO monoamine oxidase

MAOI monoamine oxidase inhibitor

MAP mean arterial pressure; modified American plan

MAPI [Microsoft's] Messaging Application Programming Interface

M-appeal man appeal

MAPs microtubule-associated proteins

MAPS measuring air pollution from space; mesoscale analysis and prediction system; Meteorological and Aeronautical Presentation System

MAPW Medical Association for Prevention of War

mar. maritime; married

Mar. March

MAR major acquisition review; Mid-Atlantic Ridge

MARAD Maritime Administration

MARC machine readable cataloging

March. marchioness

Marecs Maritime European Communications Satellite

MARF Medical Acupuncture Research Foundation

marg. margin; marginal

MARIC Marine Resources Information Center

MARS multicast address resolution server

Mart. Martinique

MARV maneuverable reentry vehicle

MAS mobile atmospheric spectrometer

masc. masculine

maser microwave amplification by stimulated emission of radiation

MASH Mobile Army Surgical Hospital

maspin mammary associated serine protease inhibitor

Mass. Massachusetts

MAST military antishock trousers

MAT Master of Arts in Teaching

mat. matinee

MATC maximum acceptable toxicant concentration

math mathematics

math. mathematical; mathematician

MATIP mapping of airline traffic over IP

Matt. Matthew

MATV master antenna television

MATZ military air traffic zone

MAU media attachment unit; multistation access unit

MAV micro air vehicle

MAWS missile approach warning system

max maximum

MAX Cinemax

max. maximum

MAXX Maximum Access to Diagnosis and Therapy (The Electronic Library of Medicine)

mayo mayonnaise

mb millibar

Mb megabit

MB Manitoba; *Latin* Medicinae Baccalaureus (Bachelor of Medicine); megabyte

MBA married but available; Hewlett-Packard Co.

MBAA Mortgage Bankers Association of America

MBAS methylene blue active substance

MBC maximum breathing capacity

MBCI Medical Books for China International

mbd million barrels per day

MBD minimal brain dysfunction

MBDA Minority Business Development Agency
MBE Member of the Order of the British Empire; minority business enterprise; molecular beam epitaxy
MBFR mutual and balanced force reduction
MBHO Managed Behavioral Healthcare Organization
Mbits/s megabits per second
MBL marine boundary layer
MBNA Monument Builders of North America
MBO management by objective
Mbone multicast backbone
Mbps megabits per second
MBR master bedroom; master boot record
MBret. Middle Breton
MBS maximum burst size; mortgage-backed security; Mutual Broadcasting System
MBT mother's blood type
MBTA Massachusetts Bay Transit Authority
MBTI Myers-Briggs [personality] Type Indicator
MBV model-based vision
Mbyte megabyte
mc millicurie
Mc Maccabees; megacycle
MC Marine Corps; Maritime Commission; Master Card; master of ceremonies; Medical Corps; megacycle; Member of Congress; Monaco (international vehicle ID)
.mc Monaco
m/c miscarriage
MCA microchannel architecture; middle cerebral artery; motorcycle accident

MCAT Medical College Admissions Test
MCB maximum buoyancy can
MCBF mean cycles between failures
MCC mid-course correction; Midwest Climate Center; Mission Control Center
MCCA Medicare Catastrophic Coverage Act
MCD McDonald's Corp.; minimum cost design
MCDV maximum cell delay variation
mcf thousand cubic feet
mcg microgram
MCGA multicolor graphics array
MCh Magister Chirurgiae, Master of Surgery
MCH mean corpuscular hemoglobin
MCHB Maternal and Child Health Bureau
MCHC mean corpuscular hemoglobin concentration
MCHPRC Maternal and Child Health Policy Research Center
mCi millicurie
MCI Kansas City International Airport; Microwave Communications Inc. (formerly)
MCIC Managed Care Information Center
MCL Marine Corps League; Master of Civil Law; Master of Comparative Law; [Environmental Protection Agency] maximum contaminant level; medial collateral ligament
MCLG [Environmental Protection Agency] maximum contaminant level goal

MCM mechanical current meter; multichip module

MCMI Millon clinical multiaxial inventory

MCN molecular and cellular neuroscience

MCO managed care organization; Orlando International Airport

MCP male chauvinist pig; metacarpophalangeal joint; microchannel plate

MCP-1 monocyte chemoattractant protein-1

MCPI medical consumer price index

MCPO master chief petty officer

MCR medical cost ratio; metabolic clearance rate; minimum cell rate

MCS mesoscale convective system; multiple chemical sensitivity

M-CSF macrophage colony-stimulating factor

MCT metal-oxide-semiconductor controlled transistor

MCTD maximum cell transfer delay

MCU multipoint control unit

MCV mean corpuscular volume; mesoscale convectively generated vortices

Md mendelevium

MD mail drop; Maryland; mediation device; Medical Department; *Latin* Medicinae Doctor (Doctor of Medicine); Middle Dutch; minidisc; Moldova (international vehicle ID); muscular dystrophy

Md. Maryland

.md Moldova

m/d months after date

MDA methylenedioxy amphetamine; monochrome display adapter; Muscular Dystrophy Association

MDa. Middle Danish

M-day mobilization day

MDC more developed country

MDD major depressive disorder

MDE motor drive electronics

MDF Macular Degeneration Foundation

MDI metered dose inhaler; multiple document interface

m. dict. *Latin* more dicto (as directed)

MDiv Master of Divinity

MDL Moldova—leu (currency)

MDLP Mobile Data Link Protocol

Mdm. Madam

MDMA methylenedioxy-methamphetamine

MDN message disposition notification

MDNCF monocyte-derived neutrophil chemotactic factor

mdnt. midnight

MDR minimum daily requirement

MDS Master of Dental Surgery; Message Delivery Service

mdse. merchandise

mds rm maid's room

MDT Harrisburg International Airport; Mountain Daylight Time

MDu. Middle Dutch

MDW Chicago Midway Airport

MDY month/day/year

ME Maine; medical examiner; Middle English

Me. Maine

M.E. mechanical engineer; mechanical engineering; mining engineer; mining engineering; mission engineer

meas. measurable; measure

mech. mechanical; mechanics; mechanism

MECO main engine cutoff

med medical

MEd Master of Education

MED minimum effective dose; Office of Medical Services (State)

med. medial; median; medication; medicine; medieval; medium

Med. Mediterranean

MEDEA Measurements of Earth Data for Environmental Analysis

medfly Mediterranean fruit fly

Med. Gk Medieval Greek

Med. Gr. Medieval Greek

Medicaid medical aid insurance

Medicare medical care insurance

Medit. Mediterranean

Med. L Medieval Latin

MEDLARS Medical Literature Analysis and Retrieval System

Med. Lat. Medieval Latin

MEDLINE MEDLARS Online

meds medications

MEDS Meteorological and Environmental Data Services

meg megabyte; megohm

MEG magnetoencephalogram

MEGO my eyes glaze over

MEI Medicare Economic Index

MEK methyl ethyl ketone

MEL Melbourne [Australia] Airport (Tullamarine Airport)

MELICA medium energy ion composition analyzer

MEM Eagle's minimum essential medium

mem. member; memoir; memorandum; memorial

memo memorandum

MEMS microelectromechanical systems

MEN Mensa (constellation)

MEng Master of Engineering

mep mean effective pressure

MEP member of the European Parliament

MEPED medium energy proton and electron detector

mEq milliequivalent

MEQ/L milliequivalents per liter

mer. meridian

merc. mercantile; mercury; Mercury

Mercosur *Spanish* Mercado Común del Cono Sur (Southern Cone Common Market)

MES main engine start

MESA microsurgical epididymal sperm aspiration

MeSH Medical Subject Headings

MESI modified, exclusive, shared, and invalid [data]

Messrs. Messieurs

Met New York Metropolitan Opera Company; New York Metropolitan Opera House

MET metabolic equivalent

met. metaphysics; metropolitan

metal. metallurgic; metallurgy

metall. metallurgic; metallurgy

metaph. metaphor; metaphoric; metaphysics

METCON Metropolitan Consortium for Minorities in Science and Engineering

meteor. meteorological; meteorology

meteorol. meteorology

meth methamphetamine

Meth. Methodist

metHb methemoglobin

metMb myoglobin

METO Middle East Treaty Organization

mets metastasis

METs metabolic equivalents

METSAT meteorological satellite

MeV million electron-volts

MEWA multiple employer welfare arrangements

MEX Benito Juárez International Airport (Mexico City, Mexico); Mexico (international vehicle ID)

Mex. Mexican; Mexico

Mex. Sp. Mexican Spanish

mezz. mezzanine

mf medium frequency; mezzo forte

mF millifarad

MF medium frequency; Middle French; mother fucker

MFA Master of Fine Arts

MFBI major fuel burning installation

MFCMA Magnuson Fishery Conservation and Management Act

MFD multifunction display

mfd. manufactured

MFE McAllen [TX] Miller International Airport

mfg. manufacture; manufacturing; manufactured

MFH Master of Fox Hounds

MFIB Medicare Fraud Investigations Branch

MFJ married filing jointly

MFlem. Middle Flemish

MFM modified frequency modulation

MFN most-favored nation

MFP major frame pulse; mean free path; mobile flux platform

MFR Rogue Valley International-Medford [OR] Airport

mfr. manufacture; manufacturer

MFS Medicare fee schedule

MFT master file table

mg Malagasy; milligram

Mg magnesium

MG machine gun; major general; military government

.mg Madagascar

MGA Augusto César Sandino Airport (Managua, Nicaragua); monochrome graphics adapter

mgal milligal

mGal milligal

MGB *Russian* Ministerstvo Gosudarstvennoj Bezopasnosti (Ministry of State Security)

mgd million gallons per day

MGE Minneapolis Grain Exchange

MGES Multispecialty Group Executive Society

MGF Madagascar—Malagasy franc (currency)

MGk Middle Greek

MGL Mongolia (international vehicle ID)

MG/L milligrams per liter

mgm milligram

MGM Metro-Goldwyn-Mayer; Montgomery [AL] Regional/Dannelly Field Airport

MGMA Medical Group Management Association

mgmt. management

MGP matrix Gla protein

mgr. manager

Mgr. Monseigneur; Monsignor

MGS Mars Global Surveyor

mgt. management

MGySgt master gunnery sergeant

mh millihenry

MH Medal of Honor; medical history; mental health

.mh Marshall Islands

MHA Master of Hospital Administration; Mental Health Association

MHAUS Malignant Hyperthermia Association of the United States

MHBFY my heart bleeds for you

MHC major histocompatibility complex; Mental Health Commission

MHD magnetohydrodynamic

MHG Middle High German

MHL Master of Hebrew Literature

MHN Mental Health Net

MHOTY my hat's off to you

MHP Multimedia Home Platform

MHS message handling system; Military Health System

MHSS Military Health Services System

MHT Manchester [NH] Airport

MHW mean high water

MHz megahertz

mi Maori

Mi Micah

MI mentally impaired; Michigan; military intelligence; mitral insufficiency; mode indicator; multiple intelligences; myocardial infarction

mi. mile; mill

MIA Miami Dolphins; Miami International Airport; missing in action

MIB Medical Information Bureau; Management Information Base

MIBK methyl isobutyl ketone

mic microphone

MIC media interface connector; message integrity check; methyl isocyanate; Microscopium (constellation); military-industrial complex; minimal inhibitory concentration

Mic. Micah

MICA medical intensive care unit; mentally ill chemical abuser; mentally ill chronic abuser; modem ISDN channel aggregation

Mich. Michigan

MICIS Midwestern Climate Information System

MICLP Medical Informatics Cultural Literacy Project

MICR magnetic ink character recognition

MICS macro interpretive commands

micro. microcomputer; microprocessor; microscopic

microbiol. microbiology

mid. middle

MID message identifier; Military Intelligence Division; minimal infecting dose

MIDI musical instrument digital interface

Midn. midshipman

MIDP Mobile Information Device Profile

MIF migration-inhibitory factor

MIGA Multilateral Investment Guarantee Agency

MIH melanotropin release-inhibiting hormone

MII media independent interface

mil million

MIL military; Milwaukee Brewers; mother-in-law

mil. military; militia

.mil military organization

MILF mother I'd like to fuck

milit. military

MILO magnetically insulated line oscillator

MILSTAR military strategic and tactical relay satellite

MIM *Mendelian Inheritance in Man*

mim. mimeograph

MIME multipurpose Internet mail extensions

mimeo mimeograph

MIMIC microwave/millimeter wave monolithic integrated circuit

MIN Minnesota Twins; Minnesota Vikings

min. mineralogy; minim; minimum; mining; minister; minor; minute

Minn. Minnesota

MINURSO *French* la Mission des Nations Unies pour l'organisation d'un référendum au Sahara occidental (United Nations Mission for the Referendum in Western Sahara)

MIO minimal identifiable odor

MIP monthly investment plan

MIPS million instructions per second

MIr Middle Irish

MIR microwave imaging radiometer

MIRA Media Image Resource Alliance

MIRP Manipulated Information Rate Processor

MIRV multiple independently targeted reentry vehicle

MIS management information services; management information system; manager of information services

misc. miscellaneous

MISR multiangle imaging spectrometer

Miss. Mississippi

mistr. mistranslation; mistranslating

mit mitigating circumstance

MIT Massachusetts Institute of Technology

MIT/LL Massachusetts Institute of Technology—Lincoln Laboratory

MIX multiservice interchange

MIZ marginal ice zone

mk Macedonian

Mk Mark

MK Macedonia (international vehicle ID); make (shortwave transmission); menaquinone

mk. mark; markka

.mk Macedonia

MK-6 menaquinone-6

MK-7 menaquinone-7

MKD Macedonia—denar (currency)

MKE General Mitchell International Airport (Milwaukee, Wisconsin)

MKG Muskegon County [MI] Airport

MKK Molokai Airport (Kaunakakai, HI)

mks meter-kilogram-second

mksA meter-kilogram-second-ampere

MKSAP Medical Knowledge Self-Assessment Program

mkt. market

mktg. marketing

ml Malayalam; milliliter

mL millilambert

Ml Malachi

ML Medieval Latin; Middle Latin

M-L mediolateral

.ml Mali

MLA Medical Library Association; Member of the Legislative Assembly; Modern Language Association

MLB Melbourne, Florida, International Airport

MLC Marginal Line Calculus Index

MLD median lethal dose; minimum lethal dose

MLDT mean logistics delay time

MLE midline episiotomy

MLF multilateral force

MLG Middle Low German

MLI multilayer insulation; Quad City International Airport (Moline, IL)

Mlle Mademoiselle

Mlles Mesdemoiselles

mlRNA messenger-like RNA

MLS Master of Library Science; multilayer switching; Multiple Listing Service

MLSS mixed liquor suspended solids

MLV medium launch vehicle

MLVSS mixed liquor volatile suspended solids

MLW mean low water

mm millimeter

MM mesoscale model

.mm Myanmar

m.m. *Latin* mutatis mutandis (with the necessary changes)

M.M. Messieurs

MMC Marine Mammal Commission

MMCC Medicare Managed Care Contract

MMD mass median diameter

MMDS Multichannel Multipoint Distribution Service

Mme Madame

Mmes Mesdames

mmf magnetomotive force

MMF multimode fiber

MMH monomethyl hydrazine

mmHg millimeters of mercury

MMI man-machine interface

MMIC monolithic microwave integrated circuit

MMK Myanmar—kyat (currency)

MML Man-Machine Language

MMM mesoscale and microscale meteorology; Minnesota Mining & Manufacturing Co.

MMMT malignant mixed müllerian tumor; malignant mixed mesodermal tumor

mmol millimole

MMPA Marine Mammal Protection Act

MMPI Minnesota Multiphasic Personality Inventory

MMR measles, mumps, rubella

MMS Minerals Management Service

MMT million metric tons; multiple mirror telescope

MMU manned maneuvering unit; memory-management unit

MMW millimeter wave

MMX multimedia extensions

mn Mongolian

Mn manganese

MN magnetic north; Minnesota

.mn Mongolia

MNC multinational corporation

MND motor neuron disease

MNDA Motor Neurone Disease Association

mngr. manager

MNL Ninoy Aquino International Airport (Manila, Philippines)

MNP Microcom Network Protocol

MnSOD manganese superoxide dismutase

MNT medical nutrition therapy; Mongolia—tugrik (currency)

mo Moldavian

Mo molybdenum

MO magnetooptical; mail order; medical officer; Missouri; *Latin* modus operandi (way of working); money order; Philip Morris Cos.

mo. month

Mo. Missouri

.mo Macau

MOA market opportunity analysis; memorandum of agreement

MoAb monoclonal antibody

MOB medical office building; mother of the bride

MOBA Museum of Bad Art [of Boston]

moc moccasin

MOC market on close [order]; Mozambique (international vehicle ID)

mod modern

MOD mesiodistocclusal

mod. moderate; moderato; modern; modulo; modulus

Mod. Da. Modern Danish

modem modulator demodulator

Mod. Du. Modern Dutch

Mod. E. Modern English

Mod. Fr. Modern French

Mod. G Modern German

Mod. Gk Modern Greek

Mod. Gr. Modern Greek

Mod. Heb. Modern Hebrew

Mod. Icel. Modern Icelandic

modif modification

Mod. Ir. Modern Irish

MODIS moderate resolution imaging spectroradiometer

Mod. L. Modern Latin

Mod. Prov. Modern Provençal

Mod. Skt Modern Sanskrit

MOF magneto-optical filter

MOG mother of the groom

Moho Mohorovicic discontinuity

MOI memorandum of intent

MOIL Marine Operations and Instrumentation Laboratory

MOL Manned Orbital Laboratory

mol. molecular; molecule

mol. wt. molecular weight

MOM Militia of Montana; milk of magnesia

m.o.m. middle of month

MOMA Museum of Modern Art

MOMV manned orbital maneuvering vehicle

MON Monoceros; Montreal Expos

mon. monastery; monetary

Mon. Monday

Mong. Mongolia

mono monaural; mononucleosis; monophonic

Mont. Montana

MOO Milkbottles Only Organization; MUD, object oriented

MOP Macau—pataca (currency)

MOPA master oscillator power amplifier

MOR middle-of-the-road; monthly operating review

mor. morocco; mortar

Mor. Morocco; Moroccan

mor. dict. *Latin* more dicto (as directed)

MORE Minority Outreach Research and Education

MorF male or female

morn. morning

morph metamorphose; morphine

morph. morphological; morphology

mor. sol. *Latin* more solito (as usual, as customary)

MOS margin of safety; member of the opposite sex; metal-oxide semiconductor; military occupational specialty

mos. months

MOSFET metal oxide semiconductor field effect transistor

MOST magneto-optical storage technology

mot. motion

MOTAS member of the appropriate sex

MoTD message of the day

MOTOS member of the opposite sex

MOTSS member of the same sex

MOTV manned orbital transfer vehicle

MOU memorandum of understanding

Mountie mounted policeman; member of the Royal Canadian Mounted Police

MOVE Mobility Opportunities Via Education

MOW movie of the week

MOZ Mozambique

Moz. Mozambique

mp melting point; mezzo piano

MP member of Parliament; military police; military police officer; mounted police

.mp Northern Mariana Islands

m.p. *Latin* modo praescripto (in the manner prescribed)

MPA Master of Public Administration; Master of Public Accounting; microscopic particulate analysis

MPAA Motion Picture Association of America

MPC Multimedia Personal Computer

MPCA The Media Photographers' Copyright Agency

MPD maximum permissible dose; minimum peripheral dose

MPE malignant pleural effusion; Master of Public Education

MPEG Moving Picture Experts Group

MPer. Middle Persian

mpg miles per gallon

mph miles per hour

MPH Master of Public Health

MPhil master of philosophy

MPI marine pollution incident

MPLC Motion Picture Licensing Corporation

Mpls. Minneapolis

mpm meters per minute

MPM malignant pleural mesothelioma; microwave power module

MPN most probable number

MPP massively parallel processor

MPPDA Medicine-Pediatrics Program Directors Association

MPR mannose-6-phosphate receptors; monthly program review

MPRSA Marine Protection, Research, and Sanctuaries Act

mps meters per second

MPS Medical Protection Society; mononuclear phagocyte system

MPX multiplex

.mq Martinique

MQP mandatory quote period

MQT Marquette County [MI] Airport

mr Marathi; milliradian

mR milliroentgen

MR medium rate; mental retardation; metabolic rate; mitral regurgitation

Mr. mister (Used as a courtesy title for a man)

.mr Mauritania

MRA minimum retirement age

MRAA Mental Retardation Association of America

MRC Medical Research Council

MRCP magnetic resonance cholangiopancreatography; Member of the Royal College of Physicians

MRCP(E) Member of the Royal College of Physicians (Edinburgh)

MRCP(I) Member of the Royal College of Physicians (Ireland)

MRCS Member of the Royal College of Surgeons

MRCS(E) Member of the Royal College of Surgeons (Edinburgh)

MRCS(I) Member of the Royal College of Surgeons (Ireland)

MRCVS Member of the Royal College of Veterinary Surgeons

MRD minimal reacting dose

MRE Meals Ready to Eat

mrem millirem

MRF medium-range forecast; melanotropin-releasing factor

MRH melanotropin-releasing hormone

MRI machine-readable information; magnetic resonance imaging; Mystery Readers International

MRIN marriage record identification number

MRIPS Multimodality Radiological Image Processing System

MRK Merck & Co. Inc.

MRMC Medical Research Modernization Committee

mRNA messenger RNA

MRO Mauritania—ouguiya (currency); Medical Review Officer

MROCC Medical Review Officer Certification Council

MRP material requirements planning

Mrs. Used as a courtesy title for a married or widowed woman (from "mistress")

MRS media recognition system ; medical review systems

MRSA methicillin-resistant Staphylococcus aureus

MRY Monterey Peninsula Airport

ms Malay; manuscript; millisecond; mitral stenosis

Ms Used as courtesy title for a woman, regardless of marital status (a blend of Miss and Mrs.)

MS *Latin* Magister Scientiae (Master of Science); mail stop; mass spectrometer; mass spectrometry; Mauritius (international vehicle ID); Microsoft; microwave scanner; Mississippi; mitral stenosis; multiple sclerosis

Ms. Miss/Mrs.

.ms Montserrat

MSA management services agreement; Master of Science in Agriculture; medical savings account; methane sulfonic acid; Metropolitan Statistical Area

MSAFP maternal serum alpha-fetoprotein

MSB most significant bit; most significant byte

MSc *Latin* Magister Scientiae (Master of Science)

MSC most significant character

MSCI Morgan Stanley Capital Index

MSD most significant digit

MS-DOS Microsoft Disk Operating System

msec millisecond

MSEN Multiple Sclerosis Education Network

MSF Multiple Sclerosis Foundation

MSFC Marshall Space Flight Center; Medical Students for Choice

MSFT Microsoft Corp.

MSG monosodium glutamate

msg. message

Msgr. Monseigneur; Monsignor

M.Sgt. master sergeant

MSH melanocyte-stimulating hormone

MSHA Mine Safety and Health Administration

MSI minority-serving institution; multispectral imager

MS in LS Master of Science in Library Science

MSJ message (shortwave transmission)

MSKCC Memorial Sloan-Kettering Cancer Center

MSL maximum stress load; mean sea level

MSLT Multiple Sleep Latency Test

MSN Dane County [WI] Regional Airport-Truax Field; Master of Science in Nursing; MSNBC

MSNBC Microsoft/National Broadcasting Company

MSO management service organization

MSP Minneapolis-St. Paul Airport/Wold-Chamberlain Field Airport; most significant portion

MSPB Merit Systems Protection Board

MSR measure (shortwave transmission); monthly status report

MSRC Marine Sciences Research Center

mss manuscripts

MSS management support system; message switching system; multispectral scanner

MSS. manuscripts

MSSD Model Secondary School for the Deaf

MST mesosphere-stratosphere-troposphere; Mountain Standard Time

mstr. br. master bedroom

MSTS Military Sea Transportation Service

MSU Michigan State University; microwave sounding unit; Minnesota State University; Mississippi State University; Montana State University

MSUD Maple Syrup Urine Disease

MSW Master of Social Welfare; Master of Social Work

MSw. Middle Swedish

MSY New Orleans International Airport/Moisant Field

mt Maltese

Mt Matthew; meitnerium

MT empty; machine translation; massage therapy; megaton; metric ton; Montana; Mountain Time

mt. maintenance

Mt. mount; mountain

.mt Malta

MTA material transfer agreement; message transfer agent; Metropolitan Transportation Authority

MTB Materials Transportation Bureau

MTBE methyl tertiary butyl ether

MTBF mean time between failures

mtc. maintenance

MTCR Missile Technology Control Regime

MTD maximum tolerated dose

mtDNA mitochondrial deoxyribonucleic acid

MTF modulation transfer function

mtg. meeting; mortgage

mtge. mortgage

mth. month

mthly. monthly

MTL Malta—lira

Mtn. mountain

MTO Mediterranean Theater of Operations

MTPPI Medical Technology and Practice Patterns Institute

MTPR miniature temperature pressure recorder

MTR magnetic tape recorder; miniature temperature recorder

MTS Musculoskeletal Tumor Society

Mts. mountains

MTSO mobile telephone switching office

MTTR mean-time-to-restore; mean-time-to-repair

MTU maximum transmission unit

MTV Music Television

MTY General Mariano Escobedo International Airport (Monterrey, Mexico)

MU multiple unit

.mu Mauritius

m.u. mouse unit

MUC Munich Franz Josef Strauss International Airport

MUD multiuser dimension; multiuser domain; multiuser dungeon

MUDOS [Digital Research's] Multiuser Distributed Operating System

MUFON Mutual UFO Network, [Inc.]

multi-CSF multicolonystimulating factor

mun. municipal

muni municipal bond

munic. municipal

Mur muramic acid

MUR Mauritius—rupee (currency)

MUS Musca (constellation)

mus. museum; music; musical; musician

MusB *Latin* Musicae Baccalaureus (Bachelor of Music)

MusD *Latin* Musicae Doctor (Doctor of Music)

MusDr *Latin* Musicae Doctor (Doctor of Music)

MusM *Latin* Musicae Magister (Master of Music)

mux multiplexer

mV millivolt

MV mean variation; megavolt; mitral valve

.mv Maldives

MVA motor vehicle accident

MVD *Russian* Ministerstvo Vnutrennikh Del (Ministry of Internal Affairs)

MVMA Motor Vehicle Manufacturers Association

MVP most valuable player; mitral valve prolapse

MVPS medical volume performance standard; Medicare volume performance standard

MVR Maldives—rufiyaa (currency); mitral valve replacement

MVS [IBM's] Multiple Virtual System

MVV maximum voluntary ventilation

mW milliwatt

MW Malawi (international vehicle ID); molecular weight

.mw Malawi

MWC married with children

MWC model Monod-Wyman-Changeux model

MWe megawatts electric

MWF Monday-Wednesday-Friday

MWK Malawi—kwacha (currency)

MWS major weapon system; microwave spectrometer

MWSR microwave water substance radiometer

mx metastases

Mx maxwell

MX Merry Christmas; motocross

.mx Mexico

mxd. mixed

MXP Mexico—peso; Milano-Malpensa International Airport

my Burmese; million years

My. May

.my Malaysia

MYA million years ago

myc. mycological; mycology

mycol. mycological; mycology

MYOB Mind your own business!

MYR Malaysia—ringgit (currency); Myrtle Beach International Airport

myth. mythological; mythology

mythol. mythological; mythology

.mz Mozambique

MZM Mozambique—metical (currency)

MZT General Rafael Bueina [Airport] (Mazatlan, Mexico)

N

n indefinite number; neuter; neutron; new; normal; note

N en; knight; name; needs improvement; Newton; New York Stock Exchange; nitrogen; no (shortwave transmission); nominative; noon; north; northern; Norway (international vehicle ID); not (shortwave transmission); noun

n. footnote; *Latin* natus (born); net; note; noun

N. Norse

na Nauru

Na Nahum; sodium

NA Narcotics Anonymous; Native American (as in personal ads); Netherlands Antilles (international vehicle ID); not allowed; not applicable; not available

Na. Nahum

.na Namibia

n.a. *Latin* non allocatur (it is not allowed)

N.A. North America

N/A not applicable; not available

NAA National Academy on Aging; National Aeronautic Association; Neurosciences Administration Assembly; next available agent

NAACP National Association for the Advancement of Colored People

NAADD National Association on Alcohol, Drugs and Disability

NAAF National Alopecia Areata Foundation

NAAFA National Association to Advance Fat Acceptance

NAAP National Association of Activity Professionals

NAAR National Alliance for Autism Research

NAAWP National Association for Advancement of White People

NAB National Association of Broadcasters; *New American Bible*

NABCO National Alliance of Breast Cancer Organizations

nabe neighborhood

NABR National Association for Biomedical Research

NAC National Advisory Council; National AIDS Clearinghouse; National Asbestos Council

NACA National Advisory Committee for Aeronautics

NACAA National Association of Consumer Agency Administrators

NACB National Academy of Clinical Biochemistry

NACC North Atlantic Cooperation Council

NACCHO National Association of County and City Health Officials

NACD National Association of Computer Dealers; National Association of Conservation Districts

NACHRI National Association of Children's Hospitals and Related Institutions

NACM National Association of Credit Management

NACO National Association of Counties

NACoA National Association for Children of Alcoholics

NACOA National Advisory Committee on Oceans and Atmosphere

NACS National Association of College Stores

NACU National Association of Colleges and Universities

NAD Namibia—dollar; National Academy of Design; National Association of the Deaf; nicotinamide adenine dinucleotide; no acute distress; no apparent distress; no appreciable disease

NADA National Automobile Dealers Association

NADC Naval Air Development Center

NADF National Adrenal Diseases Foundation; North American Directory Forum

NADH nicotinamide adenine dinucleotide (reduced form)

NADL National Association of Dental Laboratories

NADN nearest active downstream neighbor

NADONA/LTC National Association of Directors of Nursing Administration in Long Term Care

NADP nicotinamide adenine dinucleotide phosphate

NADPH nicotinamide adenine dinucleotide phosphate (reduced form)

NAD+ nicotinamide adenine dinucleotide (oxidized form)

NADP+ nicotinamide adenine dinucleotide phosphate (oxidized form)

nads testicles (from "gonads")

NADS National Association for Down Syndrome; *Newsletter of the American Dialect Society*

NADT National Association for Drama Therapy

NAE National Academy of Engineering

NAELA National Academy of Elder Law Attorneys

NAEMSE National Association of Emergency Medical Service Educators

NAEMSP National Association of Emergency Medical Service Physicians

NAEMT National Association of Emergency Medical Technicians

NAEP National Assessment of Educational Progress

NAEPP National Asthma Education and Prevention Program

NAER National Association for Emergency Response

NAF National Abortion Foundation; National Anxiety Foundation; National Ataxia Foundation; Naval Air Facility; neutrophil activating factor

NAFA Nordic Association for Andrology

NAFAC National Association for Ambulatory Care

NAFC National Association for Continence

NAFO Northwest Atlantic Fisheries Organization

N. Afr. North Africa

NAFTA North American Free Trade Agreement

NAG N-acetylglutamate

NAGARA National Association of Government Archives and Records Administrators

Nah. Nahum

NAHAT National Association of Health Authorities and Trusts

NAHB National Association of Home Builders

NAHC National Association for Home Care

NAHDO National Association of Health Data Organizations

NAHN National Association of Hispanic Nurses

NAHQ National Association of Health Quality

NAHRO National Association of Housing and Redevelopment Officials

NAHS North American Hyperthermia Society

NAIA National Association of Intercollegiate Athletes

NAIC National Aging Information Center; National Association of Insurance Commissioners

NAICS North American Industry Classification System

Nairu nonaccelerating inflation rate of unemployment

NAK negative acknowledgment

NALC National Association of Letter Carriers

Nam Vietnam

NAM Namibia (international vehicle ID); National Association of Manufacturers

N. Am. North America; North American

NAMA National Alliance of Methadone Advocates

NAMAC National Alliance for Media Arts and Culture

NAMCP National Association of Managed Care Physicians

NAMCS National Ambulatory Medical Care Survey

NAME National Association of Miniature Enthusiasts

N. Amer. North America; North American

NAMES National Association for Medical Equipment Services

NAMF National Association of Metal Finishers

NAMH National Association for Mental Health

NAMI National Alliance for the Mentally Ill

NAMIEP National AIDS Minority Information and Education Program

NAMSS National Association Medical Staff Services

NAMT National Association for Music Therapy

NANAD National Association of Anorexia Nervosa and Associated Disorders

NANBNC hepatitis non-A, non-B, non-C hepatitis

NANC neuron nonadrenergic, noncholinergic neuron

NANCO National Association of Noise Control Officials

NAND NOT AND (logical operator)

NANDA North American Nursing Diagnosis Association

N & V nausea and vomiting

NANP North American Numbering Plan

NANMT National Association of Nurse Massage Therapists

NANN National Association of Neonatal Nurses

NANOS North American Neuro-Ophthalmology Society

NANPRH National Association of Nurse Practitioners in Reproductive Health

NAOMA National Acupuncture and Oriental Medicine Alliance

NAON National Association of Orthopaedic Nurses

NAOTD National Alliance of the Disabled

NAP Napoli-Capodichino Airport; network access point; neutrophil activating protein

NAPA National Academy of Public Administration; National Association of Performing Artists

NAPAFASA National Asian Pacific American Families Against Substance Abuse

napalm naphthene + palmitate

NAPAP National Acid Precipitation Assessment Program

NAPBC National Action Plan on Breast Cancer

NAPCAN National Association for Prevention of Child Abuse and Neglect

NAPCRG North American Primary Care Research Group

NAPE National Association of Physicians for the Environment

NAPH National Association of Public Hospitals and Health Systems

naph. naphtha

NAPHO National Association of Physician Hospital Organization

NAPHSIS National Association for Public Health Statistics and Information Systems

NAPIA National Association of Professional Insurance Agents

NAPNAP National Association of Pediatric Nurse Associates and Practitioners

NAPNES National Association for Practical Nurse Education and Service

NAPS National Association of Personnel Services

NAPSA North American Pediatric Subspecialty Association

NAPWA National Association of People Living with HIV/AIDS

NAR National Association of Realtors

nar. narrow

NARA National Air Resources Act; National Archives and Records Administration

NARAL National Abortion and Reproductive Rights Action League

NARAS National Academy of Recording Arts and Sciences

narc narcotics agent

narc. narcotic; narcotics

narco narcotics agent

NARCOMS North American Research Consortium on Multiple Sclerosis

NAREB National Association of Real Estate Boards

NARFE National Association of Retired Federal Employees

NARHP National Adolescent Reproductive Health Partnership

NARIC National Rehabilitation Information Center

NARMC North Atlantic Regional Medical Center

NARP National Association of Railroad Passengers

NARPPS National Association of Rehabilitation Professionals in the Private Sector

narr. *Latin* narratio (narrative, that is, declaration in a legal action); narrator

NARSD National Alliance for Research on Schizophrenia and Depression

NAS Nassau [Bahamas] International Airport; National Academy of Sciences; National Airspace System; National Audubon Society; naval air station; network access server; no added salt; nonindigenous aquatic species

NASA National Aeronautics and Space Administration

NASAA North American Securities Administrators Association

NASA DFRC National Aeronautics and Space Administration—Dryden Flight Research Center

NASCAR National Association of Stock Car Auto Racing

NASCI North American Society for Cardiac Imaging

NASD National Association of Securities Dealers

Nasdaq National Association of Securities Dealers Automated Quotation System

NASEMSD National Association of State Emergency Medical Service Directors

NaSGIM National Study of Graduate Education in Internal Medicine

NASK nuclear attack survival kit

NASL North American Soccer League

NASM National Academy of Sports Medicine; National Air and Space Museum

NASN National Association of School Nurses

NASOG National Association of Specialist Obstetricians and Gynaecologists

NASP National Aerospace Plane

NASPGN North American Society for Pediatric Gastroenterology and Nutrition

NASS National Agricultural Statistics Service; North American Spine Society

NASTAT North American Society of Teachers of the Alexander Technique

NAU Nauru (international vehicle ID); network access unit; network addressable unit

NASUCA National Association of State Utility Consumer Advocates

NASW National Association of Science Writers; National Association of Social Workers

NAT network address translation

nat. national; native; natural

NATA North American Telephone Association

NATCA National Air Traffic Controllers Association

natch naturally

NATE National Association of Teachers of English

NATICH National Air Toxics Information Clearinghouse

natl. national

NATO North Atlantic Treaty Organization

Nau. Nauru

NAUN nearest active upstream neighbor

naut. nautical

NAV net asset value

nav. naval; navigable; navigation

Nav. Navajo

N.A.V Net asset value

navaid navigation aid

NAVAIR Naval Air Systems command headquarters

NAVH National Association for the Visually Handicapped

navig. navigation

NAVS North American Vegetarian Society

NAVSAT navigation satellite

NAVTA North American Veterinary Technician Association

NAWAS National Warning System

NAWC Naval Air Warfare Center

NAWHO National Asian Women's Health Organization

NAWHP National Association of Women's Health Professionals

Nazi *German* Nationalsozialistische [deutsche Arbeiter-Partei] (National Socialist [German Workers' Party])

nb Norwegian Bokmal

Nb niobium; Numbers

NB New Brunswick; northbound

Nb. Numbers

n.b. *Latin* nota bene (note well)

NBA National Basketball Association; National Boxing Association

NBAC National Bioethics Advisory Commission

NBC National Broadcasting Company

NBCC National Board for Certified Counselors; National Breast Cancer Coalition

NBCCEDP National Breast and Cervical Cancer Early Detection Program

NBCDI National Black Child Development Institute

NBCHN National Board for Certification of Hospice Nurses

NBD no big deal

NbE north by east

nbg no bloody good

NBM nothing by mouth

NBMA nonbroadcast multiaccess

NBME National Board of Medical Examiners

NBN National Banking Network

NBNA National Black Nurses Association

NBNSC National Board of Nutrition Support Certification

NBO Jomo Kenyatta International Airport (Nairobi, Kenya)

NBOME National Board of Osteopathic Medical Examiners

NBP Name Binding Protocol; National Braille Press

NBS National Biological Survey; National Bureau of Standards (now **NIST:** National Institute of Standards and Technology)

NBT nitroblue tetrazolium

NBT test nitroblue tetrazolium test

NBVF National Burn Victim Foundation

NbW north by west

NC network computer; no charge; no credit; noncallable; noncarcinogen; Nordic Council; normocephalic; North Carolina

.nc New Caledonia

N.C. North Carolina

NC-17 No children under 17 admitted

NCA National Coal Association; Noise Control Act

NCAA National Collegiate Athletic Association

NCADD National Council on Alcoholism and Drug Dependence

NCADI National Clearinghouse for Alcohol and Drug Information

NCADV National Coalition Against Domestic Violence

NCAHF National Council Against Health Fraud

NCAI National Coalition for Adult Immunization

NCALI National Clearinghouse for Alcohol Information

NCAMP National Coalition Against the Misuse of Pesticides

NCAQ National Commission on Air Quality

NCAR National Center for Atmospheric Research

N.Car. North Carolina

NCATA National Coalition of Arts Therapies Associations

NCATT no comment at this time

NCB National Cooperative Bank

NCBDE National Certification Board for Diabetes Educators

NCBE National Clearinghouse on Bilingual Education

NCBI National Center for Biotechnology Information

NCC National Coordinating Committee; National Council of Churches

NCCA National Commission for the Certification of Acupuncturists; *Negligence and Compensation Cases Annotated*

NCCAN National Center on Child Abuse and Neglect

NCCAOM National Certification Commission for Acupuncture and Oriental Medicine

NCCDPHP National Center for Chronic Disease Prevention and Health Promotion

NCCE National Coalition for Consumer Education

NCCF National Childhood Cancer Foundation

NCCIDSA North Central Chapter Infectious Diseases Society of America

NCCLS National Committee for Clinical Laboratory Standards

NCCMHC National Council of Community Mental Health Centers

NCCN National Comprehensive Cancer Network

NCCP National Center for Children in Poverty

NCCPA National Commission on Certification of Physician Assistants

NCCS National Children's Cancer Society; National Coalition for Cancer Survivorship

NCD National Council on Disability

N.C.D. *Latin* nemine contra dicente (no one dissenting)

NCDA National Cheerleading and Dance Association

NCDB National Cancer Data Base

NCDC National Climatic Data Center

NCDRH National Center for Devices and Radiological Health

NCE Côte d'Azur Airport (Nice, France)

NCEH National Center for Environmental Health

NCEHIC National Center for Environmental Health and Injury Control

NCEMCH National Center for Education in Maternal and Child Health

NCEMI National Center for Emergency Medicine Informatics

NCEP National Centers for Environmental Prediction; National Cholesterol Education Program

NCEPOD National Confidential Enquiry into Perioperative Deaths

NCF no clean flux

NCFC National Council of Farmer Cooperatives

NCFR National Council on Family Relations

NCFST National Center for Food Safety and Technology

NCGR National Center for Genome Research

NCH National Center for Homeopathy

NCHC National Coalition on Health Care

NCHE National Center for Health Education

NCHEC National Commission for Health Education Credentialing

NCHGR National Center for Human Genome Research

NCHP National Council of Hospice Professionals

NCHS National Center for Health Statistics

NCHSR National Center for Health Services Research and Health Care Technology Assessment

NCHSTE National Consortium of Health Science and Technology Education

NCHSTP National Center for HIV, STD, and TB Prevention

NCI National Cancer Institute

NCIA native client interface architecture

NCIC National Cancer Institute of Canada; National Cartographic Information Center

NCID National Center for Infectious Diseases

NCIPC National Center for Injury Prevention and Control

NCIS Naval Criminal Investigative Service

NCJRS National Criminal Justice Reference Service

NCL National Consumers League

NCLF National Children's Leukemia Foundation

NCM National Coastal Monitoring

NCND National Center for Nutrition and Dietetics

NCO noncommissioned officer

NCOA National Council on the Aging

NCOD National Coming Out Day

NCOFF National Center on Fathers and Families

NCOIC noncommissioned officer in charge

NCP [Environmental Protection Agency] National Contingency Plan; network control program; Network Control Protocol

NCPC National Capital Planning Commission

NCPCA National Committee to Prevent Child Abuse

NCPIE National Council on Patient Information and Education

NCPOA National Chronic Pain Outreach Association

NCQA National Committee for Quality Assurance

NCQHA National Committee for Quality Health Care

NCRA National Cancer Registrars Association

NCRP National Council on Radiation Protection and Measurements

NCRR National Center for Research Resources

NCRW National Council for Research on Women

NCS National Cemetery System; National Center for Stuttering

NCSA National Center for Supercomputing Applications

NCSBN National Council of State Boards of Nursing

NCSC National Council of Senior Citizens

NCSU North Carolina State University

NCTE National Council of Teachers of English

NCTM National Council of Teachers of Mathematics

NCTR National Center for Toxicological Research

NCUA National Credit Union Administration

NCV nerve conduction velocity

n.c.v. no commercial value

NCWM National Conference of Weights and Measures

NCWQ National Commission on Water Quality

NCYD National Center for Youth with Disabilities

Nd neodymium

ND Doctor of Naturopathy; North Dakota; Notre Dame

n.d. no date [of publication]

N.D. North Dakota

N/D no drinking/drugs; non drinker

NDA New Drug Application; nondisclosure agreement

NDACAN National Data Archive on Child Abuse and Neglect

N.Dak. North Dakota

NDB nondirectional beacon

NDDF National Drug Data File

NDDIC National Digestive Diseases Information Clearinghouse

NDE near-death experience

NDEA National Defense Education Act

NDEI National Diabetes Education Initiative

NDEP National Diabetes Education Program

NDGA National Depression Glass Association

NDI National Death Index

NDIC National Diabetes Information Clearinghouse

NDIS network driver interface specification

NDMA Nonprescription Drug Manufacturers Association

NDMDA National Depressive and Manic-Depressive Association

NDMS National Disaster Medical System

NDP New Democratic Party [of

Canada]; nucleoside diphosphate

NDR nondestructive readout

NDRI Naval Dental Research Institute

NDRO nondestructive readout

NDSC National Down Syndrome Congress

NDSS National Down Syndrome Society

NDSU North Dakota State University

NDT nondestructive testing

NDU National Defense University

NDVI normalized difference vegetation index

ne Nepali

Ne Nehemiah; neon

NE Nebraska; network element; New England; New England Patriots; northeast; northeastern; not equal to

Ne. Nehemiah

.ne Niger

NEA National Education Association; National Endowment for the Arts; Nuclear Energy Agency

NEB *New English Bible*

Neb. Nebraska

NEbE northeast by east

NEbN northeast by north

Nebr. Nebraska

nebul. nebula

NEC Nuclear Energy Commission

NED *New English Dictionary* (now **OED**: *Oxford English Dictionary*)

NEDARC National Emergency Medical Services for Children Data Analysis Resource Center

NEEP negative end-expiratory pressure

neg. negative; negotiable

NegAM negative amortization

negl. negligible

NEH National Endowment for the Humanities

Neh. Nehemiah

NEHA National Environmental Health Association

NEHAP National Environmental Health Action Plan

NEHEP National Eye Health Education Program

NEI National Eye Institute

n.e.i. not elsewhere included

NEIC National Earthquake Information Center; National Electronic Information Corporation

NEIS National Earthquake Information Service

NEJM *New England Journal of Medicine*

NEL National Engineering Laboratory

NEMA National Electrical Manufacturers Association; National Emergency Medicine Association

nem con *Latin* nemine contra dicente (no one contradicting)

nem diss *Latin* nemine dissentiente (no one dissenting)

NEMO North East Map Organization

NEMPAC National Emergency Medicine Political Action Committee

NEMSA National Emergency Medical Service Alliance

neo newborn (from "neonate")

NEP National Energy Plan;

Nepal (international vehicle ID); New Economic Policy; non-English proficient

Nep. Nepal

NEPA National Environmental Policy Act

NEPP National Early Psychosis Project

NERL National Exposure Research Laboratory

NES National Enuresis Society

n.e.s. not elsewhere specified

NESDIS National Environmental Satellite, Data and Information Services

NESDRES National Environmental Data Referral Service

NESS National Environmental Satellite Service

NEST non-surgical embryonic selective thinning

Net Internet

NET National Educational Television

.net network provider

Neth. Netherlands

netiquette [Inter]net etiquette

NeuAc N-acetylneuraminic acid

neur. neurological; neurology

neurol. neurology; neurosurgery

neut. neuter; neutral

Nev. Nevada

NewEng. New England

Newf. Newfoundland

Newfie resident of Newfoundland; Newfoundland (breed of dog)

New Hebr. New Hebrides

New Test. New Testament

NewZeal. New Zealand

NEX Navy exchange

NEXRAD [National Weather Service] Next Generation Weather Radar

NF National Formulary; neurofibromatosis; Newfoundland; no funds

.nf Norfolk Island

n/f no funds

NFA National Fire Academy; National Futures Association

NFAS Non-Facility Associated Signaling

NFB National Federation for the Blind

NFC National Finance Center; National Football Conference

NFCC National Foundation for Consumer Credit

NFCVP National Funding Collaborative on Violence Prevention

NFD network flow diagrams

NFDC National Flight Data Center

NFED National Foundation for Ectodermal Dysplasias

NFFE National Federation of Federal Employees

NFFR National Foundation for Facial Reconstruction

NFI National Fisheries Center

NFIA National Families in Action

NFID National Foundation for Infectious Diseases

NFL National Football League

NFIP National Flood Insurance Program

Nfld. Newfoundland

NFNA National Flight Nurses Association

NFP natural family planning

NFPA National Flight Paramedics Association

NFPRHA National Family Planning and Reproductive Health Association

NFr. Northern French

NFris. Northern Frisian

NFS National Forest Service; network file system

NFW no fucking way

NFWF National Fish and Wildlife Foundation

ng nanogram

NG nasogastric; National Guard; natural gas; newsgroup; no good; nose guard; not good

.ng Nigeria

NGA National Governors Association; Natural Gas Association

NGB National Guard Bureau

NGDC National Geophysical Data Center

NGF National Golf Foundation; nerve growth factor

NGk. New Greek

NGLTF National Gay and Lesbian Task Force

NHeb. New Hebrew

NGI Next Generation Internet

ngm nanogram

NGN Nigeria—naira (currency)

NGNA National Gerontological Nursing Association

NGO Komaki Airport (Nagoya, Japan); nongovernmental organization

NGRI not guilty by reason of insanity

NGS National Genealogical Society; National Geodetic Survey; National Geographic Society

NGSP National Glycohemoglobin Standardization Program

NGU nongonococcal urethritis

NGVD National Geodetic Vertical Datum

NH New Hampshire; Northern Hemisphere

N.H. New Hampshire

NHAAP National Heart Attack Alert Program

NHANES National Health and Nutrition Examination Survey

NHBPEP National High Blood Pressure Education Program

NHC National Health Council; National Hurricane Center

NHCSSP National Health Care Skill Standards Project

NHDS National Hospital Discharge Survey

N.Hebr. New Hebrides

NHeLP National Health Law Program

NHES National Health Examination Survey

NHF National Hemophilia Foundation

NHGRI National Human Genome Research Institute

NHHCS National Home and Hospice Survey

NHI National Health Insurance; National Highway Institute

NHIC National Health Information Center

NHIK National Health Information Knowledgebase

NHIRC National Health Information Resource Center

NHIS National Health Interview Survey

NHL National Hockey League

NHLBI National Heart, Lung, and Blood Institute

NHLBI OEI National Heart,

Lung, and Blood Institute Obesity Education Initiative

NHMRC National Health and Medical Research Council

NHNA New Hampshire Nurses' Association

NHO National Hospice Organization

NHPA National Historic Preservation Act

NHPC Natural Holistic Pet Care

NHPF National Health Policy Forum

NHPI National Health Provider Inventory

NHPRC National Historical Publications and Records Commission

NHRC Naval Health Research Center

NHRP Next Hop Resolution Protocol

NHS National Health Service; National Honor Society; Next Hop Server

NHSA National Healthcare Staffing Association

NHSC National Health Service Corps

NHSDA National Household Survey on Drug Abuse

NHTSA National Highway Traffic Safety Administration

Ni nickel

NI night (shortwave transmission)

.ni Nicaragua

NIA National Institute on Aging

NIAAA National Institute on Alcohol Abuse and Alcoholism

NIAD National Institute of Art and Disabilities

NIAID National Institute of Allergy and Infectious Diseases

NIAMS National Institute of Arthritis and Musculoskeletal and Skin Diseases

NIB National Industries for the Blind; Nordic Investment Bank

NIC National Ice Center; National Institute of Corrections; network interface card; newly industrializing country; Nicaragua (international vehicle ID)

Nic. Nicaragua; Nicaraguan

NiCad nickel-cadmium [battery]

NICBDAT nothing is certain but death and taxes

NICD National Information Center on Deafness

NICE National Institute for Consumer Education

NFIC National Fraud Information Center

NICHCY National Information Center for Children and Youth with Disabilities

NICHHD National Institute of Child Health and Human Development

NICHSR National Information Center on Health Services Research and Health Care Technology

NICK Nickelodeon (cable television channel)

NICO National Insurance Consumer Organization

NICS National Institute for Chemical Studies

NICU neonatal intensive care unit

NICWA National Indian Child Welfare Association

NID Iraq–dinar

NIDA National Institute on Drug Abuse

NIDCD National Institute on Deafness and Other Communication Disorders

NIDDK National Institute of Diabetes and Digestive and Kidney Diseases

NIDDM non-insulin-dependent diabetes mellitus

NIDR National Institute of Dental Research

NIDRR National Institute on Disability and Rehabilitation Research

NIE National Institute of Education; newly industrializing economy

NIEHS National Institute of Environmental Health Sciences

NIFO next in, first out

NIFOC nude in front of computer

NIG National Institute of Genetics

Nig. Nigeria; Nigerian

nightie nightgown

NIGMS National Institute of General Medical Sciences

NIH National Institutes of Health

NIHB National Indian Health Board

NIHECS National Institutes of Health Electronic Computer Store

NIHM National Institutes of Mental Health

NII National Information Infrastructure

NIJ National Institute of Justice

NIK Nickelodeon channel

NIL nothing, I have nothing

for you (shortwave transmission)

NIMBY not in my backyard

NiMH nickel-metal hydride

NIMH National Institute of Mental Health

NIMR National Institute for Medical Research

NIMS National Infant Mortality Survey

NIMTO not in my term of office

NINDS National Institute of Neurological Disorders and Stroke

NINE National Institute of Nutritional Education

NINR National Institute of Nursing Research

NIO Nicaragua—cordoba oro (currency)

NIOSH National Institute for Occupational Safety and Health

NIOSHTIC National Institute for Occupational Safety and Health Technical Information Center

NIP National Immunization Program

NIPAW National Inhalants and Poisons Awareness Week

NIPC National Inhalant Prevention Coalition

NIPF National Incontinentia Pigmenti Foundation

NIPS National Institute for Physiological Sciences

NIR near infrared

N. Ir Northern Ireland; Northern Irish

N. Ire. Northern Ireland

NIRS National Institute of Radiological Science

NIS Naval Investigative Service; network information service; Newly Independent States

NIST National Institute of Standards and Technology

NISU National Injury Surveillance Unit

NIT National Intelligence Test; National Invitational Tournament

nitro nitroglycerin

NIV noninvasive ventilation

NJ New Jersey

N.J. New Jersey

NK none known; not known

NKA no known allergy; now known as

nkat nanokatal

NKCF National Keratoconus Foundation

NKDA no known drug allergy

NKF National Kidney Foundation

NKSF natural killer cell stimulating factor

NKUDIC National Kidney and Urologic Diseases Information Clearinghouse

NKVD *Russian* Narodnyj Kommissariat Vnutrennikh Del (Peoples' Commissariat of Internal Affairs)

nl Dutch

NL National League; Netherlands (international vehicle ID); Newfoundland and Labrador; new line; New Latin

.nl Netherlands

n.l. *Latin* non licet (not permitted); *Latin* non liquet (not clear)

NLADA National Legal Aid and Defender Association

NLC node line card

NLCS National League Championship Series

NLDS National League Division Series

NLDTD National Library of Digital Theses and Dissertations

Nle norleucine

NLESO Network-level Extended Security Option

NLF National Liberation Front

NLG The Netherlands—guilder

NLGHA National Lesbian and Gay Health Association

NLHE no limit hold 'em

NLM National Library of Medicine

NLM SIS National Library of Medicine Specialized Information Services

NLN National League for Nursing

NLO nonlinear optics

NLOS non-line-of-sight

NLQ near letter quality

NLRA National Labor Relations Act

NLRB National Labor Relations Board

NLRI Network Layer Reachability Information

NLSC National Logistics Supply Center

NLSR Natural Language Speech Recognition

NLT night letter; not later than

NLTN National Laboratory Training Network

nm nanometer; nautical mile; nuclear magneton

nM nanomolar

NM near mint; New Mexico; neuromuscular

N.M. New Mexico

NMA National Medical Association

NMC National Marine Center; National Meteorological Center

NMCHC National Maternal and Child Health Clearinghouse

NMCS National Military Command System

NMCUES National Medical Care Utilization and Expenditure Survey

NMDA N-methyl D-aspartate excitotoxic amino acid

NMDC National Medical Device Coalition

NMEA National Marine Electronics Association

NMES National Medical Expenditure Survey

N.Mex. New Mexico

NMF National Marfan Foundation

NMFI National Master Facility Inventory

NMFS National Marine Fisheries Service

NMHA National Mental Health Association

NMHC nonmethane hydrocarbon

NMHF National Mental Health Foundation

NMHID National Mental Health Institute on Deafness

NMHS National Mental Health Strategy

NMI National Measurement Institute; National Metrology Institute; no middle initial

NMIHS National Maternal and Infant Health Survey

NMIMC Naval Medical Information Management Center

NMIMT New Mexico Institute of Mining and Technology

NMIS Network Medical Information Services

NML National Measurement Laboratory

NMRDC Naval Medical Research and Development Command

NMMSA National Minority Medical Suppliers Association

NMN nicotinamide mononucleotide

NMOC nonmethane organic compound

NMP Network Management Processor; not my problem; nucleoside 5c-monophosphate

NMPIS National Marine Pollution Information Systems

NMR nuclear magnetic resonance

NMS National Mortality Survey; network management system

NMSS National Multiple Sclerosis Society

NMT Nordic Mobile Telephone

NMU National Maritime Union

NMVT network management vector transport

NN National Number; network node; Neural Network; no news

nn Norwegian Nynorsk

nn. footnotes; names; notes; nouns

NN2R no need to reply

NNBA National Nurses in Business Association

NNDSS National Notifiable Diseases Surveillance System

NNE north-northeast

NNFF National Neurofibromatosis Foundation

NNHS National Nursing Home Survey

NNHSF National Nursing Home Survey Followup

NNI network node interface

NN/LM National Network of Libraries of Medicine

NNM NASDAQ National Market

NNR National Narcolepsy Registry

NNS National Natality Survey

NNSA National Nurses Society on Addictions

NNSDO National Nursing Staff Development Organization

NNT nearest neighbor tool (mathematical method)

NNTP Network News Transfer Protocol

NNW north-northwest

no Norwegian

No nobelium

NO New Orleans Saints

no. north; northern; number

.no Norway

NOA Nature of Address

NOAA National Oceanic and Atmospheric Administration

NOAASIS National Oceanic and Atmospheric Administration Satellite Information System

NOAEL no observed adverse effect level

NOAH Network of Animal Health

NOAO National Optical Astronomy Observatories

NOARL Naval Ocean and Atmosphere Research Laboratory

NOB notes over bonds

NOC network operations center

NOCIRC National Organization of Circumcision Information Resource Centers

NOCR Network for Oncology Communication and Research

noct. maneq. *Latin* nocte maneque (at night and in the morning)

No.Dak. North Dakota

NODC National Oceanographic Data Center

NOE nuclear Overhauser effect

NOED *New Oxford English Dictionary*

NOEL no observable effects level

NOF National Osteoporosis Foundation

NOFAS National Organization on Fetal Alcohol Syndrome

NOHARMM National Organization to Halt the Abuse and Routine Mutilation of Males

NOHIC National Oral Health Information Clearinghouse

NoHo North of Houston [Street] (Manhattan neighborhood)

NOHSCP [Environmental Protection Agency] National Oil and Hazardous Substances Contingency Plan

NOI Nation of Islam

n.o.i.b.n. not otherwise indexed by name

NOK Norway—krone (currency)

NOL net operating loss

NOLF Nursing Organization Liaison Forum

NoLita North of Little Italy (Manhattan neighborhood)

nolo nolo contendere

nol. pros. nolle prosequi

NOLTP National Organization of Lung Transplant Patients

nom. nominative

NOMAD Navy Oceanographic Meteorological Association

NOMIC National Organization for Mentally Ill Children

NoMSG National Organization Mobilized to Stop Glutamate

non nonsmoking (area of restaurant)

noncom noncommissioned officer

non obs. *Latin* non obstante (notwithstanding)

non obst. *Latin* non obstante (notwithstanding)

non pros. *Latin* non prosequitur (he or she does not follow up)

non seq. *Latin* non sequitur (it does not follow)

nonstand. nonstandard

non-U non upper class

NOP not operational; not our publication

n.o.p. not otherwise provided for

NOPE network operations engineer

NOR Norma (constellation); NOT OR (logical operator)

Nor. Norman; north; northern; Norway; Norwegian

NORA National Oil Recyclers Association

NORAD North American Aerospace Defense Command (formerly North American Air Defense Command)

Noraid Irish Northern Aid Committee

NORC naturally occurring retirement community

NORD National Organization for Rare Disorders

Norf. Norfolk

NORIF nonstimulated oocyte retrieval in (office) fertilization

norm standard; model; pattern

norm. normal

Norm. Norman

NORML National Organization for the Reform of Marijuana Laws

north. northern

Northumb. Northumbrian

N or V nausea or vomiting

Norw. Norway; Norwegian

NOS National Ocean Service; network operating system

nos. numbers

n.o.s. not otherwise specified

NOSB National Organic Standards Board

NOSS National Oceanic Satellite System

NO synthase nitric oxide synthase

NOTT Nocturnal Oxygen Therapy Trial

Notts. Nottinghamshire

Nov. November

N.O.V *Latin* non obstante veredicto (notwithstanding the verdict)

NOVA Nurses Organization of Veterans Affairs

NOW National Organization for Women

N.O.W. account negotiable order of withdrawal account

Nox nitrogen oxide

NOx nitrous oxide

NOYB none of your business

n.p. no pagination; no place [of publication]

np no problem

Np neptunium

NP neuropsychiatry; notary public; not palpable; noun phrase; number of pitches; nurse practitioner

.np Nepal

NPA National Pediculosis Association; National Perinatal Association; National Prostate Association

NPAA Noise Pollution and Abatement Act

NPACE Nurse Practitioner Association for Continuing Education

n. pag. no pagination

NPC National Petroleum Council

NPCA National Parks and Conservation Association

NPCMCH National Parent Consortium on Maternal and Child Health

NPCR National Program of Cancer Registries

NPDES [Environmental Protection Agency] National Pollutant Discharge Elimination System

NPDWR [Environmental Protection Agency] National Primary Drinking Water Regulations

NPF National Parkinson Foundation; National Psoriasis Foundation

n.p.f. not provided for

NPG negative population growth

NPH normal pressure hydrocephalus

NPI National Provider Identifier

NPL [Environmental Protection Agency] National Priorities List ("Superfund" List)

n. pl. plural noun

NPM National Poetry Month

NPN nonprotein nitrogen

NPND National Parent Network on Disabilities

n.p.o. *Latin* non per os (not by mouth); *Latin* nil per os (nothing by mouth)

NPP non-physician practitioner

NPPC National Pork Producers Council

NPPHCN National Progressive Primary Health Care Network

NPPSIS National Parent to Parent Support and Information System

NPPV noninvasive positive pressure ventilation

NPR National Public Radio; Nepal—Nepalese rupee

NPRH Nurse Practitioners in Reproductive Health

Nps nitrophenylsulfenyl

NPS National Park Service; nonpoint source [pollution]

NPT Non-Proliferation Treaty

NPTN National Pesticides Telecommunications Network

NPV negative pressure ventilation

NQF National Quality Forum

nr near

NR not rated; number (shortwave transmission)

.nr Nauru

N.R. nonresident; not reported

NRA National Recovery Administration; National Rifle Association; Naval Reserve Association

NRAO National Radio Astronomy Observatory

NRC National Recycling Coalition; National Research Council; [United States Coast Guard] National Response Center; nonreusable container; Nuclear Regulatory Commission

NRCC National Registry in Clinical Chemistry

NRCCSA National Resource Center on Child Sexual Abuse

NRCS Natural Resources Conservation Service

NRDC Natural Resources Defense Council

NREM non-rapid eye movement

NREMT National Registry of Emergency Medical Technicians

NREN National Research and Education Network

NRFB never removed from box

NRG energy

NRHA National Rural Health Association

NRID National Registry of Interpreters for the Deaf

NRL Naval Research Laboratory

NRM Network Resource Management; normal response mode

NRMP National Resident Matching Program

NRN no reply necessary

nRNA nuclear RNA

NRO National Reconnaissance Office

NRPF National Retinitis Pigmentosa Foundation (now Foundation Fighting Blindness)

NRSP National Remote Sensing Program

NRT Narita International Airport (Tokyo, Japan); [Environmental Protection Agency]

National Response Team; near real-time

NRTA National Retired Teachers Association

NRWA National Rural Water Association

NRZ nonreturn [to] zero

NRZ-L nonreturn [to] zero level

ns nanosecond

Ns nimbostratus

NS nervous system; neurosurgery; New Style (calendar); nonsmoking section; normal saline; no smoking allowed; Nova Scotia; nuclear sclerosis; nuclear ship

n.s. new series; not specified

n/s not sufficient

N/S nonsmoker

NSA National Security Agency; National Skating Association; National Ski Association; National Standards Association; National Stroke Association; National Student Association; non-service affecting; nonsurgical sperm aspiration

NSAC National Society for Autistic Children

NSA/CSS National Security Agency/Central Security Service

NSAID nonsteroidal antiinflammatory drug

NSAP network service access point

NSAW National Sleep Awareness Week

NSAWI National Substance Abuse Web Index

NSB National Science Board

NSBRI National Space Biomedical Research Institute

NSC NASDAQ Small Capitalization; National Safety Council; National Security Council; Neuroscience Center

NSCLC non-small cell lung cancer

NSDWR National Secondary Drinking Water Regulations

NSE National Stock Exchange

nsec nanosecond

NSERC Natural Sciences and Engineering Research Council

NSF National Science Foundation; National Sleep Foundation; not sufficient funds

n.s.f. not sufficient funds

NSFG National Survey of Family Growth

NSFNET National Science Foundation Network

NSFW not safe for work; not suitable for work

NSG Nuclear Suppliers Group

NSGC National Society of Genetic Counselors, Inc.

NSIDC National Snow and Ice Data Center

NSILA nonsuppressible insulin-like activity

NSMS National Sheet Music Society

NSO National Solar Observatory

NSP neurological shellfish poisoning

NSPCA National Society for the Prevention of Cruelty to Animals

NSPHPC National Survey of Personal Health Practices and Consequences

NSPS [Environmental Protection Agency] New Source Performance Standards

NSR nasoseptal reconstruction; normal sinus rhythm

NSSA National Sjogren's Syndrome Association

NSSDC National Space Science Data Center

NSSFC National Severe Storms Forecast Center

NSSLHA National Student Speech Language Hearing Association

NST non-stress test

NSTA National Science Teachers Association

NSTC National Science and Technology Council

NSTL National Space Technology Laboratories

NSVD normal spontaneous vaginal delivery

NSW New South Wales

NT nasotracheal; New Testament; Northwest Territories

nt. night

NTDBWY nice to do business with you

NTDRA National Tire Dealers and Retreaders Association

NTE not to exceed

NTF National Turkey Federation

NTG nitroglycerin; nothing (shortwave transmission)

Nthb. Northumberland

NTIA National Telecommunications and Information Administration

NTID National Technical Institute for the Deaf

NTIS National Technical Information Service

NTMI nontransmural myocardial infarction

NTNG nontoxic nodular goiter

NTP Network Time Protocol; normal temperature and pressure

NTR nuclear thermal rocket

NTS nucleus tractus solitarii

NTSB National Transportation Safety Board

NTSC National Television Standards Committee

NTTAWWT not that there's anything wrong with that

NTU nephelometric turbidity unit; network terminating unit

nt.wt. net weight

NTYMI now that you mention it

NTZ Neutral Zone

NU name unknown

.nu Niue

Nuc nucleoside

NUG necrotizing ulcerative gingivitis

NUI Network User Identification; notebook user interface

nuke a nuclear device or weapon; a nuclear-powered electric generating plant

num. number; numeral

Num. Numbers

numb. numbered

numis. numismatic; numismatics

Num Lock numeric lock key

nv Navajo

NV Nevada; never (shortwave transmission); not voting

N-V neurovascular

Nva norvaline

NVA net value added

NVCA National Valentine Collectors Association

N/V/D nausea-vomiting-diarrhea

NVE network-visible entity

NVG Night Vision Goggles

NVHA National Voluntary Health Agencies

NVIC National Vaccine Information Center

NVP nominal velocity of propagation

NVRAM nonvolatile random access memory

NVS nonvolatile solids

NVSS nonvolatile suspended solids

NW northwest; northwestern; now (shortwave transmission)

NWAV(E) New Ways of Analyzing Variation (in English and other languages)

NWB non-weight-bearing

NWbN northwest by north

NWbW northwest by west

NWC National War College

NWDA National Wholesale Druggists Association

NWDC National Wildlife Defense Council

NWHIC National Women's Health Information Center

NWHRC National Women's Health Resource Center

NWIC National Water Information Clearinghouse

NWO New World Order

NWP numerical weather prediction

NWR National Oceanic and Atmospheric Administration Weather Radio; National Wildlife Refuge [System]

NWRC National Women's Resource Center

NWS National Weather Service

NWSFO National Weather Service Forecast Office

NWT Northwest Territories

n.wt. net weight

NWU National Writers Union

NX next (shortwave transmission)

ny Chichewa

NY New York

N.Y. New York

NYBID New York interbank bid rate

NYBOR New York interbank offered rate

NYC New York City

NYCE New York Cotton Exchange

NYCTMI now you come to mention it

NYFE New York Futures Exchange

NYG New York Giants

NYJ New York Jets

NYM New York Mets

NYMEX New York Mercantile Exchange

NYP not yet published

NYPD New York Police Department

NYS New York State

NYSE New York Stock Exchange

NYT *New York Times*

NYU New York University

NYY New York Yankees

NZ New Zealand (international vehicle ID)

.nz New Zealand

N.Z. New Zealand

NZD New Zealand—dollar

NZDSF non-zero dispersion-shifted fiber

n₀ Loschmidt's number

O

o *Latin* octarius (pint); octavo; ohm

O old; Oriental (as in personal ads, but usually **A**, Asian); out; outstanding

O. ocean; Ohio

OA office automation; Office of Administration; operations agreement; Ophthalmology Assembly; osteoarthritis

o/a on or about

OAA Obstetric Anaesthetists Association; Otolaryngology Administration Assembly

OADM Obstetric Anaesthetists Association; optical add/drop multiplexer; Otolaryngology Administration Assembly

OAK Metropolitan Oakland [CA] International Airport; Oakland Athletics; Oakland Raiders

OAL over-all length

OAM [National Institute of Health] Office of Alternative Medicine; operation, administration, and maintenance

OAM & P operations, administration, management, and provisioning

O & M operations and maintenance

OAO orbiting astronomical observatory

OAPEC Organization of Arab Petroleum Exporting Countries

OAPO Eastern Pacific Tuna Fishing Organization

OAPP Office of Adolescent Pregnancy Programs

OAR [National Oceanic and Atmospheric Administration Office of] Oceanic and Atmospheric Research

OAS Organization of American States

OASDHI Old Age, Survivors, Disability, and Health Insurance

OASDI Old Age, Survivors' and Disability Insurance

OASIS Obstetric Anesthesia Safety Improvement Study; On-Line Asperger Syndrome Information and Support

OASTP Office of the Assistant Secretary for Technology Policy

OATUS on a totally unrelated subject

OAU Organization of African Unity

OAUS on an unrelated subject

ob obvious

OB obstetric; obstetrics; obstetrician; off Broadway

ob. *Latin* obiit (he or she died); *Latin* obiter (incidentally); oboe

Ob. Obadiah

OBC on board computer

OBE Order of the British Empire

OBGA Obstetrics and Gynecology Assembly

OB/GYN obstetrician/gynecologist; obstetrics/gynecology

OBIC optical beam induced current

Obie OB (that is, off Broadway)

OBIGGS on-board inert gas generating system

obit obituary

obit. *Latin* obitus (death, that is, obituary)

obj. object; objective

obl. oblique; oblong

obno obnoxious

OBO or best offer; order book official

o/b/o or best offer

OBOGS on-board oxygen generation system

OBP on-base percentage

OBRA Omnibus Budget Reconciliation Act

OBS organic brain syndrome

obs. obscene; observation; observatory; obsolete; obstetrics

OBS/GYN obstetrics/gynecology

obstet. obstetric; obstetrics

OBT on-board time

obv. obverse

oc Occitan

Oc. ocean

OC Officer Commanding; Old Catholic; open-captioned; optical carrier; Orphan's Court

o.c. *Latin* opere citato (in the work cited)

o/c overcharge

OCA Obsessive Compulsive Anonymous

OCAS Organization of Central American States

OCC Options Clearing Corporation

occ. occident; occidental; occupation

occas. occasional; occasionally

OCD obsessive compulsive disorder

oceanogr. oceanography

OCF Obsessive-Compulsive Foundation

OCHAMPUS Office of Civilian Health and Medical Program of the Uniformed Services

OCO one cancels the other order

OCorn. Old Cornish

OCP obligatory contour principle; oral contraceptive pill

OCR Office of Civil Rights; optical character reader; optical character recognition

OCRM Office of Coastal Resource Management

OCS Office of Community Services; Officer Candidate School; Old Church Slavonic; outer continental shelf

OCSE Office of Child Support Enforcement

OCST Office of Commercial Space Transportation

OCT Octans (constellation)

oct. octavo

Oct. October

OC-VU ocean view

OD Doctor of Optometry; officer of the day; overdose; overdraft; overdrawn

o.d. *Latin* oculus dexter (right eye); olive drab; on demand; outside diameter

ODA official development assistance; Open Document Architecture

ODBC open database connectivity

ODI open data-link interface

ODIHR Office for Democratic Institutions and Human Rights

ODM oil debris monitoring

ODP ozone depletion potential

ODPHP Office of Disease Prevention and Health Promotion

ODS ozone-depleting substance

Oe oersted

OE Old English

OECD Organization for Economic Cooperation and Development

OECS Organization of Eastern Caribbean States

OED *Oxford English Dictionary*

OEM original equipment manufacturer

OEMP Office of Environmental Monitoring and Prediction

OEO Office of Economic Opportunity

OEP Office of Emergency Preparedness; Office of Environmental Policy; open enrollment period

OER officer efficiency report

OES Office of Employment Security

OETA original estimated time of arrival

OF Oriental female; outfield; outfielder

OFA Office of Family Assistance; optical fiber amplifier

ofc office

OFCC Office of Federal Contract Compliance

OFCCP Office of Federal Contract Compliance Programs

OFDM Orthogonal Frequency Division Multiplexing

off. office; officer; official

offic. official

OFM Office of Financial Management; Order of Friars Minor

OFP Office of Family Planning

OFPP Office of Federal Procurement Policy

OFr Old French

OFR Office of the Federal Register

ofr. offer

OFris. Old Frisian

OFS office (shortwave transmission)

OG officer of the guard

OGE Office of Government Ethics

OGG Kahului [HI] Airport

OGOD one gene, one disorder

OGPS Office of Grants and Program Systems

OGPU *Russian* Ob"edinennoe Gosudarstvennoe Politcheskoe Upravlenie (United State Political Administration)

OH off hand; Ohio; open house (real estate)

OHD organic heart disease

OHG Old High German

OHI Oral Hygiene Index

OHI-S Simplified Oral Hygiene Index

OHMO Office of Health Maintenance Organizations

OHMS On Her (or His) Majesty's Service

OHRE Office of Human Radiation Experiments (Department of Energy)

OHS Office of Homeland Security

OI Office of Investigator; optimum interpolation; osteogenesis imperfecta

OIC Office of Independent Counsel; officer in charge; oh, I see

OID object identifier

OIE Overseas Investment Exchange

OIF Osteogenesis Imperfecta Foundation

OIG Office of Inspector General

OIP official index period

OIR online insertion and removal

OIr. Old Irish

OIS Osteopathic Information Service

OIT Office of International Trade

OIt. Old Italian

OJ orange juice

OJJDP Office of Juvenile Justice and Delinquency Prevention

OJP Office of Justice Programs

OJT on-the-job training

OK Oklahoma

O.K. oll korrect

OKC Will Rogers World Airport (Oklahoma City, OK)

Okie Oklahoman

Okla. Oklahoma

OL Old Latin

OLAP Online Analytical Processing

OLB offensive linebacker; outside linebacker

Old Ch. Slav. Old Church Slavonic

OLE object linking and embedding

oleo oleomargarine

OLFrank. Old Low Frankish

OLG Old Low German

OLI/HMD Online Images from the History of Medicine Division

OLL online love

OLR outgoing longwave radiation

OLS ordinary least squares

OLSNA Orthopaedic Laser Society of North America

OM Order of Merit; Oriental male; otitis media; outcomes management

Om. Oman

.om Oman

OMA Occupational Management and Budget

OM & R operations, maintenance, and replacement

OMB Office of Management and Budget

OMC optimum moisture content

OMD *Online Medical Dictionary*

OMDB over my dead body

OMEC Online Medical Employment Center

OMG Object Management Group; oh my God

OMH Office of Minority Health

OMH-RC Office of Minority Health Resource Center

OMIK open mouth, insert keyboard

OMIM Online Mendelian Inheritance in Man

OMIS Office of Management and Information Systems

omn. hor. *Latin* omni hora (every hour)

OMNI Organizing Medical Networked Information

OMO Office of Marine Operations

OMP oligo-N-methylmorpholinium propylene oxide; orotidylic acid; orotidylate; orotidine 5c-monophosphate

OMPA octamethyl pyrophosphoramide

OMR Oman—rial (currency)

OMS orbital maneuvering system; organic mental syndrome; outcomes management system

OMT object modeling technique

ON Old Norse; Ontario

ONC open network computing

ONFr. Old Northern French

ONI Office of Naval Intelligence

ONNA oh no, not again

ONR Office of Naval Research

ONS Oncology Nursing Society

ONT Ontario [CA] International Airport

Ont. Ontario

OO object-oriented

OOA out of area

OOB out of bed

OOD officer of the deck

OODB object-oriented database

OODP object-oriented data processing

OOF other official flows

OOH *Occupational Outlook Handbook*; on one hand

OOI out of interest

OOO out of office

OOOS object-oriented operating system

OOP object-oriented programming; out of print

OOPL object-oriented programming language

OOS out of service

OOT object-oriented technology

OOTB out of the box (that is, brand new)

OOTC obligatory on-topic comment

op operation; operative; operator; opportunity

Op operation; op[tical] art

OP observation post; operate (shortwave transmission); operator (shortwave transmission); Order of Preachers; out of print; outpatient

op. opus

o.p. out of print

O/P out of print

OPA Office of Population Affairs; Orthopedic Practice Assembly

OPANAL *Spanish* Organismo para la Proscripción de las Armas Nucleares en la América Latina y el Caribe (Agency for the Prohibition of Nuclear Weapons in Latin America and the Caribbean)

OPC organic photoconductor; origination point code; own point code

op. cit. *Latin* opere citato (in the work cited)

OPD outpatient department

OPDIN Ocean Pollution Data Center

OPEC Organization of Petroleum Exporting Countries

Op-Ed opposite the editorial page

OPEN Online Public Education Network

OPers. Old Persian

OPFI Office of Program and Fiscal Integrity

OPFT other than permanent full time

OPg. Old Portuguese

oph Ordered to be Printed House [of Representatives]

OPH Ophiuchus (constellation)

OPHS Office of Public Health and Science

OPI overall performance index

OPIC Overseas Private Investment Corporation

OPK ovulation predictor kit

OPL [White House] Office of Public Liaison

OPM Office of Personnel Management; other people's money

OPO organ procurement organization

OPol. Old Polish

OPP Object Push Profile

opp. opposed; opposite

oppies older professional parents

oppo opposition research

OPPTS [Environmental Protection Agency] Office of Prevention, Pesticides, and Toxic Substances

OProv. Old Provençal

OPRR Office for Protection from Research Risks

OPruss. Old Prussian

ops Ordered to be Printed Senate

OPS Ophthalmic Photographers' Society

opt. optative; optical; optional

OPV oral poliovirus vaccine

or Oriya

OR open reduction; operating room; operations research; Oregon; owner's risk

Or. Oregon

ORA Orthopaedic Rehabilitation Association

ORBD~NRC Osteoporosis and Related Bone Diseases ~ National Resource Center

orch. orchestra

ORD Chicago-O'Hare International Airport; [National Institutes of Health] Office of Rare Diseases; optical rotatory dispersion

ord. order; ordinal; ordinance; ordnance

ordn. ordnance

Ore. Oregon

Oreg. Oregon

ORF Norfolk [VA] International Airport

org. organic; organization; organized

.org organization

ORHP Office of Rural Health Policy

ORI Orion

ORIF open reduction internal fixation

orig. origin; original; originally

Ork. Orkney Islands

ORM Office of Regional Management

ornith. ornithologic; ornithological; ornithology

ORNL Oak Ridge National Laboratory

OROM optical read-only memory

ORP ordinary, reasonable, and prudent

ORR Office of Refugee Relief; Office of Refugee Resettlement

ORS Orthopaedic Research Society

ORSA Operations Research Society of America

O-R system oxidation reduction system

orth. orthopedic; orthopedics

ORTHO American Orthopsychiatric Association

ORuss. Old Russian

ORV off-road vehicle

ORY Orly Airport (Paris, France)

Os osmium

OS offscreen; Old Saxon; Old Style (calendar); operating system; ordinary seaman; out of stock

o.s. *Latin* oculus sinister (left eye); old series; out of stock

OS/2 [IBM] Operating System Two

OSA obstructive sleep apnea; Optical Society of America; Order of Saint Augustine

OSB Order of Saint Benedict

OSC Office of Space Communications; Office of Special Counsel

OSCAR Orbiting Satellite Carrying Amateur Radio

OSCE Organization on Security and Cooperation in Europe

OSD operational system development

OSDBU Office of Small and Disadvantaged Business Utilization

OSE Operations Simulations Engineer

OSEP Office of Special Education Programs

OSERS Office of Special Education and Rehabilitative Services

OSF Office of Space Flight; Order of Saint Francis

OSGR Office of State Government Relations

OSH Office on Smoking and Health,

OSHA Occupational Safety and Health Administration

OSHRC Occupational Safety and Health Review Commission

OSI open system interconnection; out of stock indefinitely

OSL Gardemoen Airport (Oslo, Norway)

OSM Office of Surface Mining Reclamation and Enforcement

OSN Ocular Surgery News

OSO   Orbiting Solar Observatory

OSp.   Old Spanish

OSPF   open shortest path first

OSS   Office of Space Science;
Office of Strategic Services

OSSA   Office of Space Science
and Applications

OSSD   Office of Space Systems
Development

OST   ocean surface temperature

OSTP   Office of Science and
Technology Policy

OSU   Oklahoma State Universi-
ty; Oregon State University;
The Ohio State University;
Order of Saint Ursula

OSV   object-subject-verb

OSw.   Old Swedish

OT   occupational therapy; offensive tackle; Office of Telecommunications; Office of
Transportation; off topic; old
terminology; Old Testament;
optical thickness; optimality
theory; overtime

OTA   Office of Technology Assessment; Office of Technical
Assistance; Orthopaedic Trauma Association

OTAA   Office of Trade Adjustment Assistance

OT & E   operational testing and
evaluation

OTB   off-track betting

OTC   Officers' Training Corps;
over-the-counter; Ozone Transport Commission

OTEC   ocean thermal energy
conversion

OTH   over the horizon

OTHB   over the horizon
backscatter

OTL   out to lunch

OTO   otolaryngology

OTOH   on the other hand

otol.   otology

OTP   Bucharest Otopeni Airport

OTR   Occupational Therapist,
Registered; other (shortwave
transmission)

OTS   Office of Thrift Supervision; Officers' Training School

OTT   over the top; over the tran-
som

OTTH   on the third hand

OTTOMH   off the top of my head

OTurk.   Old Turkish

OTV   orbital transfer vehicle

O.U.   *Latin* oculus uterque (each
eye; both eyes)

OUI   operation of motor vehicle
while under influence of liquor
or drugs

OUP   Oxford University Press

OUR   oxygen utilization rate

OV   office visit; orbital vehicle;
over (shortwave transmission)

OVC   Office for Victims of
Crime

OVI   Office of Voluntarism Initiatives

OVS   object-verb-subject

OW   Old Welsh; one way

OWB   Owensboro-Daviess County [KY] Airport

OWBO   Office of Women's Business Ownership

OWelsh   Old Welsh

OWEP   Oily Waste Extraction
Program

OWH   [Centers for Disease Control and Prevention] Office of
Women's Health

OWI   Office of War Information;
operating [a vehicle] while intoxicated

OWL Orthopaedic Web Links
OWTTE or words to that effect
Ox. Oxford
Oxbridge Oxford and Cambridge [Universities]
Oxfam Oxford Committee for Famine Relief
Oxon *Medieval Latin* Oxonia (Oxford, Oxfordshire); *Latin* Oxoniensis (of Oxford)
OXR Oxnard [CA] Airport
OXT oxytocin
OY operating year; optimum yield
oz. ounce; ounces
oz. ap. apothecaries' ounce
oz. av. avoirdupois ounce
ozs. ounces
oz. t. troy ounce

P

p momentum; piano (musical direction); proton; punctuation
P pale; parental generation; parity; parking available; pass; pawn; petite; phosphorus; poor; Portugal (international vehicle ID); pressure; professional (as in personal ads); punter
p. page; part; participle; past; penny; peseta; peso; pint; pipe; pole; population; principal; purl
P. Peter
p- para-
P2P path to profitability; peer to peer
pa pulmonary artery; Punjabi
Pa pascal; protactinium
PA Palestinian Authority; Panama (international vehicle ID); Pennsylvania; physician's assistant; plate appearances (baseball); power of attorney; press agent; professional association; prosecuting attorney; public-address system; public affairs
P-A postero-anterior
Pa. past
.pa Panama
p.a. per annum
PAA Pediatric Administration Assembly
PAB Panama—balboa (currency)
PABA para-aminobenzoic acid
PABX private automatic branch exchange
PAC political action committee; premature atrial contraction
Pac. Pacific
PAC-10 Pacific Athletic Conference
Pacif. Pacific
PACOR packet processor
PACS picture archiving and communication system
PACU post anesthesia care unit
PAD packet assembler/disassembler; pressure anomaly detection
PADC Pennsylvania Avenue Development Corporation
PADS planned arrival and departure system; Publications of the American Dialect Society
PAF paroxysmal atrial fibrillation; platelet-aggregating factor
PaG. Pennsylvania German
PAGE polyacrylamide gel electrophoresis
PAH p-aminohippuric acid; polararomatic hydrocarbon; poly-

PASA | 215

cyclic aromatic hydrocarbon
PAHCOM Professional Association of Health Care Office Managers
PAHO Pan American Health Organization
PAI Population Action International
PAIGE Patient Instruction Generator
PAIRO Professional Association of Interns and Residents
PAIS Public Affairs Information Service
Pak. Pakistan; Pakistani
Paki *offensive* Pakistani
PAL phase alternation line; Police Athletic League
Pal. Palestine; Palestinian
paleogr. paleography
paleont. paleontology
PALS pediatric advanced life support
PAM pulse amplitude modulation
pam. pamphlet
PAMA Pan American Medical Association
PAMM Program Against Micronutrient Malnutrition
PAMs polyacrylamides
PAN peroxyacetyl nitrate; personal area network
Pan. Panama; Panamanian
P & A percussion and auscultation; protection and advocacy
P & H postage and handling
p & i principle and interest
P & L profit and loss
P & S purchase and sale
P & W *Poets & Writers Magazine*
pano panoramic
PANS pretty awesome new stuff

PAO Pediatric Assessment Online
PaO2 alveolar oxygen pressure
Pap Papanicolao smear; Papanicolao test
PAP Password Authentication Protocol; peroxidase antiperoxidase complex; pulmonary artery pressure
PAPP p-aminopropiophenone
pa. ppl passive participle; past participial
pa. pple passive participle; past participial
PAPS adenosine 3c-phosphate 5c-phosphosulfate; 3c-phosphoadenosine 5c-phosphosulfate
Pap smear Papanicolaou test
PAR post-anesthesia room; preferred arrival route
par. paragraph; parallel; parenthesis; parish
Par. Paraguay; Paraguayan
para paragraph
PARC [Xerox Corporation's] Palo Alto Research Center
PARCA Patient Access to Responsible Care Act
paren. parenthesis
Parl. Parliament
parsec parallax second
part. participle; particle; partitive
part. aeq. *Latin* partes aequales (in equal parts)
part. vic. *Latin* partes vicibus (in divided doses)
PAS para-aminosalicylic acid; periodic acid-Schiff stain; pseudo aircraft simulation; pulmonary artery systolic pressure
PASA para-aminosalicylic acid

pass. passage; *Latin* passim (throughout); passive

PAT point after touchdown

pat. patent

pa. t. past tense

PATCH planned approach to community health

patd. patented

PATH Port Authority Trans-Hudson; Program for Appropriate Technology in Health

path. pathological; pathology

pathol. pathological; pathology

PATOS payment at time of service

pat. pend. patent pending

PATV public access television

PAU Pan American Union

PAV Pavo (constellation)

PAYE pay as you earn; pay as you enter

payt. payment

pb paperback [book]

Pb lead

PB paperback [book]; passbook; peanut butter; petabyte; prayer book

P/B playback

PBA Professional Bowlers Association

PB & J peanut butter and jelly [sandwich]

PBB polybrominated biphenyl

PBG porphobilinogen

PBGC Pension Benefit Guaranty Corporation

PBI Palm Beach International Airport; protein-bound iodine

PBIS Performance Based Incentive System

PBJ peanut butter and jelly [sandwich]

PBL planetary boundary layer;

preamble (shortwave transmission)

PBM prescription benefit manager

PBO paperback original

PBOT Philadelphia Board of Trade

PBR Pabst Blue Ribbon [beer]; photobioreactor

PBS Public Broadcasting Service; Public Buildings Service

PBX private branch exchange

PC partly cloudy; Past Commander; penal code; personal computer; photoconductive; police constable; post commander; political correctness; politically correct; professional corporation; pulverized coal

pc parallax second

pc. piece

p.c. percent; personal communication; *Latin* post cibum (after meals)

P.C. Privy Council

p/c petty cash; prices current

PCA Paperweight Collectors Association; patient-controlled analgesia; Permanent Court of Arbitration; personal care aide

PCAST President's Council of Advisors on Science and Technology

PCB polychlorinated biphenyl; printed circuit board

PCC Panama Canal Commission; patient care coordinator

PCCAL Pharmacy Consortium for Computer Aided Learning

PCCU postcoronary care unit

PCD polycrystalline diamond

PCDD polychlorinated dibenzo-dioxin

PCDF polychlorinated dibenzo-furan

PC-DOS Personal Computer Disk Operating System

PCE perchloroethylene

pcg. picogram

PCGRIDS Personal Computer Gridded Interactive Display and Diagnostic System

pch Placed on Calendar House [of Representatives]

PCI Peripheral Component Interconnect; prophylactic cranial irradiation

pCi/l picocuries per liter

PCIS patient care information system

PCL posterior cruciate ligament; [Hewlett-Packard Laserjet] Printer Control Language

PCM pulse code modulation

PCMB p-chloromercuribenzoate

PCMCIA Personal Computer Memory Card International Association

PCMI President's Council on Management Improvement

PCN personal communication network; primary care network

PCO2 carbon dioxide concentration

PCOD polycystic ovary disease

PCON *Primary Care Optometry News*

PCOS Polycystic Ovarian Sydrome

PCP personal care physician; phencyclidine; pneumocystis pneumonia; primary care physician; primary care provider; Progressive-Conservative Party

PCPM per contract per month

PCR physician contingency reserve; polymerase chain reaction

PCS personal communications service; Placed on Calendar Senate; predefined command sequence; programmable character set

PCSD President's Council on Sustainable Development

PCT patient care technician; post coital test

pct. percent

PCU power control unit; progressive care unit

PCV packed cell volume

PCVS Professional Credentials Verification Service

PCWP pulmonary capillary wedge pressure

Pd palladium

PD plumbing damage; police department; position description; postal district; potential difference; program director; public defender; public domain; pulse Doppler [radar]; pupillary distance

pd. paid

p.d. per diem

PDA patent ductus arteriosus; personal digital assistant; public display of affection

PDAS photodiode array spectrophotometer

PdB *Latin* Pedagogiae Baccalaureus (Bachelor of Pedagogy)

PDB project data base

PDC preexisting condition

PdD *Latin* Pedagogiae Doctor (Doctor of Pedagogy)

PDD pervasive developmental disorder; program design document

PDF Parkinson's Disease Foundation; portable document file; precision direction finder; programmable data formatter

PDGF platelet-derived growth factor

PDI Periodontal Disease Index

PDL page description language

PDLL poorly differentiated lymphocytic lymphoma

PdM *Latin* Pedagogiae Magister (Master of Pedagogy)

PDN private duty nurse

PDO portable distributed objects

PDOMA pulled directly out of my ass

PDP program development plan

PDQ Physicians Data Query (of the NCI); pretty damn quick

PDR *Physicians' Desk Reference*; preliminary design review

PDRY People's Democratic Republic of Yemen

PDS partitioned data set

PDT Pacific Daylight Time

PDU power distribution unit

PDX Portland [OR] International Airport; probable diagnosis

pe printer's error

PE Peru (international vehicle ID); physical education; physical examination; pleural effusion; Prince Edward Island; probable error; pulmonary edema; pulmonary embolism

.pe Peru

P.E. professional engineer

P/E ratio price/earnings ratio

PEBA polyether block amide

PEBB power electronic building block

PEBCAK problem exists between chair and keyboard

pec pectoral muscle

pecs pectoral muscles

PECUSA Protestant Episcopal Church of the United States of America

Ped pedestrian

PedNSS Pediatric Nutrition Surveillance System

pee piss

PEEP positive end-expiratory pressure

PEER Performance Efficiency Evaluation Report; Program for Extraordinary Experience Research

PEF peak expiratory flow

PEFR peak expiratory flow rate

PEG Pegasus (constellation); polyethylene glycol

P.E.I. Prince Edward Island

PEK Beijing Capital International Airport

pel picture element

PEL permissible exposure limit

PEM paste-eating moron

pen penitentiary

PEN International Association of Poets, Editors, Essayists, and Novelists; Peru—nuevo sol (currency)

Pen. peninsula

Penn. Pennsylvania

Penna. Pennsylvania

PENS Pediatric Endocrinology Nursing Society

PEP Parkinson's Educational Program

PER Perseus (constellation)

per. period; person

Per. Persian

perc has passed soil percolation test

per cent. *Latin* per centum (by the hundred)

perf. perfect; perforated; perforation; performance; performed by; performer

perh. perhaps

peri pericardial; pericardium

PERI Pharmaceutical Education and Research Institute

perk perquisite

perm permanent; permanent wave

perm. permanent

perp perpetrator

perp. perpendicular

PERRLA pupils equal round, react to light and accommodation

PERS personal emergency response system

pers. person; personal

Pers. Persia; Persian

PERT program evaluation and review technique

pert. pertaining

PES programmable electronic system

PESA percutaneous epididymal sperm aspiration

PET polyethylene terephthalate; positron emission tomography

pet. petroleum

Pet. Peter

PETA People for the Ethical Treatment of Animals

PETE polyethylene terephthalate

PETN pentaerythritol tetranitrate

petrog. petrography

petrol. petrology

PEU processing electronics unit

PF power factor; pianoforte; Prostatitis Foundation; protection factor

pf. preferred; pfennig

.pf French Polynesia

PFC perfluorocarbon; persistent fetal circulation; private first class

PFD personal flotation device

pfd. preferred

PFFD proximal femoral focal deficiency

pfg. pfennig

PFLAG Parents, Families, and Friends of Lesbians and Gays

PFOB perfluorooctyl bromide

PFP Partnership for Peace

PFT permanent full time; pulmonary function test

PG parental guidance; paying guest; postgraduate; pregnant; Procter & Gamble Co.

pg. page; picogram

Pg. Portuguese

.pg Papua New Guinea

PG-13 parental guidance for children under 13

PGA Professional Golfers' Association

PGC professional graphics controller

PgDn page down

PGH paragraph (shortwave transmission)

PGK Papua New Guinea—kina (currency)

PGML Precision Graphics Markup Language

PGP prepaid group practice; pretty good privacy

PGR psychogalvanic response

PGT preimplantation genetic testing

PgUp page up
PGY post graduate year
pH potential of hydrogen (0 to 14 scale—0, very acidic; 7, neutral; 14, very alkaline)
Ph Philippians
PH penthouse; public health; Purple Heart
ph. phase; phone number
.ph Philippines
PHA potentially hazardous asteroid; Public Housing Administration; Public Housing Authority
phar. pharmaceutical; pharmacist; pharmacopoeia; pharmacy
PharB *Latin* Pharmaciae Baccalaureus (Bachelor of Pharmacy)
PharD *Latin* Pharmaciae Doctor (Doctor of Pharmacy)
PharM *Latin* Pharmaciae Magister (Master of Pharmacy)
pharm. pharmaceutical; pharmacist; pharmacology; pharmacopoeia; pharmacy
PharmD Doctor of Pharmacy
PhB *Latin* Philosophiae Baccalaureus (Bachelor of Philosophy)
PhC pharmaceutical chemist
PHCSG Primary Health Care Specialist Group
PhD *Latin* Philosophiae Doctor (Doctor of Philosophy)
PHD pulse height discriminators
PHE Phoenix (constellation)
phenom someone or something that is phenomenal
PHERP Public Health Education and Research Program
PHF Public Health Foundation

PhG Graduate in Pharmacy
PHI Philidelphia Eagles; Philidelphia Phillies
PHID Project for Health Information Dissemination
phil. philological; philology; philosopher; philosophical; philosophy
Phil. Philippians; Philippines
Phila. Philadelphia
Phil. I. Philippine Islands
Phil. Is. Philippine Islands
Philly Philadelphia
philol. philological; philology
philos. philosopher; philosophical; philosophy
PhilSp. Philippine Spanish
Phl Philippians
PHL Philadelphia International Airport
PHLI Public Health Leadership Institutes
Phlm. Philemon
PHLS Public Health Laboratory Service
PHLX Philadelphia Stock Exchange
Phm Philemon
PhM *Latin* Philosophiae Magister (Master of Philosophy)
PHN postherpetic neuralgia; Public Health Network
PHO physician-hospital organization
phon. phonetic; phonetics; phonology
phonet. phonetic; phonetically; phonetics
phono phonograph
phonol. phonology
photo. photograph
photog. photograph; photographic; photography

photogr. photography

photom. photometry

photo op photographic opportunity

PHP Parents Helping Parents; Philippines—peso; prepaid health plan

PHPES Program for Health Policy in Economies under Stress

PHPPO Public Health Practice Program Office

phr. phrase

phren. phrenology

phrenol. phrenology

PhRMA Pharmaceutical Research and Manufacturers of America

PHS Public Health Service

PHS & T packaging, handling, storage, and transportation

PHSS Population Health Summary System

PHTM Public Health and Tropical Medicine

PHTN Public Health Training Network

p.h.v. *Latin* pro hac vice (for this purpose)

phy ed physical education

phys. physical; physician; physicist; physics; physiological; physiology

phys ed physical education

physiol. physiological; physiology

PHz petahertz

pi Pali

P$_i$ inorganic phosphate

PI performance indicator; politically incorrect; present illness; primary infertility; principal investigator; private investigator

PIA Greater Peoria Regional Airport; practicably irrigable acreage

pic [motion] picture

PIC Pictor (constellation); pressurized ion chamber; Public Information Center

PICC peripherally inserted central catheter

PICO Polio Information Center Online

PICS Platform for Internet Content Selection

PID pelvic inflammatory disease; Poisons Information Database; process identifier

PIE Proto-Indo-European

PIF program information file

PIGLET Personalized Intelligently Generated Explanatory Text

PIGS passive infrared guidance system

PIH prolactin-inhibiting hormone

PIK payment in kind

PIL publishing interchange language

PILOT phased integrated laser optics technology

PIM personal information manager

PIMP peeing in my pants

PIN personal identification number

PING Packet Internet Groper

PINS persons in need of supervision

pinx. *Latin* pinxit (he or she painted it)

pion pi-meson

PIP picture [with]in picture; program implementation plan;

proximal interphalangeal [joint]

PIPES piperazine diethanesulfonic acid

PIP₂ phosphatidylinositol 4,5-bisphosphate

PIREPS pilot reports

PIRG Public Interest Research Group

PIS psychiatric information services

PIT Greater Pittsburgh International Airport; Pittsburgh Pirates; Pittsburgh Steelers

PITA pain in the ass

PITC phenylisothiocyanate

PITI principal, interest, taxes, and insurance

pix pictures

pixel picture element

pixelsat picture element satellite

pizz. pizzicato

PJ presiding justice

PJ's pajamas

PK Pakistan (international vehicle ID); penalty kick; placekicker; preacher's kid; psychokinesis

pk. park; peak; peck

.pk Pakistan

pkat picokatal

pkg. package; parking

PKI Public Key Infrastructure

PKR Pakistan—rupee (currency)

pkt. packet

PKU phenylketonuria

pkV peak kilovoltage

Pkwy parkway

Pky parkway

PKZIP Phil Katz's Zip (file compression and/or archiving program)

pl Polish

PL partial loss; Poland (international vehicle ID); private line; public law

pl. plate; plural

Pl. place

.pl Poland

PL/1 Programming Language 1

plat. plateau; platoon

PLBB Patent Licensing Bulletin Board

PLC public limited company

PLCO [National Cancer Institute] Prostate, Lung, Colorectal, and Ovarian [Cancer Screening Trial]

plf. plaintiff

PLI paternal leukocyte immunization

PLLO phase-locked loop oscillators

PLM payload module; polarized light microscopy; product lifecycle management

PLMD periodic limb movements disorder

PLMK please let me know

pln. plain

PLO Palestine Liberation Organization

PLOKTA press lots of keys to abort

PLP pyridoxal 5c-phosphate; parathyroid hormonelike protein

PLS please (shortwave transmission)

pls. please

PLSS portable life-support system; public land survey system

PLU Pacific Lutheran University

plu. plural

plur. plural

PLZ Poland—zloty (currency)

pm phase modulated; phase modulation

pM picomolar

Pm promethium

PM particulate matter; past master; police magistrate; postmaster; postmenopausal; postmistress; postmortem; prime minister; private message; provost marshal

pm. premium; premolar

.pm Saint Pierre and Miquelon

p.m. *Latin* post meridiem (after noon)

P.M. *Latin* post meridiem (after noon)

PMA Photo Marketing Association; positive mental attitude

PM & R physical medicine and rehabilitation

PMC Pacific Marine Center; permanently manned capability

PMCIA Personal Computer Memory Card International Association

PME personnel management evaluation

PMEL Pacific Marine Environmental Laboratory

PMF pardon my French; probable maximum flood; product master file

PMFJI pardon me for jumping in

PMG postmaster general; primary medical group

PMH past medical history

PMI private mortgage insurance

PMIGBOM put mind in gear before opening mouth

PMJI pardon my jumping in

pmk. postmark

PML progressive multifocal leukoencephalopathy

PMMA polymethylmethacrylate

PMMW passive millimeter wave

PMN polymorphonuclear leukocytes

pmol picomole

PMP parts, material, and process; previous menstrual period

PMPM per member per month

PMR proportional mortality ratio

PMRA Physical Medicine and Rehabilitation Alliance

PMS Pantone Matching System; premenstrual syndrome

PMSA Primary Metropolitan Statistical Area

PMSG pregnant mare's serum gonadotropin

PMT photomultiplier tube; premenstrual tension

pmt. payment

PMW position mode wavelength

PN practical nurse; pseudo noise

.pn Pitcairn

p.n. promissory note

P/N part number; promissory note

PNA personal needs allowance

PNAs polynuclear aromatic hydrocarbons

PNC premature nodal contraction; prenatal care

PND paroxysmal nocturnal dyspnea

pneum. pneumatic; pneumatics

PNG Papua New Guinea (international vehicle ID);

portable network graphics

p.n.g. *Latin* persona non grata (undesirable person)

PNHP Physicians for a National Health Program

PNMT phenylethanolamine N-methyltransferase

PNNI private network-to-network interface

pno. piano

PNP party and play; psychogenic nocturnal polydipsia

PnP plug and play

PNPB positive-negative pressure breathing

PNS Pensacola Regional Airport; peripheral nervous system

PNSS Pregnancy Nutrition Surveillance System

PNTY pantry

pnxt *Latin* pinxit (he or she painted it)

po putout

Po polonium

PO personnel officer; petty officer; physician organization; piss off ; postal order; post office; purchase order

p.o. *Latin* per os (by mouth)

P/O police officer

POA plan of action

POB post office box

POC particulate organic carbon; point of compliance; port of call; product of combustion

POD payable on delivery; post office department; postoperative day; print on demand; probability of detection; proton omnidirectional detector

PO'd pissed off

PODS pools of doctors

POE point-of-entry; point of exposure; port of entry

POES Polar-orbiting Operational Environmental Satellite

poet. poetic; poetical; poetry

POF premature ovarian failure

POGO Polar Orbiting Geophysical Observatories; privately-owned/government-operated

POHC principal organic hazardous constituent

POHI physically and otherwise health impaired

pol politician

POL petroleum, oil, and lubricants; physician office laboratories

pol. polite; political; politics

Pol. Poland; Polish

POLAR Polar Plasma Laboratory

poli sci political science

polit. political; politician; politics

po. lo. suo. *Latin* ponit loco suo (puts in his place)

poly polyester fiber

poly(A) poly-adenylic acid

poly(u) poly-uridylic acid

POM particulate organic matter; polycyclic organic matter; public order member

POMC pro-opiomelanocortin

pomo postmodern; postmodernism

POMP Purinethol, Oncovin, methotrexate, and prednisone

POMR problem-oriented medical record

POMS Polar Operational Meteorological Satellite

PON particulate organic nitrogen

pon. pontoon

PONA person of no account

pop popular

PoP point of presence

POP Post Office Protocol; proof of purchase

pop. popular; popularly; population

POPIN [United Nations] Population Information Network

Pop. L Popular Latin

POPLINE Population Information Online

POR problem-oriented record

por. portrait

p.o.r. pay on return; price on request

porn pornography

porno pornographic; pornography

port. portable; portrait

Port. Portugal; Portuguese

POS parent over shoulder; part of speech; point of sale; point of service; polar orbiting satellite

pos. position; positive

POSH prevention of sexual harassment; probability of severe hail; the claim that POSH stands for "port out, starboard home" is without foundation

POSIX Portable Operating System Interface for UNIX

POSNA Pediatric Orthopaedic Society of North America

poss. possession; possessive; possible

possess. possessive

POSSLQ person of the opposite sex sharing living quarters

POST power-on self test

post. posterior

post-mod post-modern

post-obit. *Latin* post obitum (after death)

post-op post-operative

POSW privately owned stored water

pot. potential

POTS plain old telephone service

POTUS President of the United States

POU point of use

POV point of view; privately owned vehicle

POW prisoner of war

pp pianissimo

PP parcel post; partly paid; past participle; postpaid; postpartum; prepositional phrase

pp. pages; prepaid; postpaid

p.p. *Latin* per procurationem (by proxy)

P.p. *Latin* punctum proximum (near point)

P.P. *Latin* propria persona (in his own person)

PPA phenylpropanolamine; preferred provider arrangement

p.p.a. per power of attorney

PPAC Practicing Physicians Advisory Council

PPAG Pediatric Pharmacy Advocacy Group

ppb parts per billion

PPB paper, printing, and binding

PPBS Planning, Program, and Budgeting System

PPC pay-per-click

PPCA proserum prothrombin conversion accelerator

PPCF plasmin prothrombins conversion factor

PPCP PowerPC platform

PPD purified protein derivative (of tuberculin)

ppd. postpaid; prepaid

PPE Personal Protection Equipment

PPF plasma protein fraction

PPFA Planned Parenthood Federation of America

p-p factor pellagra-preventing factor

PPG primary provider group

PPH primary pulmonary hypertension

pph. pamphlet

PP$_i$ inorganic pyrophosphate

PPI plan position indicator; policy proof of interest; producer price index

ppl participial

ppl a. participial adjective

pple participle

PPLO pleuropneumonia-like organism

ppm page per minute; parts per million

PPMC physician practice management company

ppmv parts per million by volume

PPO preferred provider organization

PPP Point to Point Protocol; purchasing power parity

PPQ Plant Protection and Quarantine

PPRC Physician Payment Review Commission

PPRibp 5-phospho-α-D-ribosyl 1-pyrophosphate

Pps pulses per second

PPS packet per second; pay-per-sale; prospective payment system; prospective pricing system; protected payments system

P.P.S. *Latin* post postscriptum (additional postscript)

ppt parts per thousand; parts per trillion; precipitate

PPT permanent part time

ppth parts per thousand

pptn. precipitation

PPV pay-per-view; positive pressure ventilation

PQ Parti Québecois; Quebec (two-letter postal code); photosynthetic quotient; previous question

PQ-9 plastoquinone-9

PQA palm query application

PQI personal quality improvement

pr preferences

Pr praseodymium; propyl; Proverbs

PR payroll; proportional representation; public relations; Puerto Rico

pr. pair; present; printed; printing; pronoun

.pr Puerto Rico

p.r. *Latin* punctum remotum (far point)

PRA Paperwork Reduction Act; plasma renin activity

PRAM parameter random access memory

PRAMS Pregnancy Risk Assessment Monitoring System

PRB Population Reference Bureau

PRBC packed red blood cell

PRC People's Republic of China; Postal Rate Commission

PRCA Professional Rodeo Cowboys Association

PRD presidential review directive

PRE progressive resistive exercise

preamp preamplifier

prec. preceding

pred. predicate; predicative; predicatively

pred. a. predicative adjective

preemie prematurely born infant

pref. preface; preferred; prefix

prefab prefabricated

prelim preliminary; preliminary examination

prem. premium

pre-med pre-medical college undergraduate major

premie prematurely born infant

PR enzyme phosphorylase-rupturing enzyme; photoreactivating enzyme

pre-op pre [sex-change] operation; pre-operative

prep preparatory

PREP Pediatrics Review and Education Program

prep. preposition; prepositional

prepd. prepared

prepn. preparation

preppie a student at or a graduate of a preparatory school

preppy a student at or a graduate of a preparatory school

pres. present; president

Presb. Presbyterian

Presby. Presbyterian

pres. ppl present participial

pres. pple present participle

pres. t. present tense

pret. preterit

prev. previous; previously

PREVLINE Prevention Online

prexy president

prez president

PRF pulse recurrence frequency; pulse repetition frequency

prf. proof

PRG Ruzyně Airport (Prague, Czech Republic)

PRH prolactin-releasing hormone

PRI primary rate interface; Public Radio International

prim. primary; primitive

prin. principal; principle

print. printing

priv. private; privative

PRK photorefractive keratotomy

prkg. parking

PRL Polar Research Laboratory; prolactin

PRM Bureau of Population, Refugees, and Migration

PRN printer

p.r.n. *Latin* pro re nata (as the situation demands)

pro professional; prostitute

PRO peer review organization; professional review organization; pronoun; public relations officer

pro. pronoun

prob. probable; probably; probate; problem

proc. proceeding; proceedings; process

PROCAARE Program for Collaboration Against AIDS and Related Epidemics

procto proctoscopy

prod. produce; produced; product; production

Prof professional
prof. professional
Prof. Professor
Prof'l professional
prog. program
proj project; projector
Project DARE Drug Abuse Resistance Education
prole proletarian
prom a dance (from "promenade")
PROM passive range of motion; premature rupture of membranes; programmable read-only memory
prom. promontory
ProMED Program for Monitoring Emerging Diseases
promo promotional announcement
pron. pronominal; pronoun; pronounced; pronunciation
pronunc. pronunciation
prop propeller
prop. proper; property; proposition; proprietor; proprietress
ProPAC Prospective Payment Assessment Commission
propr. proprietor; proprietress
prop. reg. proposed regulation
pro rat. aet. *Latin* pro ratione aetatis (according to [patient's] age)
pros. prosody
Pros. Atty. prosecuting attorney
Prot. Protestant
protec. protectorate
pro tem *Latin* pro tempore (for the time being)
prov. province; provisional; provost
Prov. Provençal; Proverbs

prox. *Latin* proximo [mense] (next [month])
PrP prion protein
PRP potentially responsible party
prp. present participle
PRPP 5-phospho-α-D-ribosyl 1-pyrophosphate
PRS price reporting system
PRT personal rapid transit; platinum resistance thermometers
PRTC priority real time command
Pruss. Prussian
Prv Proverbs
prvt private
prwr prewar (usually before World War II)
ps Pashto; picosecond
PS passenger steamer; photosystem; PostScript; point source (of pollution); police sergeant; polystyrene; public school; public statutes
Ps. Psalm; Psalms
P.S. postscript
PSA Piscis Austrinus (constellation); prostate-specific antigen; public service announcement
Psa. Psalms
PSAP Pharmacotherapy Self-Assessment Program
PSC Pisces; polar stratospheric cloud; Tri-Cities Airport (Pasco, WA)
PSCU Private Sector Casemix Unit
PSDA Patient Self-Determination Act
PSE Mercedita Airport (Ponce, PR); Pacific Stock Exchange; please (shortwave transmission); power supply electronics

psec. picosecond

PSEF Plastic Surgery Educational Foundation

pseud. pseudonym

PSF point spread function

psf. pounds per square foot

PSG platoon sergeant

psi pounds per square inch

psia pounds per square inch absolute

psid pounds per square inch differential

psig pounds per square inch gauge

PSIMPLE Problem Solving in Medical Physiology, Logically Explained

PSIS Plastic Surgery Information Service

PSL polystyrene latex

PSK phase shift keying

PSM project security manager

PSN packet-switched network

PSO physician services organization

PSP Palm Springs International Airport; Paralytic Shellfish Poisoning; phenolsulfonphthalein; program segment prefix; progressive supranuclear palsy

PSPA Physician Services Practice Analysis

PSPDN packet switched public data network

PSR Physicians for Social Responsibility; premature separation and rupture; program status review; pulsar

PSRAM pseudo-static random-access memory

PSRO professional standards review organization

PST Pacific Standard Time

PSU Pennsylvania State University; Portland State University; power supply unit

PSVT paroxysmal supraventricular tachycardia

psych psychoanalyze

psych. psychiatric; psychiatry; psychological; psychologist; psychology

psycho psychopath

psychol. psychological; psychologist; psychology

psywar psychological warfare

pt [hospital] patient; Portuguese

Pt Peter; platinum

PT Pacific Time; patrol torpedo; physical therapist; physical therapy; physical training; proficiency testing

pt. part; payment; pint; preterit

Pt. point; port

.pt Portugal

p.t. pro tempore

P/T part time; psychotherapist

PTA Parent-Teacher Association; prior to [hospital] admission

pta. peseta

PTAH phosphotungstic acid hematoxylin

PTC phenylthiocarbamide

PTCA percutaneous transluminal coronary angioplasty

PtCT patient care technologies

Ptd phosphatidyl

PtdCho phosphatidylcholine

PtdEth phosphatidylethanolamine

PtdIns phosphatidylinositol

PtdSer phosphatidylserine

PTE Portugal—escudo (currency); pulmonary thromboembolism; pulmonary thromboendarterectomy

PTEA pulmonary thromboendarterectomy

PTFE polytetrafluoroethylene (Teflon)

PTF plasma thromboplastin factor

ptg. printing

PTGS post-transcriptional gene silencing

PTH parathyroid hormone

PTHC percutaneous transhepatic cholangiography

PTI previously taxed income

P.T.I. pretrial intervention

PTL Praise the Lord

PTMA phenyltrimethylammonium

PTMPTY per thousand members per year

PTO Parent-Teacher Organization; Patent and Trademark Office; power takeoff

p.t.o. please turn over

PTR problem trouble report; program technical report

PTSA Parent-Teacher-Student Association

PTSD posttraumatic stress disorder

PTSO Parent-Teacher-Student Organization

PTT partial thromboplastin time

PTU propylthiouracil

PTV pay television; public television

pty. proprietary

Pu plutonium

PU pickup

P.U. Used to indicate a bad or offensive smell (from "phew")

pub. public; publication; published; publisher

publ. publication; published; publisher

P.U.C. Public Utilities Commission

PUD peptic ulcer disease; planned unit development

PUK Patriotic Union of Kurdistan

PUL pulmonary metastases

pulm. pulmonary

pulv. *Latin* pulvis (powder)

PUO pyrexia of unknown/uncertain origin

PUP Puppis (constellation)

Pur purine

PUR *Public Utility Reports*

PUSH People United to Serve Humanity

PV photovoltaic; plasma volume; polyvinyl; potential vorticity

PVA polyvinyl acetate

PVC permanent virtual circuit; polyvinyl chloride; premature ventricular contraction

PVD peripheral vascular disease; T.F. Green Airport (Providence, RI)

PVL parameter value language

PVM parallel virtual machine

PVO private voluntary organization

PVP polyvinylpyrrolidone

PVR Gustavo D. Ordaz International Airport (Puerto Vallarta, Mexico); personal video recorder

PVT private

pvt. private

PW puncture wound

.pw Palau

P/W prewar (usually before World War II)

PWA People with AIDS Coalition; person with AIDS; Public Works Administration

P-wave pressure wave

PWBA Pension and Welfare Benefits Administration

PWC National Organization of Physicians Who Care

PWD person with disability

PWM pokeweed mitogen; Portland (ME) International Jetport Airport

PWR power (shortwave transmission); pressurized water reactor

pwr. power

PWS public water system; public water supply

PWSA Prader-Willi Syndrome Association

pwt. pennyweight

px medical prognosis

PX physical examination; Post Exchange

pxt. *Latin* pinxit (he or she painted it)

.py Paraguay

PY Paraguay (international vehicle ID); prior year

PYG Paraguay—guarani (currency)

PYO pick your own

Pyr pyrimidine

pyro. pyrotechnics

PYX Pyxis (constellation)

PZM pressure zone microphone

PZT piezoelectric transducer

Q

q charge

Q quarter; queen

q. quart; quarter; quarterly; question; quintal; quire

Q. quarto

QA Qatar (international vehicle ID); quality assurance

.qa Qatar

QAE quality assurance engineer

QALY quality-adjusted life years

q and a question and answer

QAO quality assurance office

QAP quality assurance plan

QAR Qatar—rial (currency)

QB quarterback; queen's bishop

Q.B. Queen's Bench

Q.B.D. Queen's Bench Division

QBE query by example

QBF query by form

QBO quasi-biennial oscillation

QC quality circle; quality control

Q.C. Queen's Counsel

q.c.f. *Latin* quare clausum fregit (wherefore he broke the close, that is, trespass)

QCPP quality control program plan

q.d. *Latin* quaque die (every day)

Q.D. *Latin* quasi dictat (as if he should say)

QED Quality, Efficiency, Dependability; quantitative evaluative device; quantum electrodynamics

Q.E.D. *Latin* quod erat demonstrandum (which was to be demonstrated)

Q.E.F. *Latin* quod erat faciendum (which was to have been done)

Q.E.I. *Latin* quod erat inveniendum (which was to be found out)

Q.E.N. *Latin* quare executionem non (wherefore execution [should] not [be issued])

QF quick-firing

QGA queen's gambit accepted (chess)

QGD queen's gambit denied (chess)

q.h. *Latin* quaque die (every hour)

QI quality improvement

QIC quarter-inch cartridge

q.i.d. *Latin* quater in die (four times a day)

QIO quality improvement organization

QIT quality improvement team

QK quick (shortwave transmission)

QKt queen's knight

ql. quintal

Qld. Queensland

qlty. quality

QM quartermaster

q.m. *Latin* quaque mane (every morning)

QMAS Quality Measurement Advisory Service

QMB qualified Medicare beneficiary

QMC quartermaster corps

QMG quartermaster general

QMR Quick Medical Reference

qn. question

QNB quinuclidinyl benzilate

QNS quantity not sufficient

q._____h. *Latin* quaque _____ hora (every _____ hours)

Qo Qoheleth

Qoh. Qoheleth

QOL quality of life

QoS quality of service

QP queen's pawn

q.p. *Latin* quantum placet (as much as you please)

QPL Qualified Products List

qq. questions

Qq. quartos

qq.v. *Latin* quae vide (which [things] see)

QR queen's rook

qr. quarter; quarterly; quire

q.r. *Latin* quantum rectum (however much is correct)

q.s. *Latin* quantum sufficit (as much as suffices)

QS quarter sessions

QSO quasi-stellar object

QT cutie

qt quart

q.t. quiet

Q.T. *Latin* qui tam (who sues)

qtd. quartered

Q-TIP trust qualified terminal interest property trust

Qto. quarto

qtr. quarter

qty. quantity

qu Quechua

qu. query; question

quad quadraphonic; quadriceps (thigh muscle); quadruplet

Quad quadrangle

quad. quadrangle; quadrant; quadrilateral; quadrillion

quads quadriceps (thigh muscles)

qual. qualitative

quant. quantitative

quar. quarter; quarterly

quart. quarterly

quasar quasi-stellar object

Que. Quebec

ques. question

quint quintuplet

quot. quotation

quot. op. sit. *Latin* quoties opus sit (as often as necessary)

q.v. *Latin* quod vide (which see)

QWERTY standard computer and typewriter keyboard

QWIP quantum well infrared photodetector

QWL quality of work life

R

r correlation coefficient; radius; resistance

R gas constant; radical; rain; range; Réaumur; receiver; registered trademark; Republican; response; restricted (children under 17 must be accompanied by a parent or guardian); right; roentgen; rook; run

r. rare; recto; reigned; retired; rod; rubber; ruble; rupee

R. patented; rabbi; received as transmitted (shortwave transmission); rector; registered; *Latin* rex (king); *Latin* regina (queen); river

Ra radium

RA Argentina (international vehicle ID); rear admiral; reasonable alternative; regular army; remedial action; research assistant; research associate; resident advisor; resident assistant; rheumatoid arthritis; right ascension; right atrium; risk analysis; route analysis

Ra. range

R.A. Royal Academy

R/A room air

RAAF Royal Australian Air Force

RACH random access channel

racon radar beacon

rad radian; radiation absorbed dose; *Slang* radical (that is, excellent)

RAD Royal Academy of Dancing

rad. radical; radius; radix

RADA Royal Academy of Dramatic Art

radar radio detecting and ranging

RADM rear admiral (upper half)

RAE right atrial enlargement

RAES retail automated execution system

RAF Royal Air Force

rah Referred with Amendments House [of Representatives]

RAI radioactive iodine

RAID redundant array of inexpensive disks

RAM radar absorbing material; random-access memory; rarely adequate memory; Royal Academy of Music

RAMDAC random-access memory digital-to-analog converter

RAMP Rural Abandoned Mine Program

RAND research and development

R & B rhythm and blues

R & D research and development

R & M reliability and maintainability

R & R rest and recreation

RAO right anterior oblique

RAP recurrent abdominal pain

rap. rapid
RAPD rapid analysis of polymorphic deoxyribonucleic acid
RAPS radiologists, anesthesiologists, pathologists; regulated all-paper system
RAR revenue agent's report
RARR range and range rate
ras Referred with Amendments Senate
RAS reticular activating system; Royal Astronomical Society
RASC Royal Astronomical Society of Canada
RASER research and seeker emulation radar
RASS radio acoustic sounding system
RAT right anterior thigh
rato rocket-assisted takeoff
RAV Rous-associated virus
RAWIN radar wind sounding
Rb rubidium
RB Botswana (international vehicle ID); reciprocal beneficiary; running back
RBAY right back at ya
RBBB right bundle branch block
RBC red blood cell; red blood cell count
RBE relative biological effectiveness
RBF renal blood flow
RBI runs batted in
RBMA Radiology Business Management Association
RBRVS resource based relative value scale
RBTL read between the lines
RC red card (soccer); Red Cross; Roman Catholic; Taiwan (international vehicle ID)

R/C radio-controlled
RCA Central African Republic (international vehicle ID)
RCB Congo (international vehicle ID)
RCAF Royal Canadian Air Force
RCC Regional Climate Center
R.C. Ch. Roman Catholic Church
RCD received (shortwave transmission)
rcd. received
RCE reaction control equipment
rch Reference Change House [of Representatives]
RCH Chile (international vehicle ID)
RCL ruling case law
RCMP Royal Canadian Mounted Police
RCN Royal Canadian Navy
RCP respiratory care practitioner; Royal College of Physicians
RCPC Royal College of Physicians of Canada
RCP(E) Royal College of Physicians (Edinburgh)
RCP(I) Royal College of Physicians (Ireland)
rcpt. receipt
RCR registered commodity representative
RCRA Resource Conservation and Recovery Act
rcs Reference Change Senate
RCS radar cross section; reaction control system; Royal College of Surgeons
RCSC Royal College of Surgeons of Canada
RCS(E) Royal College of Surgeons (Edinburgh)

RCS(I) Royal College of Surgeons (Ireland)

RCT randomized controlled trial; root canal treatment

rct. recruit

RCVR receiver (shortwave transmission)

rd rod; Rutherford

RD reference document; registered dietitian; retinal degeneration; rural delivery

Rd. road

RDA recommended daily allowance; remote database access; Rural Development Administration

RDB Rare Disease Database

RDBMS relational database management system

RDF radio direction finder

RDFS ratio of decayed and filled surfaces

RDFT ratio of decayed and filled teeth

RDG Ridge (in postal abbreviations)

rdh Received in the Senate

RDH Registered Dental Hygienist

RDML rear admiral (lower half)

rDNA ribosomal deoxyribonucleic acid

RDS respiratory distress syndrome

RDU Raleigh-Durham International Airport; remote data uplink

RDX rapid detonation explosive

re Reprint of an Amendment

Re earth radii; rhenium

RE real estate; repair escrow [required]; reproductive endocrinologist; right end

Re. Rupee

.re Réunion

REA Rural Electrification Administration

reah Re-engrossed Amendment House

reb rebel

rebar reinforcing bar

rec. receipt; record; recording; recreation

recap recapitulation

recce reconnaissance

recd. received

recip. reciprocal; reciprocity

recon reconnaissance

rec. sec. recording secretary

rect. receipt; rectangle; rectangular; rectified; rector; rectory

red. reduced; reduction

redox. reduction oxidation

redupl. reduplicated; reduplication

REE rare earth element

ref referee

REF refer to (shortwave transmission)

ref. reference; referred

re. fa. lo. *Latin* recordari facias loquelam (cause the plaint to be recorded)

refash. refashioned

REFCORP Resolution Funding Corporation

refl. reflection; reflective; reflex; reflexive

refr. refraction

refrig refrigerating; refrigeration

reg regulation

reg. regent; regiment; region; register; registered; registration; registrar; registry; regular; regularly; regulation

regd. registered

reg. gen. *Latin* regula generalis (a general rule [of court])

reg. jud. *Latin* registrum judiciale (the register of judicial writs)

reg. pl. *Latin* regula placitandi (rule of pleading)

regs regulations

regt. regent; regiment

rehab rehabilitation

REIT real estate investment trust

rel. related; relating; relative; relatively; released; religion; religious

relig. religion

relo relocation

rem roentgen equivalent in man

REM rapid eye movement; remark

rem. remittance

REMIC real estate mortgage investment conduit

renov renovated

ren. sem. *Latin* renovetur semel (shall be renewed [only] once)

rep repertory; repetition; representative; reputation

rep. repair; repetition; report; reporter; represent; representative; reprint; republic

Rep. representative; republic; Republican

repl. replace; replaced; replacement; replacing

REPNZ repeat while not zero

repo repossessed merchandise or property; repossession of merchandise or property; repurchase agreement

repr. representative; represented; representing; representation; reprint; reprinted

repro reproduction

rept. report

Repub. Republic; Republican

REPZ repeat while zero

req. require; required; requisition

reqd. required

reqmt. requirement

res Re-engrossed Amendment Senate

RES reticuloendothial system

res. reservation; reserve; reservoir; residence; resolution

Res. reservation; reservoir

resid residual

resp. respective; respectively

RESPA Real Estate Settlement Procedures Act

respirs respirations

RET Reticulum (constellation)

ret. retired; return

retcon retroactive continuity

retd retained; retired; returned

RETRF Rural Electrification and Telephone Revolving Fund

retro *French* rétro (French clipping for rétrospectif, that is, retrospective)

retro. retroactive

re-up re-sign up, that is, to enlist again

rev. revenue; reverse; reversed; review; revised; revision; revolution

Rev Reverend

Rev. Revelation; reverend

rev'd reversed

reverb reverberation

rev'g reversing

rev. proc. revenue procedure

rev. rul. revenue ruling

Rev. Ver. Revised Version

rew rewind

Rf rutherfordium

RF radio frequency; response factor; rheumatic fever; right field; right fielder

rf. reef; refund

RFA Radio Free Asia; request for applications; right frontoanterior (position)

RFB request for bid

RFC Reconstruction Finance Corporation; request for comments; river forecast center

RFCA Reconstruction Finance Corporation Act

RFCM radio frequency countermeasure

RFD rural free delivery

RFDU radio frequency distribution unit

RFE Radio Free Europe

rfh Referred in House [of Representatives]

rfhr Referred in House [of Representatives]—Reprint

rfi radio frequency interference

RFI ready for inspection; request for information

RFID radio frequency identification

RFK Robert Francis Kennedy

RFLP restriction fragment length polymorphism

RFP request for proposal; request for proposals; right frontoposterior (position)

RFQ request for quotation; request for quotations; request for quote; request for quotes

rfs Referred in Senate

RFS remote file system

rfsr Referred in Senate—Reprint

RFT registered floor trader (stock market); right frontotransverse (position)

Rg roentgenium

RG Guinea (international vehicle ID); relational grammar; retrograde; right guard; Rio Group

R.G. *Latin* regula generalis (general rule, or order [of a court])

RGB red, green, blue

rh Reported in House [of Representatives]; rheumatic

Rh Rhesus factor; rhodium

RH Haiti (international vehicle ID); relative humidity; releasing hormone; right hand

Rha. L-rhamnose

rhbdr. rhombohedron

RHCC Rural Health Care Corporation

RHCS regional health care system

RHD rheumatic heart disease

rheo. rheostat

rhet. rhetoric; rhetorical

R-hFSH recombinant human follicle stimulating hormone

RHIN Regional Health Information Network

rhino rhinoceros

rhinos. rhinoceros

RHIP rank has its privileges

RHIS REUTERS Health Information Services

rhomb. rhombic

rhp rated horsepower

RHP Rainforest Health Project

rhr Reported in House [of Representatives]—Reprint

RI Indonesia (international vehicle ID); reproductive immunologist; Rhode Island

R.I. Rhode Island

RIA radioimmunoassay; Research Institute on Addictions

RIATT Research Institute for Assistive and Training Technologies

RIC Radon Information Council; Richmond International Airport/Byrd Field

RICHS Rural Information Center Health Service

RICO Racketeer Influenced and Corrupt Organizations Act [of 1970]

RID radial immunodiffusion; Registry of Interpreters for the Deaf

ridic ridiculous

RIF reduction in force; resistance-inducing factor

RIG station equipment (short-wave transmission)

rih Referral Instructions House [of Representatives]

RIJ right internal jugular

rIL-2 recombinant interleukin-2

RIM Mauritania (international vehicle ID)

RIN record identification number; relative intensity noise

RIO radar intercept officer

RIP raster image processor; reproductive immunophynotype

R.I.P. *Latin* requiescat in pace (may he or she rest in peace); *Latin* requiescant in pace (may they rest in peace)

ris Referral Instructions Senate

RISA radioiodinated serum albumin

RISC reduced instruction set computer

RISP runners in scoring position

RIST radioimmunosorbent test

RIT Rochester Institute of Technology

RITA relocation income tax allowance

rit. ritardando

riv. river

RJ radial jerk (reflex); road junction

RJE remote job entry

RJOS Ruth Jackson Orthopaedic Society

RK radial keratectomy; radial keratotomy

RL Lebanon (international vehicle ID); Radio Liberty; real life (that is, as opposed to virtual reality, as on the Internet); Roman law

R.L. revised laws

R>L right greater than left

RLE right lower extremity; run-length encoded

RLG ring laser gyro

RLL right lower lobe; run length limited

RLN remote local area network node

RLO Returned Letter Office

RLQ right lower quadrant

RLS restless legs syndrome; Robert Louis Stevenson

rm Rhaeto-Romance

Rm Romans

RM Madagascar (international vehicle ID); reconfiguration module; reichsmark; room

rm. ream; room

RMA reliability-maintainability-availability; right mentoanterior (position); risk management agency

RMB *Chinese* renminbi (people's currency)

RMCL recommended maximum containment level

rmdr remainder

RMI Republic of the Marshall Islands

RML right middle lobe

RMM Mali (international vehicle ID)

RMMS remote maintenance monitoring system

RMN Richard Milhous Nixon

RMP right mentoposterior (position)

rms root mean square

RMS Railway Mail Service; remote manipulator system; Royal Mail Service; Royal Mail Steamship

RMSF Rocky Mountain spotted fever

RMT right mentotransverse (position)

RMV respiratory minute volume

rn Kirundi

Rn radon

RN Niger (international vehicle ID); registered nurse; Royal Navy

RNA ribonucleic acid

RNAase ribonuclease

RNase ribonuclease

RNase D ribonuclease D

RNAi RNA interference

RNC Republican National Committee

rnd around

rnd. round

RNN recurrent neural network

RNO Reno/Tahoe International Airport

RNP ribonucleoprotein

RNR Zambia (international vehicle ID)

RNS Respiratory Nursing Society

RNZAF Royal New Zealand Air Force

ro Romanian

RO read only; revenue officer; Romania (international vehicle ID)

ro. recto; rood

.ro Romania

R/O receiver only; rule out

r-o run-on

ROA return on assets; right occipitoanterior (position); Roanoke Regional Airport/Woodrum Field

ROC Greater Rochester [NY] International Airport; Republic of China (Taiwan); rest of Canada (other than Quebec)

ROE residue on evaporation; return on equity

ROFL rolling on floor laughing

ROG reactive organic gas

r.o.g. receipt of goods

ROI return on investment

ROK Republic of Korea (South Korea); South Korea (international vehicle ID)

ROL Romania—leu (currency)

rom roman

ROM range of motion; range of movement; read-only memory

Rom. Roman; Romance; Romania; Romanian; Romans

ROM BIOS read-only memory basic input/output system

romcom romantic comedy

roo kangaroo

ROP record of production; right occipitoposterior (position); run of paper; run of press

ROR release on own recognizance

ROS review of systems

Ros. Roscommon

ROT registered options trader; right occipitotransverse (position)

rot. rotating; rotation

ROTC Reserve Officers' Training Corps

ROTF rolling on the floor

ROTFL rolling on the floor laughing

ROTFLMAO rolling on the floor laughing my ass off

ROTFLMAOPIMP rolling on the floor, laughing my ass off, peeing in my pants

ROTFLOL rolling on the floor laughing out loud

ROTM right on the money

roto rotogravure

ROU Uruguay (international vehicle ID)

ROV remotely operated vehicle; rover

ROY G. BIV red, orange, yellow, green, blue, indigo, violet (the colors of the spectrum)

RP Philippines (international vehicle ID); Received Pronunciation; repairs in progress; retinitis pigmentosa; responsible party

RPA random phase approximation

RPB recognized professional body

RPC remote procedure call

RPD Rapid (in postal abbreviations)

RPDS Rapids (in postal abbreviations)

RPF renal plasma flow

RPG report program generator; rocket-propelled grenade; role playing game

RPh Registered Pharmacist

RPI retail price index

RPL recurrent pregnancy loss

rpm revolutions per minute

RPN reverse Polish notation

RPO railway post office; Royal Philharmonic Orchestra

RPR remote procedure request

rps revolutions per second

RPT repeat; I repeat (shortwave transmission)

rpt. repeat; report

RPU remote pickup

RPV remotely piloted vehicle

RQ respiratory quotient

RR railroad; recovery room; respiration rate; rural route

R.R. right reverend

RRB Railroad Retirement Board

RRC residency review committee

rRNA ribosomal RNA

RRS Radiation Research Society

RRT Registered Respiratory Therapist

rs Reported in Senate

Rs Solar Radius

RS recording secretary; Royal Society

R.S. Revised Statutes

RSA recurrent spontaneous abortion; Rehabilitation Services Administration

RSC residual sodium carbonate; Royal Shakespeare Company

RSD reflex sympathetic dystrophy

RSDL reverse spiral dual layer

RSFSR *Russian* Rossijskaja Sovetskaja Federativnaja Sotsialisticheskaja Respublika (Russian Soviet Federated Socialist Republic)

RSI relative strength indicator; repetitive strain injury; repetitive stress injury

RSM San Marino (international vehicle ID)

RSN radio supernova; real soon now (sometimes sarcastic); record sequencing number

RSNA Radiological Society of North America

RSP right sacroposterior (position)

RSPA Research and Special Programs Administration

rsr Reported in Senate—Reprint

RSR regular sinus rhythm; rotating shadowband radiometer

RSS Really Simple Syndication; root sum square

RST right sacrotransverse (position); Rochester [MN] Municipal Airport

RSV Revised Standard Version

RSVP *French* répondez s'il vous plaît (respond if you please—that is, a response is expected); Resource Reservation Protocol; Retired and Seniors Volunteers Program

RSW Southwest Florida International Airport

RSWC right side up with care

Rt Ruth

RT radiation therapy; radio technician; radiotelephone; respiratory therapist; response time; return ticket; right tackle; room temperature

rt. right

Rt. route

R/T real-time

RTA ready to assemble; renal tubular acidosis

RTB Rural Telephone Bank

RTC real time clock; Resolution Trust Corporation

RTD return to duty

Rte. route

RTECS Registry of Toxic Effects of Chemical Substances

RTF [Microsoft's] Rich Text Format

RTFFAQ read the fucking FAQ

RTFI read the fucking instructions

RTFM read the fucking manual

RTG radioisotope thermal generator

rth Referred to Committee House [of Representatives]

RtH right-handed

Rt. Hon. Right Honorable

RTK Net The Right-To-Know Network

RTM read the manual

rTMP ribothymidylic acid

RTP Rapid Transport Protocol; Real-Time Transport Protocol; Routing Table Protocol

r-TPA recombinant tissue plasminogen activator

RT-PCR reverse transcriptase-polymerase chain reaction

RTOG Radiation Therapy Oncology Group

Rt. Rev. Right Reverend

rts Referred to Committee Senate

RTS request to send

RTSC read the source code

RTSMP real-time symmetric multiprocessor

RTSP Real-Time Streaming Protocol

RTT round-trip time

RTTY radio-teletype

RTU remote terminal unit

RTV rough-terrain vehicle

RTW ready-to-wear

rty. rarity

ru Russian

Ru Ruth; ruthenium

RU Burundi (international vehicle ID)

.ru Russian Federation

RU-486 Roussel-Uclaf-486 (mifepristone)

RUC rapid update cycle

RUE right upper extremity

RUG resource utilization group

RUL right upper lobe

Rum. Rumania; Rumanian

RUQ right upper quadrant

RUR Russia—ruble

RUS Rural Utilities Service; Russian Federation (international vehicle ID)

Rus. Russia; Russian

Russ. Russia; Russian

RUST Remote User Scheduling Terminal

RV recreational vehicle; reentry vehicle; residual volume; Revised Version; right ventricle

R/V Research Vessel

Rv. Revelation

RVE right ventricular enlargement

RVH right ventrical hypertrophy

RVR runway visual range

RVS relative value scale

RVU relative value unit

rw Kinyarwanda

RW radiological warfare; relief wins

.rw Rwanda

R.W. Right Worshipful; Right Worthy

R/W read/write

RWA Rwanda (international vehicle ID)

RWE Ralph Waldo Emerson

RWF Rwanda—franc

RWJF The Robert Wood Johnson Foundation

RWM read write memory

RWR radar warning receiver

rwy. railway

Rx *Latin* recipe (take)[that is, a medical prescription]; remedy

RX receive

ry. railway

S

s second; second; split; stere; strange quark

S entropy; safety; Samuel; satisfactory; Saturday; Senate; send (shortwave transmission); sentence; sexual [situations] (television rating); siemens; single (as in personal ads); small; smoking section; soprano; south; southern; straight (as in personal ads); strike; sulfur; Sunday; sunny; superior; Sweden (international vehicle ID)

s. shilling; singular; sire; solo; son; substantive

S. saint; sea; signature; signor; signore; statute

S3T sequentially sampling sediment trap

sa Sanskrit

Sa Saturday

SA Saudi Arabia (international vehicle ID); seaman apprentice; seasonally adjusted; semen analysis; sex appeal; solar array; subject to approval

.sa Saudi Arabia

s.a. *Latin* sine anno (without year—that is, undated)

S.A. Salvation Army; *Spanish* Sociedad Anónima (Corporation); South Africa; South America; South Australia

S-A sinuatrial

SAA solar azimuth angle; [IBM's] System Application Architecture

SAAAPA Student Academy of the American Academy of Physician Assistants

SAARC South Asian Association for Regional Cooperation

SAB spontaneous abortion

Sab. Sabbath

SAC single-attached concentrator; Strategic Air Command

sac. sacrifice

SACEUR Supreme Allied Commander, Europe

SACT sinoatrial conduction time

SACU Southern African Customs Union

SAD seasonal affective disorder

SADC Southern African Development Community

SADCC Southern African Development Coordination Conference

SADD Students Against Drunk Driving

SADHA Student's American Dental Hygienists Association

SAE seasonal application efficiency; self-addressed envelope; Society of Automotive Engineers

SAED selected-area electron diffraction

SAEM Society for Academic Emergency Medicine

saf safety

SAF single Asian female; soon as feasible (shortwave transmission)

SAFE simulation analysis of financial exposure; Smokefree Air for Everyone

SAFER spectral application of finite element representation

SAFETY Sun Awareness for Educating Today's Youth

SAFPA Society of Air Force Physician Assistants

S. Afr. South Africa; South African

SAG Sagittarius; Screen Actors Guild

SAGE Russian-American Gallium Experiment (formerly Soviet-American Gallium Experiment)

SAGRI Substance Abuse, Growth, and Recovery Institute

SAH Society of Automotive Historians; systemic arterial hypertension

SAIDI spaced antenna imaging Doppler interferometer

SAIF Savings Association Insurance Fund

SAL semiactive laser

sal. salary

SALT Strategic Arms Limitation Talks; Strategic Arms Limitation Treaty

SAM sequential access method; single Asian male; surface-to-air missile

Sam. Samuel

SAMBA Society of Ambulatory Anesthesia

SAMDS Serbian American Medical and Dental Society

S. Amer. South America; South American

SAMHSA Substance Abuse and Mental Health Services Administration

Saml. Samuel

sAMP adenylosuccinic acid

san sanatorium

SAN San Diego International Airport/Lindbergh Field; storage area network

S & E salaries and expenses

S & H shipping and handling

S & L savings and loan association

S & M sadomasochism

S & P 500 Standard and Poor's 500-Stock Price Index

S & T science and technology

SANE sulfur and nitrogen emissions

sanit. sanitary; sanitation

S-A node sinoatrial node

SANS small angle neutron scattering

SAO Smithsonian Astrophysical Observatory

SaO2 arterial oxygen saturation

SAP service access point; soon as possible (shortwave transmission)

s.ap. apothecaries' scruple

SAPA Society of Army Physician Assistants

Sar sarcosine

SAR Saudi Arabia—riyal (currency); search and rescue; segmentation and reassembly; sodium adsorption ratio; Sons of the American Revolution; special access required; specific absorption rate; synthetic aperture radar

SAREC Science of Anticipation Recognition Evaluation Control [of Health Risks]

SAREX Shuttle Amateur Radio Experiment

SARSAT search and rescue satellite-aided tracking

SART sinoatrial recovery time; Society of Assisted Reproductive Technology

sas Additional Sponsors Senate

SAS Scandinavian Airline Systems; single attachment station; Society for Applied Spectroscopy; soil absorption system; space activity suit; space adaptation syndrome; Statistical Analysis System

SASE self-addressed stamped envelope

Sask. Saskatchewan

sat saturated

SAT Samoa—tala (currency); San Antonio International Airport; a trademark used for a set of standardized college entrance examinations (originally Scholastic Aptitude Test)

sat. saturate; saturated

Sat. Saturday

SATA Society for Advanced Telecommunications in Anesthesia

satbot satellite robot

SATCOM satellite communication

satd. saturated

SATH Society for the Advancement of Travel for the Handicapped

sat. sol. saturated solution

sat. soln. saturated solution

S. Aust. South Australia

SAV Savannah International Airport; state-of-the-atmosphere variables

SAVE Systematic Alien Verification for Entitlement

SAWS Silent Attack Warning System

sax saxophone

Sax. Saxon

Sb antimony

SB *Latin* Scientiae Baccalaureus (Bachelor of Science); sedimentation basin; simultaneous broadcast; small bowel; stolen base; southbound

sb. substantive

.sb Solomon Islands

S.B. [United States] Senate bill

SBA Santa Barbara Municipal Airport; Small Business Administration

SBAA Spina Bifida Association of America

SBC SBC Communications Inc.; Southern Baptist Convention

SBCS Single Byte Character Set

SBD silent but deadly [flatulent emission]; Solomon Islands—dollar

SbE south by east

SBE Society of Broadcast Engineers; subacute bacterial endocarditis

SBF single Black female

SBIC Small Business Investment Company

SBIR small business innovative research

SBIRS space-based infrared system

SBL Society of Biblical Literature; space-based laser

SBM single Black male; Society of Behavioral Medicine

SBN South Bend/Michiana Regional Airport; Standard Book Number

SBO small bowel obstruction

SBP Society of Biological Psychiatry

SBR sequencing batch reactors; spectral band replication

SBS sick building syndrome

SBUV solar backscatter ultraviolet

SbW south by west

sc Sponsor Change House [of Representatives]

Sc scandium

SC Security Council; Sisters of Charity; South Carolina; Supreme Court

sc. scale; scene; *Latin* scilicet (that is to say); scruple; *Latin* sculpsit (carved by)

Sc. Scotch; Scots; Scottish

.sc Seychelles

s.c. small capital (letter); subcutaneous; subcutaneously

S.C. South Carolina

S/C spacecraft

SCA Sexual Compulsives Anonymous; shuttle carrier aircraft; Society for Creative Achronisms

Scand. Scandinavia; Scandinavian

SCAR Society for Computer Applications in Radiology

S.Car. South Carolina

SCARD Society of Chairmen of Academic Radiology Departments

SCAT School and College Ability Test; special crimes action team; supersonic commercial air transport

SCATA Society for Computing and Technology in Anaesthesia

ScB *Latin* Scientiae Baccalaureus (Bachelor of Science)

SCBNP Society for the Collecting of Brand-Name Pencils

SCBT/MR Society of Computed Body Tomography and Magnetic Resonance

SCC serial communications controller; storage connecting circuit

SCCA Sports Car Club of America

SCCCPMA Society for Computing in Critical Care, Pulmonary Medicine, and Anesthesia

SCCM Society of Critical Care Medicine

SCCS source code control system

ScD *Latin* Scientiae Doctor (Doctor of Science)

SCD sickle cell disease; sudden cardiac death

SCET spacecraft event time

SCF satellite control facility; single Christian female

ScGael. Scottish Gaelic

sch. school

schizo a schizophrenic person

sci. science; scientific

SCI *Science Citation Index*

SCIA Society for Computers in Anesthesia

SCID severe combined immunodeficiency; spacecraft identification

sci-fi science fiction

scil. *Latin* scilicet (surely, to wit)

SCL Sculptor (constellation)

SCLC small cell lung cancer; Southern Christian Leadership Conference

SCLK spacecraft clock

SCM single Christian male; supply chain management

ScM *Latin* Scientiae Magister (Master of Science)

SCO Scorpio

S.Con.Res. Senate Concurrent Resolution

SCORIF stimulated cycle oocyte retrieval in [office] fertilization

Scot. Scotch; Scotland; Scottish

SCP single-cell protein

SCPO senior chief petty officer

SCR Seychelles—rupee (currency); skin conductance response; standard class rate; stripchart recorder; sustainable cell rate

scr. scruple

SCRES [United States] Senate concurrent resolution

script. manuscript; prescription

Script. Scriptural; Scripture

SCS Soil Conservation Service

SCSI small computer system interface

SCSU South Carolina State University

SCT Scutum (Constellation); Society for Clinical Trials

S.Ct. *Supreme Court Reporter*

sctd scattered

SCTE serial clock transmit external; Society of Cable Television Engineers

SCU special care unit

scuba self-contained underwater breathing apparatus

sculp. sculptor; sculptress; sculpture

SCV Sons of Confederate Veterans

SCVIR Society of Cardiovascular and Interventional Radiology

SCVP Society for Cardiovascular Pathology

sd said; sewed; Sindhi

SD San Diego; San Diego Chargers; San Diego Giants; *Latin* Scientiæ Doctor (Doctor of Science); should (shortwave transmission); sight draft; software development; South Dakota; Southern District; special delivery; standard deviation; Swaziland (international vehicle ID)

sd. sound

Sd. sound

.sd Sudan

s.d. *Latin* sine die (without day, indefinitely)

S.D. South Dakota

SDA specific dynamic action

S.Dak. South Dakota

SDB Society for Developmental Biology

SDBE Small and Disadvantaged Business Enterprise

S/D B/L sight draft, bill of lading attached

SDBP Society for Developmental and Behavioral Pediatrics

SDD software design document; Sudan—dinar (currency)

SDEV standard deviation

SDF Louisville [KY] International Airport/Standiford Field

SDH subdural hematoma

SDI Strategic Defense Initiative

SDILINE Selective Dissemination of Information Online

SDK software development kit

SDLC synchronous data link control

SDMS Society of Diagnostic Medical Sonographers

S. Doc. Senate Document

SDP software development plan

SDPA Society of Dermatology Physician Assistants

SDQ Aeropuerto de las Americas (Santo Domingo, Dominican Republic)

SDR sensor data record; special drawing rights; system design review

SDRAM synchronous dynamic random access memory

SDS Students for a Democratic Society; Synchronous Data Set; System Design Specification

SDSL single-line digital subscriber line; Synchronous Data Set

SDSU San Diego State University

SDT small-diameter timber; system design team; systems development team

SDU service data unit

SDWA Safe Drinking Water Act

Se selenium

SE southeast; southeastern; split end; stock exchange; system engineer

.se Sweden

SEA Seattle Mariners; Seattle

Seahawks; Seattle-Tacoma International Airport; solar elevation angle

SEAHP Southeast Asian Health Project

SEAL sea, air, land [team]

SEAS Shipboard Environmental Data Acquisition System

SEATO Southeast Asia Treaty Organization

SEbE southeast by east

SEbS southeast by south

sec secant; second; secretary

SEC Securities and Exchange Commission; security deposit

sec. second; secretary; section; sector; *Latin* secundum (according to); security

sech hyperbolic secant

SECSG Southeastern Cancer Study Group

sect. section; sectional

secy. secretary

SED said (shortwave transmission)

SEDAC Socioeconomic Data and Applications Center

sed. sediment; sedimentation

SEER surveillance, epidemiology, and end results

SEG Society of Exploration Geophysicists

SEI systems engineering and integration

seismol seismology

SEIU Service Employees International Union

SEK Sweden—krona (currency)

SEL Kimpo Airport (Seoul, South Korea); Space Environment Laboratory

sel. select; selected; selectivity

SELA *Spanish* Sistema Económi-

co Latinoamericana (Latin American Economic System)

SEM scanning electron microscope

sem. seminary

Sem. Semitic

semi semifinal; semitrailer

SEMI subendocardial myocardial infarction

semilog semilogarithmic

semipro semiprofessional

SEMPA Society of Emergency Medicine Physician Assistants

sen. senate; senator; senior

SENFAS Support and Education Network for Fetal Alcohol Syndrome Parents and Caregivers

SEOS synchronous earth observatory satellite

SEP simplified employee pension

sep. separate; separation

Sep. September

sepd. separated

sepn. separation

SEPP Society for the Education of Physicians and Patients

Sept. September

SEPTA Southeastern Pennsylvania Transportation Authority

seq. sequel; *Latin* sequens (the following)

seqq. *Latin* sequentia (the following [things])

SER Serpens (constellation); somatosensory evoked response

ser. serial; series; sermon

Serb. Serbia; Serbian

SERC Smithsonian Environmental Research Center

SERE survival, evasion, resistance, escape

Serg. sergeant

Sergt. sergeant

SERHOLD Serials Holdings

SERLINE Serials Online

SERM selective estrogen receptor modulator

serv. service

servo servomechanism; servomotor

SES severely errored second; says (shortwave transmission); socioeconomic status

SESAP Surgical Education and Self-Assessment Program

SESPA Scientists and Engineers for Social and Political Action

sess. session

SET Secure Electronic Transaction

SETE smiling ear-to-ear

SETI Search for Extraterrestrial Intelligence

SETS Statistical Export and Tabulation System

SEU single event upset

SEX Sextans (constellation)

sf sforzando; square feet

SF sacrifice fly; San Francisco; San Francisco 49ers; San Francisco Giants; scarlet fever; science fiction; single female; sinking fund; special forces

SFF small form factor

SFX sound effects; special effects

SFAIAA so far as I am aware

SFC sergeant first class

SFDU standard formatted data unit

SFE supercritical fluid extraction

SFHA special flood hazard area

SFIP standard flood insurance policy

SFMR stepped frequency microwave radiometer

SFN Society for Neuroscience

SFO San Francisco International Airport; subfornical organ

SFRY Socialist Federal Republic of Yugoslavia

s.f.s. *Latin* sine fraude sua (without fraud on his or her part)

SFSR Soviet Federated Socialist Republic

SFT system fault tolerance

SFTAH Society for the Autistically Handicapped

sfz sforzando

sg specific gravity

Sg seaborgium; Song of Songs

SG senior grade; signaling gateway; solicitor general; Surgeon General

sg. singular

.sg Singapore

SGA small for gestational age

SGC soft gel cap

SGD Singapore—dollar

sgd. signed

SGE Sagitta (constellation)

SGF Springfield-Branson [MO] Regional Airport

SGI Silicon Graphics Inc.

SGIM Society of General Internal Medicine

SGL static groundwater level

SGLI Servicemen's Group Life Insurance

SGM sergeant major

SGML Standard Generalized Markup Language

SGN suprachiasmatic nuclei

SGNA Society of Gastroenterology Nurses and Associates

SGO Society of Gynecologic

Oncologists; Surgeon General's Office

SGOT serum glutamic-oxaloacetic transaminase

SGP Singapore (international vehicle ID); southern Great Plains

SGPT serum glutamic-pyruvic transaminase

SGR Sagittarius; Society of Gastrointestinal Radiologists

SGS Strategy Gaming Society

SGSS solar generator subsystem

SGT sergeat; Shattered Globe Theatre

Sgt. sergeant

Sgt.Maj. sergeant major

sh Serbo-Croatian

SH sacrifice hit; social history

sh. share; sheet

.sh Saint Helena

Shak. Shakespeare

Shakes. Shakespeare

SHAPE Supreme Headquarters Allied Powers, Europe

SHARP Skinheads Against Racial Prejudice

SHAZAM Solomon—wisdom of, Hercules—strength of, Atlas—stamina of, Zeus—power of, Achilles—great courage of, Mercury—speed of (from original Cap'n Marvel)

SHBG sex hormone-binding globulin

SHCA Society for Healthcare Consumer Advocacy

shd should

SHEA Society for Healthcare Epidemiology of America

Sheiiba Safety, Health, and Environment Intra Industry Benchmarking Association

Shet. Shetland

SHF single Hispanic female; superhigh frequency

SHH speech/hearing handicapped

SHHH Self Help for Hard of Hearing People

shipt. shipment

SHM single Hispanic male

SHMO social health maintenance organization

SHO Showtime

shoran short-range navigation

shp shaft horsepower

SHP Saint Helena—pound (currency)

shpt. shipment

SHR significant hydrologic resources

shr. share

SHRS School Health Resource Services

SHS Society for Human Sexuality

SHSRR Society for Health Services Research in Radiology

sht. sheet

shtg. shortage

SHTTP Secure HTTP

SHU Scoville Heat Unit

SHV Shreveport Regional Airport

Shy Shy-Drager syndrome

si Sinhalese

sI 6-mercaptopurine ribonucleoside

Si silicon; Wisdom of Jesus, the Son of Sirach

SI sacroiliac joint; secondary infertility; Smithsonian Institution; *French* Système International [d'Unités] (International System [of Units])

.si Slovenia

Sia sialic acids

SIADH syndrome of inappropriate secretion of antidiuretic hormone

sib. sibling

Sib. Siberia; Siberian

SIC standard industry classification

Sic. Sicilian; Sicily

SICP Society of Invasive Cardiovascular Professionals

SICU surgical intensive care unit

SID state inpatient database; sudden ionospheric disturbance

SIDS sudden infant death syndrome

SIECUS Sexuality Information and Education Council of the United States

SIF somatotropin release-inhibiting factor

SIG signal (shortwave transmission); signature (shortwave transmission); special interest group

sig. signal; signature

Sig. *Latin* signa (mark or label); signature; *Latin* signetur (let it be marked or labeled); signor; signore

sigill. *Latin* sigillum (seal)

SIH somatotropin release-inhibiting hormone

SIL sister-in-law; Summer Institute of Linguistics

SIM simulator; Society for the Internet in Medicine; solar irradiance monitor; subscriber identity module

SIMM single in-line memory modules

simp simpleton

SIMS stable isotope mass spectrometer

simsubs simultaneous submissions

SIMV spontaneous intermittent mandatory ventilation, synchronized intermittent mandatory ventilation

sin sine

SIN Changi International Airport (Singapore)

SINE sign, that is, operator's personal initials (shortwave transmission)

SINES short interspersed elements

sing. singular

sinh hyperbolic sine

SINK single income, no kids

SIOP Society for Industrial and Organizational Psychology

si op. sit *Latin* si opus sit (if needed)

SIP serial interface processor; session initiation protocol; single in-line package; system implementation plan

SIPC Securities Investors Protection Corporation

SIPP single in-line pin package

SIR shuttle imaging radar

Sir. Wisdom of Jesus, the Son of Sirach

siRNA small interfering RNA

SIS National Library of Medicine [Specialized Information Services]

SISO single input, single output

SIT Slovenia—tolar (currency)

sitcom situation comedy

SITD still in the dark

SITES Smithsonian Institution Traveling Exhibition Service

.sj Svalbard and Jan Mayen Islands

SJ Society of Jesus

SJC San Jose [CA] International Airport

SJD *Latin* Scientiae Juridicae Doctor (Doctor of Juridical Science)

SJF single Jewish female

SJM single Jewish male

S.J.Res. Senate Joint Resolution

SJT San Angelo [TX] Regional Airport/Mathis Field Airport

SJU Luis Muñoz Marin International Airport (San Juan, Puerto Rico)

sk Slovak

SK Saskatchewan; Slovakia (international vehicle ID)

sk. sack

.sk Slovakia

SKED schedule (shortwave transmission)

SKI spending the kids' inheritance

SKK Slovakia—koruna

Skr. Sanskrit

SKS seeks

Skt. Sanskrit

SKU stock keeping unit

sl Slovenian

SL salvage loss; sea level; sign language [interpretation]; source language; south latitude; SpaceLab; sublingual

sl. slightly; slow

.sl Sierra Leone

s.l. *Latin* sine loco (without place [of publication])

S.L. session laws

SLA second language acquisition; Symbionese Liberation Army

s.l.a.n. *Latin* sine loco, anno, vel nomine (without place, year, or name of publication)

slanguage slangy language

SLAPP Strategic Lawsuit Against Public Participation

SLAR sideways-looking airborne radar

Slav. Slavic; Slavonic

SLBM submarine-launched ballistic missile

SLC signaling link code; space launch complex

SLCM submarine-launched cruise missile

SLCS software life cycle support

sld. sailed; sealed; sold

SLE systemic lupus erythematosus

SLG slugging percentage (baseball)

slimnastics slimming gymnastics

SLIP Serial Line Internet Protocol

SLL Sierra Leone—leone

SLMA Student Loan Marketing Association

SLO Slovenia (international vehicle ID)

slo-mo slow motion

SLORC State Law and Order Restoration Council (of Myanmar)

SLP sea-level pressure

slpr sofa sleeper sofa

SLR sea-level rise; single-lens reflex camera; straight leg raising

SLS Saint Lawrence Seaway [Development Corporation]

SLSI super-large-scale integration

SLT single lung transplantation

SLV standard launch vehicle

SLW supercooled liquid water

sm Samoan

Sm samarium; Samuel

SM *Latin* Scientiae Magister (Master of Science); sensor module; sergeant major; service mark; single male; Soldier's Medal; stage manager; stationmaster; structural model

sm. small

.sm San Marino

S/M or **S-M** sadomasochism

SMA sergeant major of the army

sma. small

S-mail United States Postal Service mail (from "snail mail")

S.Maj. sergeant major

SMATV satellite master antenna television

SMB server message block

SMC small Magellanic cloud; system maintenance console; system manager console

sm. cap. small capital (letter)

SMC-GUI system manager's console graphical user interface

SMCL secondary maximum contaminant level

SMDM Society for Medical Decision Making

SMDS Switched Multimegabit Data Service

SME Suriname (international vehicle ID)

SMF Sacramento International Airport

SMG something (shortwave transmission)

SMI severely mentally impaired

SMIL Synchronized Media Integration Language

SMMR scanning multichannel microwave radiometer

SMN seaman

smog smoke and fog

SMP symmetric multiprocessing

SMR Society of Magnetic Resonance

SMS synchronous meteorological satellite

SMSA standard metropolitan statistical area

SMSgt senior master sergeant

SMT surface mount technology

SMTP Simple Mail Transfer Protocol

SMU Southern Methodist University

SMV slow-moving vehicle

sn Shona

Sn snow; tin

SN seaman; Senegal (international vehicle ID); serial number; soon (shortwave transmission); stock number; supernova

.sn Senegal

s.n. *Latin* sine nomine (without name)

S/N ratio signal-to-noise ratio

SNA John Wayne/Orange County Airport; systems network architecture

SNACC Society for NeuroAnesthesia and Critical Care

snafu situation normal all fouled up; situation normal all fucked up

SNC since (shortwave transmission)

SNCC Student Nonviolent Coordinating Committee

SNE subacute necrotizing encephalomyelopathy

SNF skilled nursing facility

SNG substitute natural gas; synthetic natural gas

SNL Sandia National Laboratory; *Saturday Night Live*

SNM Society of Nuclear Medicine

SNMP Simple Network Management Protocol; Small Network Management Packet

SNN Shannon [Ireland] Airport

SNOMED Systematized Nomenclature of Medicine

SNR signal-to-noise ratio; supernova remnant

SNRI serotonin and norepinephrine reuptake inhibitor

snRNA small nuclear RNA

SNS sympathetic nervous system

SNU solar neutrino units

so Somali

SO seller's option; significant other; Somalia (international vehicle ID); strikeout; symphony orchestra

so. south; southern

.so Somalia

s.o. strikeout

SOA S-band omni antenna; service-oriented architecture

SoAfr. South Africa, South African

SOAP Simple Object Access Protocol; Society for Obstetric Anesthesia and Perinatology; Spectrometric Oil Analysis Program

SOB Senate Office Building; shortness of breath; son of a bitch

SOBP Society of Biological Psychiatry

SOC synthetic organic chemical

soc. social; socialist; society; sociology; socket

Soc. Socialist; society

SOCAP Society of Consumer Affairs Professionals [in Business]

Sociol sociologist; sociology

SOD superoxide dismutase

So.Dak. South Dakota

SOF sound on film; Special Operations Forces

sofar sound fixing and ranging

S. of Sol. Song of Solomon

SOFT Society of Forensic Toxicologists

SOG Special Operations Group

SOH start of header

SoHo South of Houston [Street] (Manhattan neighborhood)

SOHO Solar and Heliospheric Observatory

SOI severity of illness; solar oscillations imager

SOL shit out of luck

sol. soluble; solution

Sol. Is. Solomon Islands

soln. solution

SOLP standards of laboratory practice

SOLRAD solar radiation

Som. Somalia; Somalian

sonar sound navigation and ranging

SONET synchronous optical network

SOP standard operating procedure

sop. soprano

soph. sophomore

SorG straight or gay

SORSI Sacro Occipital Research Society International

SOS a signal of distress in Morse code; chipped beef on toast (from "shit on a shingle"); same old shit; Somalia—shilling

s.o.s. *Latin* si opus sit (if needed)

SOT Society of Toxicology

sou. south; southern

SOV subject-object-verb

sov. sovereign

Sov. Soviet

SOW statement of work

SP same point; same principle; scalable processing; self-propelled; shore patrol; single pole; specialist; speech pathologist; speech pathology; standard playback; submarine patrol

sp. specials; species; specimen; spelling

Sp. Spain; Spanish

s.p. *Latin* sine prole (without issue—that is, childless)

S/P status post

SP1 stimulatory protein 1

SP4 specialist, fourth class

SPA Society for Physicians in Administration; Software Publishers Association; sperm penetration assay

spac spacious

SPAN Small Publishers of North America; standard portfolio analysis of margin

Span. Spanish

Spanglish Spanish and English mixture

SPAR *Latin* Semper Paratus (always ready—motto of the United States Coast Guard); a member of the women's reserve of the United States Coast Guard

SPARC scalar processor architecture

Sparteca South Pacific Regional Trade and Economic Cooperation Agreement

SPC South Pacific Commission; space; specific fuel consumption

SPCA Society for the Prevention of Cruelty to Animals; Spark Plug Collectors of America

SPCC Society for the Prevention of Cruelty to Children

SPD Standardized Position Description

spd. speed

SPDR's Standard and Poor's depositary receipts

SPDT single pole, double throw

SPE secondary particulate emission; Society for Pure English

SPEBSQSA Society for the Preservation and Encouragement of Barber Shop Quartet Singing in America

spec speculation; write specifications for

spec. special; specialist; specific; specifically; specification; speculation

spec grav specific gravity

spec house a house built on speculation that a buyer will be found

specif. specific; specifically

specs specifications; spectacles (eyeglasses)

SPECT single photon emission computed tomography

sped *Offensive* special education

SPF single professional female; sun protection factor

sp gr specific gravity

sph. spherical; spherical lens

SPHCOM Society for the Preservation of Historical Coin-Operated Machines

sp ht specific heat

SPI Capital Airport (Springfield, IL)

Spiders Standard and Poor's depositary receipts

SPIE Society of Photo-Optical Instrumentation Engineers

SPL sound pressure level; special (shortwave transmission); split phase level

SPLC Southern Poverty Law Center

spm suppression and mutation (of mutants that are unstable)

SPM single professional male; software programmers manual; suspended particulate matter

SPMC Society of Paper Money Collectors

SPN shared processing network; Society of Pediatric Nurses

SPNT Society for the Promotion of Nutritional Therapy

SPO status postoperative

spool simultaneous peripheral operation online

SPOT satellite positioning and tracking

SPP Sequenced Packet Protocol; Serial Port Profile; Society for Pediatric Pathology

spp. species

SPQR *Latin* Senatus Populusque Romanus (the Senate and the people of Rome)

SPR Society for Pediatric Radiology

spr. spring

sps symbols per second

SPS Sheppard AFB/Wichita Falls Municipal Airport; solar power satellite; standby power system

s.p.s. *Latin* sine prole superstite (without surviving issue— that is, no living children)

SPSS Statistical Package for the Social Sciences

SPST single pole, single throw

spt. seaport

SPU signal processing unit; Society for Pediatric Urology

SPVS Society of Practicing Veterinary Surgeons

SPX sequenced packet exchange

sq Albanian

SQ subcutaneous

sq. squadron; square

Sq. square

SQE signal quality error

sq. ft. square feet

sq km square kilometer

SQL structured query language

sq mi square mile

SQUID superconducting quantum interference device

sr Serbian; steradian

Sr showers; strontium

SR scanning radiometer; sedimentation rate; software review; solar radiation; special relativity; stimulus response; surgical removal

sr. senior

Sr. Senior; Señor; Sister

.sr Suriname

SrA senior airman

SRA scanning radar altimeter

Sra. Señora

SRAM static random access memory

SRB solid rocket booster

SRDC State Rural Development Councils

SRE Society for Radiological Engineering

SREH storm-relative environmental helicity

S. Rept. Senate Report

S. Res. Senate Resolution

SRF somatotropin-releasing factor

SRF-A slow-reacting factor of anaphylaxis

SRG Suriname—guilder

SRH somatotropin-releasing hormone

SRI sorry (shortwave transmission)

SRIF somatotropin release-inhibiting factor

SRM solid rocket motor

sRNA soluble ribonucleic acid

SRO self-regulatory organization; single room occupancy; standing room only

SROA Society for Radiation Oncology Administrators

SROM spontaneous rupture of membranes

SRP signal recognition particle; soluble reactive phosphate; soluble reactive phosphorus

SRQ Sarasota-Bradenton International Airport

SRS Scoliosis Research Society; Sleep Research Society; slow-reacting substance

SRS-A slow-reacting substance of anaphylaxis

SRT speech reception threshold

Srta. Señorita

ss sentence structure; single-stranded; Siswati; steady state

SS saints; saline solution; Saturday-Sunday; *German* Schutzstaffel (protection echelon—the elite quasimilitary unit of the Nazi party); shortstop; short stories; snow showers; social security; Song of Solomon; steamship; Sunday school; suspended solids

ss. *Latin* scilicet (that is to say, namely); sections; *Latin* semis (one half)

s/s same size

SSA Sinatra Society of America; Social Security Administration; sole source aquifer

SSAT Society for Surgery of the Alimentary Tract

SSB small smart bomb

SSBR Social Statistics Briefing Room

SSC stainless steel crown (dentistry)

SSCI *Social Science Citation Index*

SSCP Society for a Science of Clinical Psychology

SSD solid state detector; sudden sniffing death

SSDD single sided, double density

SSDI *Social Security Death Index*

SSE south-southeast

SSF Society for the Study of Fertility

SSG staff sergeant

SSgt staff sergeant

SSH Secure Shell

SSHRC Social Sciences and Humanities Research Council

SSI small-scale integration; Supplemental Security Income; Supplemental Security Income Program

SSIEM Society for the Study of Inborn Errors of Metabolism

SSIES special sensor for ions, electrons, and scintillations

SSL Secure Sockets Layer

SSME space shuttle main engine

SSM/I special sensor microwave/imager

SSM/T special sensor microwave/temperature

SSN Social Security number; Space Surveillance Network

SSNR Society for the Study of Neuronal Regulation

SSO Society of Surgical Oncology

SSP shameless self-promotion

ssp. subspecies

SSPA solid-state power amplifier

SSPE subacute sclerosing panencephalitis

SSPM software standards and procedures manual

SSR solid state recorder; Soviet Socialist Republic

SSRC Social Science Research Council

SSRI selective serotonin reuptake inhibitor

SSRT single stage rocket technology

SSS Selective Service System; sick sinus syndrome

SST sea surface temperature; spectroscopic survey telescope; supersonic transport

SSTA sea surface temperature anomaly

SSTT small satellite thermal technologies

SSU stratospheric sounding unit

SSW south-southwest

SSWAHC Society for Social Work Administrators in Health Care

st Sesotho

ST speech therapy; standard time; stratosphere-troposphere

st. stanza; state; statute; stet; stitch; stone; strophe

St. saint; state; strait; street

.st Sao Tome and Principe

s.t. short ton

STA scheduled time of arrival; Society for Technology in Anesthesia

sta. station; stationary

stalkerazzi stalking paparazzi

staph staphylococcus

START strategic arms reduction talks

stat from *Latin* statim (immediately); statistics

STAT stratospheric tracers of atmospheric transport

stat. statistic; statistics; statuary; statute

Stat. *United States Statutes at Large*

stats statistics

STB *Latin* Sacrae Theologiae Baccalaureus (Bachelor of Sacred Theology); *Latin* Scientiae Theologicae Baccalaureus (Bachelor of Theology); set-top box; Surface Transportation Board

stbd. starboard

STC satellite test center; short-term concentration

STCC Shirley Temple Collectors Club

STD *Latin* Sacrae Theologiae Doctor (Doctor of Sacred Theology); São Tome and Principe—dobra (currency); scheduled time of departure; sexually transmitted disease

std. standard

STE septic tank effluent; suite

Ste *French* sainte (female saint)

STEL short-term exposure limit

sten. stenographer; stenography

steno stenographer; stenography

stenog. stenographer; stenography

STEP Space Test Experiment Platform

ster. sterling

stereo stereophonic

St. Ex. Stock Exchange

STFM Society of Teachers of Family Medicine

stg. sterling

st'g strong

stge. storage

STH somatotropic hormone

stip. stipend; stipulation

stk. stock

STL Lambert-St. Louis International Airport; *Latin* Sacrae Theologiae Licentiatus (Licentiate of Sacred Theology); Saint Louis Cardinals; Saint Louis Rams

St.L. St. Louis

STM *Latin* Sacrae Theologiae Magister (Master of Sacred Theology); short-term memory

STN station (shortwave transmission)

STOL short takeoff and landing

stoolie stool pigeon

STOP Safe Tables Our Priority

stor. storage

storg. storage

STOVL short takeoff and vertical landing

StP St. Paul [Minnesota]

STP Scientifically Treated Petroleum; sewage treatment plant; shielded twisted pair [of wires for electrical transmission]; standard temperature and pressure

str straight; strength

STR Stuttgart-Echterdingen Airport; synchronous transmitter receiver

str. steamer; strait; string; stringed; strings; strong; strophe

Str. strait

str8 straight

Strad Stradivarius violin

strep streptococcus

stry story

STS serologic test for syphilis; shuttle transport system; Society of Thoracic Surgeons; space transportation system; star tracker sensor

ST-SAS septic tank soil absorption system

STSG split-thickness skin graft

STSs sequence-tagged sites

STT small tactical terminal

STTR Small Business Technology Transfer Program

stu studio
STU scan timing unit; standard time unit
stud. student; studio
STV subscription television
STX start of text
su Sundanese
Su Sunday
SU sulfonylurea
SUA serum uric acid
sub submarine; substitute
sub. subaltern; suburb; suburban
SUBCOM subcommutator
subd. subdivision
subdeb subdebutante
subdiv. subdivision
subj. subject; subjective; subjunctive
subjunct. subjunctive
subord. subordinate
sub-q subcutaneous
subs. subscription
subsec. subsection
subsp. subspecies
subst. substantival; substantive; substitute
substand. substandard
SUD Sudan (international vehicle ID)
Sud. Sudan
suf. suffix
suff. suffix
Suff. Suffragan
SUI stress urinary incontinence
SUM software users manual
SUMER solar ultraviolet measurements of emitted radiation
Sun. Sunday
SUNA Society of Urologic Nurses and Associates
SUNY State University of New York

SUP Society for Ultrastructural Pathology
sup. superior; superlative; supine; supplement; supplementary; supply; *Latin* supra (above)
Sup.Ct. superior court; Supreme Court
super superintendent; supernumerary
super. superior
superl. superlative
supp. supplement; supplementary
suppl. supplement; supplementary
supr. supreme
Supt. superintendent
supvr. supervisor
SUR Society of Uroradiology
sur. surface; surplus
Sur. Suriname; Surinamese
SURFRAD surface radiation
surg. surgeon; surgery; surgical
Surg. Gen. Surgeon General
surr. surrender
surv. survey; surveying; surveyor
sus. per coll. *Latin* suspendatur per collum (let him or her be hanged by the neck)
Suss. Sussex
SUV sport utility vehicle
sux. suction
SUZI subzonal insertion
sv sailing vessel; Swedish
Sv sievert
SV saves (baseball); simian virus; sludge volume
.sv El Salvador
s.v. *Latin* sub verbo (under the word); *Latin* sub voce (under the word)

SV40 simian vacuolating virus 40

SVC El Salvador—colon (currency); superior vena cava

svc. service

svce service

SVD spontaneous vaginal delivery

SVGA super video graphics array

svgs. savings

SVI sludge volume index

SVL several (shortwave transmission)

SVM service module

SVMB Society of Vascular Medicine and Biology

SVN Society for Vascular Nursing

SVO Sheremetyevo Airport (Moscow, Russia); subject-verb-object

SVT supraventricular tachycardia

sw short wave; Swahili

SW software; southwest; southwestern

sw. switch

Sw. Sweden; Swedish

S/W software

SWAK sealed with a kiss

SWAP severe weather avoidance procedures

SWAT special weapons and tactics; special weapons attack team

Swaz. Swaziland

SWB short wheelbase

swbd. switchboard

SWbS southwest by south

SWbW southwest by west

SWC Space Warfare Center

SWCD [United States Department of Agriculture] Soil and Water Conservation District

SWCS Soil and Water Conservation Society

SWDA Solid Waste Disposal Act

SWE snow water equivalent

Swed. Sweden; Swedish

sweetie sweetheart

SWF shortwave fading; single White female

SWG standard wire gauge

SWIM solar wind interplanetary measurements

Switz. Switzerland

SWM single White male

SWON Social Work Oncology Network

S-word shit

SWP Socialist Workers Party; Swiss water process

SWS Sturge Weber Syndrome

SWZ Swaziland

sx symptoms

SXI solar x-ray imager

SY Seychelles (international vehicle ID)

.sy Syria

SYD Kingsford Smith International Airport (Sydney, Australia)

syl. syllable

syll. syllable

sym. symbol; symmetrical; symphony

syn. synonym; synonymous; synonymy

sync synchronized; synchronization

synch synchronized; synchronization

synd. syndicate

synon. synonymous

synth. synthesizer; synthetic

synthespian synthetic thespian (computer-generated virtual actor)

SYP Syria—pound (currency)

syph syphilis

syr *Latin* syrupus (syrup)

SYR Syracuse [NY] Hancock International Airport; Syria (international vehicle ID)

Syr. Syria; Syrian

sys. system

sysadmin system administrator

sysop system operator

syst. system

sz size

Sz seizures

.sz Swaziland

SZA Solar Zenith Angle

SZL Swaziland—lilangeni (currency)

T

t tense (grammar); [long] ton; top quark

T AT&T Corporation (stock symbol); temperature; tenor; tesla; Thailand (international vehicle ID); thunderstorms; Thursday; thymine; time reversal; [United States] Treasury; tritium; true; T-shirt; Tuesday

t. tare; teaspoon; teaspoonful; *Latin* tempore (in the time of); time; ton; transitive; troy

T. tablespoon; tablespoonful; township

ta Tamil

Ta tantalum

TA teaching assistant; teaching associate

TAANOS The American Academy of Neurological

and Orthopedic Surgeons

tab tablet

TAB timing and acquisition bit

tab. table

TAC Tactical Air Command; total allowable catch

TACAN tactical air navigation

tach tachometer

tach. tachycardia

TACOM [United States Army] Tank-Automotive Command

TACT total audit concept technique

TAF tumor angiogenic factor

TAG Thalassemia Action Group; The Adjutant General

Tag. Tagalog

TAH total abdominal hysterectomy

TAlk total alkalinity

tan tangent

TAN teeny area network

Tan. Tanzania

T & A time and attendance; tits and ass; tonsillectomy and adenoidectomy; tonsils and adenoids

T & E test and evaluation; travel and entertainment

T & G tongue and groove

T & M time and materials

T & T tympanotomy and tube [placement]

tangelo tangerine pomelo cross

tanh hyperbolic tangent

TANJ there ain't no justice

TANSTAAFL There ain't no such thing as a free lunch!

TAP take a picture; Technical Assistance Program; Trans-Alaskan Pipeline

TAPI telephony applications programming interface

TARDEC Tank-Automotive Research, Development and Engineering Center

TARDIS time and relative dimension in space

tarfu things are really fouled up; things are really fucked up

tarp tarpaulin

TAS telephone answering system; time addressable storage; true airspeed

Tas. Tasmania; Tasmanian

TASC The American Surrogacy Center

taser teleactive shock electronic repulsion

TAT tetanus antitoxin; Thematic Apperception Test; Transatlantic Telephone; true air temperature; turnaround time

TATCA terminal air traffic control automation

TATP triacetone triperoxide

TATRC Telemedicine and Advanced Technology Research Center

TAU Taurus

TAV transatmospheric vehicle

taxi taxicab

taxon. taxonomy

tb tablespoon; tablespoonful

Tb terbium; Tobit

TB tailback; Tampa Bay Buccaneers; Tampa Bay Devil Rays; terabyte; total bases; trial balance; tuberculosis

t.b. tubercle bacillus

TBA to be advised; to be announced; to be answered

TBB Triboro Bridge

TBC thermal barrier coating; to be confirmed; to be continued

TBCF The Breast Cancer Fund

TBD to be defined; to be delivered; to be designed; to be determined; to be developed; to be documented

TBG thyroxine-binding globulin

TBH to be honest

TBHQ tertiary butylhydroquinone

TBI total body irradiation; traumatic brain injury

T-bill United States Treasury bill

TBINET The Brain Injury Information Network

TBIRD Traumatic Brain Injury Resource Directory

tbl. table

TBM tactical ballistic missile

tBoc tert-butyloxycarbonyl

T-bond United States Treasury bond

TBP thyroxine-binding protein

TBPA thyroxine-binding prealbumin

TBR to be read; to be resolved

TBS talk between ships; to be supplied; Turner Broadcasting System

tbs. tablespoon; tablespoonful

tbsp. tablespoon; tablespoonful

TBSV tomato bushy stunt virus

TBV total blood volume

TBW total body water

TByte terabyte

tc tetracycline

Tc technetium

TC teachers college; telecommand; terra-cotta; terminal control; till countermanded; total carbon; toxic concentration

tc. tierce
.tc Turks and Caicos Islands
T.C. [United States] Tax Court
TCB taking care of business; the trouble came back
TCCA Tin Container Collectors Association
TCDD tetrachlor dibenzo dioxin
TCE thermal control electronics; trichloroethylene
T cell thymus-derived cell
TCG time compensation gain
TCH Chad (international vehicle ID)
TCI Tele-Communications Inc.
TCID tissue culture infectious dose
TCL tool command language
TCM traditional Chinese medicine; Turner Classic Movies
TCP Transmission Control Protocol; trichloropropane
TCP/IP Transmission Control Protocol/Internet Protocol
TCS thermal control system
TCXO temperature controlled crystal oscillator
Td tetanus and diphtheria
TD tank destroyer; technical director; touchdown; toxic dose; Treasury Department
.td Chad
TDA tax-deferred annuity; telecommunications and data acquisition; Trade and Development Agency
TDD telecommunications device for the deaf
TDEM time-domain electromagnetics
TDF testis-determining factor
TDI tabbed document interface
TDM time-division multiplexing

TDMA time division multiple access
TDMS Toxicology Data Management System
TDN total digestible nutrients
TDP ribothymidine 5c-diphosphate
TDR temperature data record; test discrepancy report; time domain reflectometry; *Toxicology Desk Reference*
TDS total dissolved solids
TDWR Terminal Doppler Weather Radar
TDY temporary duty
te Telugu
TE tight end
T.E. textile engineer; textile engineering
TEA torque equilibrium attitude
TEAL The Electronic Anesthesiology Library
TeBG testosterone-estradiol-binding globulin
tec detective
tec. technical; technician
tech technical person
tech. technical; technician
Tech. technology
techies technologically oriented people
technol. technology
TED Thomas Edmund Dewey; total energy detector; trawl efficiency device; turtle excluder device
TEDD total end-diastolic diameter
Te Deum *Latin* Te Deum laudamus (You, God, we praise)
tee T-shirt
TEE transesophageal echocardiography

TEFL teaching English as a foreign language
Teflon polytetrafluoroethylene
TEFRA Tax Equity and Fiscal Responsibility Act
TEG tetraethylene glycol
TEHIP Toxicology and Environmental Health Information Program
TEI Text Encoding Initiative
TEL Telescopium (constellation)
tel. telegram; telegraph; telephone
telco telephone company
telecom telecommunications
teleg. telegram; telegraph; telegraphic; telegraphy
telegr. telegraphy
teleph. telephony
TeleSCAN Telematics Services in Cancer
TELEX teletypewriter exchange
TEM transmission electron microscope; triethylenemelamine
temp temperature; temporary [employee]
TEMP test and evaluation master plan
temp. temperance; temperature; template; temporal; temporary; *Latin* tempore (in the time of)
TEN Tennessee Titans; toxic epidermal necrolysis
ten. tenor; tenuto
Tenn. Tennessee
tennies tennis shoes
TENS transcutaneous electrical nerve stimulation
TEO technology executive officer
TEPA triethylene phosphoramide

TEPC tissue equivalent proportional counter
TEPP tetraethylpyrophosphate
Ter. terrace; territory
TERA Toxicology Excellence for Risk Assessment
T/E ratio testosterone/epitestosterone ratio
TERIS Teratogen Information System
term. terminal; termination
Terr. terrace; territory
terry terry cloth
TESA testicular sperm aspiration
TESD total end-systolic diameter
TESL teaching English as a second language
TESOL Teachers of English to Speakers of Other Languages
TEST Telemedicine and Education Support Team
test. testator; testatrix; testimony
Test. Testament
TET tubal embryo transfer
Teut. Teuton; Teutonic
TeV tera-electron volts
TEX Texas Rangers
Tex. Texas
Tex-Mex Texas-Mexican
TF Territorial Force; true/false
.tf French Southern Territories
TFA Thyroid Foundation of America
TFCS Treasury Financial Communication System
TFG transfer frame generator
TFM traffic flow management
tfr. transfer
TFT temporary full time; thin

film transfer; thin film transistor

TFTP Trivial File Transfer Protocol

tg Tajik

TG Togo (international vehicle ID); transformational grammar; transgender

.tg Togo

t.g. type genus

TGC time-varied gain control; time-gain compensation

TGE transmissible gastroenteritis of swine

TGF transforming growth factor

TGFα transforming growth factor α

TGFβ transforming growth factor β

TGH telegraph (shortwave transmission)

TGIF thank God it's Friday

TGO total gross output

TGR together (shortwave transmission)

T group training group

TGS timeline generation system

tgt. target

TGV *French* Train à Grande Vitesse (high-speed French train)

th Thai

Th Thessalonians; thorium; Thursday

TH townhouse

.th Thailand

THAAD Theater High Altitude Area Defense [missile system]

Thai. Thailand

ThB *Latin* Theologiae Baccalaureus (Bachelor of Theology)

THB Thailand—baht (currency)

THC tetrahydrocannabinol;

thermohaline circulation

ThD *Latin* Theologiae Doctor (Doctor of Theology)

theat. theater; theatrical

theatr. theatrical

theol. theologian; theological; theology

therap. therapeutic; therapeutics

therm. thermometer

Thes. Thessalonians

Thess. Thessalonians

THF tetrahydrofolate

THIC The Heart Institute for Children

THIR temperature humidity infrared radiometer

ThM *Latin* Theologiae Magister (Master of Theology)

THMs trihalomethanes

tho though

ThOD theoretical oxygen demand

thoro thorough

Thos. Thomas

thou thousand

thp thrust horsepower

THR total hip replacement

3-D three dimensional

three R's reading, writing, and arithmetic

thrombo thrombophlebitis; thrombosis

thru through

Thu. Thursday

Thur. Thursday

Thurs. Thursday

Thy thymine

THz terahertz

ti Tigrinya

Ti titanium; Titus

TI time (shortwave transmission)

TIA thanks in advance; transient ischemic attack

TIAA Teachers Insurance and Annuity Association

Tib. Tibetan

TIC tongue in cheek; total inorganic carbon

t.i.d. *Latin* ter in die (three times a day)

TIE Telemedicine Information Exchange; Treatment Improvement Exchange

TIF tax increment financing

TIFF tagged image file format

TIGER Topologically Integrated Geographic Encoding and Referencing

TIGRIS Topologically Integrated Geographic Resource Information System

TIGTA Treasury Inspector General for Tax Administration

TILS tumor-infiltrating lymphocytes

TIM technical interchange meeting

Tim. Timothy

TIMS theoretical indicative margin system; Tuberculosis Information Management System

TIN taxpayer identification number; total inorganic nitrogen

TINA Truth in Negotiations Act

tinc. tincture

tinct. tincture

TINWIS that is not what I said

TIP technology investment plan; total inorganic phosphate

Tip. Tipperary

TIPPSA Technical Industrial Pharmacists and Pharmaceutical Scientists Association

TIROS Television and Infrared Operational Satellite; Television Infrared Observation Satellite

TISE take it somewhere else

tit. title

Tit. Titus

TITh 3,5,3c-triiodothyronine

tix tickets

TJ Tajikistan (international vehicle ID); triceps jerk (reflex)

.tj Tajikistan

TJR total joint replacement

TJS Tajikistan—somoni (currency)

tk Turkmen

Tk toolkit

TK take (shortwave transmission)

tk. truck

.tk Tokelau

TKE turbulent kinetic energy

TKO technical knockout; to keep [vein] open

TKR total knee replacement

tkt. ticket

tl Tagalog

Tl thallium

TL target language (that is, language being learned); total loss; tubal ligation

TLA three-letter acronym

TLB *The Living Bible*

TLC tender loving care; The Learning Channel; total lung capacity

TLD top-level domain

TLE temporal lobe epilepsy; thin-layer electrophoresis

TLH Tallahassee Regional Airport

TLM telemetry

TLO total loss only

tlr. tailor

TLT Trademark Law Treaty

TLV Ben Gurion Airport (Tel Aviv-Yafo, Israel); threshold limit value

Tm thulium; Timothy

TM telemetry; them (shortwave transmission); trademark; transcendental meditation; true mean; Turkmenistan (international vehicle ID); tympanic membrane

.tm Turkmenistan

T.M. *Tax Magazine*

TMA Toy Manufacturers of America

T-man [United States] Treasury man

TMC The Movie Channel

TMD temporomandibular joint dysfunction

TMET treadmill exercise test

TMI Three Mile Island; too much information; trainable mentally impaired; tympanic membrane intact

TMJ temporomandibular joint

TMM Turkmenistan—manat (currency)

TMO telegraph money order

TMOD Treatment and Management of Ocular Disease

TMOT trust me on this

TMP ribothymidylic acid; trimethoprim

T.M.R. *Trademark Reports*

TMV tobacco mosaic virus

TMW tomorrow (shortwave transmission)

tn Setswana

TN Tennessee; Tunisia (international vehicle ID)

tn. ton; town; train

.tn Tunisia

TNC The Nature Conservancy

TND Tunisia—dinar (currency)

TNF tumor necrosis factor

tng. training

TNK think (shortwave transmission)

TNM tumor-node-metastasis; tumor-node-metastases

TNN The Nashville Network

T-note United States Treasury note

Tnpk. turnpike

TNR *The New Republic*

TNS Transcultural Nursing Society

TNT trinitrotoluene; Turner Network Television

TNTC too numerous to count

TNX thanks

to Tonga

TO table of organization; telegraph office; tubo-ovarian; turn over

.to Tonga

t.o. turn over

Tob. Tobit

TOC table of contents; total organic carbon

Toch. Tocharian

TOCP triorthocresyl phosphate

TOD time of day; top of descent

TOEFL A trademark for a test of English as a foreign language

TOF top of file

tol. tolerance

TOL Toledo Express Airport

TOMS total ozone mapping spectrophotometer

TON threshold odor number

TONE Trial of Nonpharmacologic Interventions in the Elderly

tonn. tonnage

TOP temporarily out of print; Tonga—pa'anga (currency)

topo. topographic; topographical

topog. topography

TOPS Take Off Pounds Sensibly; transparent operating system

TOR Toronto Blue Jays

TORI totally obvious rapid information

TOS terms of service

TOT time of travel; time over target

tot. total

TOXLINE Toxicology [Information] Online

TOXLIT Toxicology Literature

TOXNET Toxicology [Data] Network

TP title pending; triple play

Tp. township

.tp East Timor

t.p. title page; toilet paper

tPA tissue plasminogen activator

TPA Tampa International Airport; third party administrator; tissue plasminogen activator; total plate appearances

TPB trade paperback

TPE Chiang Kai-Shek Airport (Taipei, Taiwan)

Tpk. turnpike

Tpke. turnpike

TPL total path length

TPN triphosphopyridine nucleotide; total parenteral nutrition

TPNH triphosphopyridine nucleotide, reduced form

TPN+ triphosphopyridine nucleotide, oxidized form

TPP thiamin pyrophosphate

TPR temperature, pulse, and respiration

TPS thermal protection system

tps. townships; troops

TPTB the powers that be

TPTH triphenyltinhydroxide

TQI total quality improvement

TQM total quality management

TPR total player rating

TPY tons per year

tr Turkish

TR Theodore Roosevelt; tons registered (of a ship); transmit-receive; Turkey (international vehicle ID)

tr. tape recorder; transitive; translated; translation; translator; transpose; transposition; treasurer; trust; trustee; turnover rate

.tr Turkey

T/R transmit/receive

TRA Triangulum Australe (constellation)

trach. tracheal; tracheotomy

TRACON terminal radar approach control

trag. tragedy; tragic

trans. transaction; transitive; translated; translation; translator; translator; transportation; transpose; transposition; transverse

transf. transfer; transferred

transl. translated; translation

transp. transportation

TRASOP Tax Reduction Act Stock Ownership Plan

trav. traveler; travels

TRC Transportation Research Center

TRDMC tears running down my cheeks

T.R.E. *Latin* Tempore Regis Edwardi (in the time of King Edward)

treas. treasurer; treasury

TRF thyrotropin-releasing factor

TRH thyroid-releasing hormone; thyrotropin-releasing hormone

TRI Toxic Release Inventory; Triangulum (constellation); Tri-Cities [TN] Regional Airport

trib. tributary

Tribeca Triangle below Canal [Street] (Manhattan neighborhood)

trig trigonometry

trigon. trigonometric; trigonometry

trike tricycle

TRIO Transplant Recipients International Organization

tripl. triplicate

TRIPP Teaching Resource for Instructors in Prehospital Pediatrics

Tris tris[hydroxymethyl]aminomethane; tris[hydroxymethyl]methylamine

trit. triturate

TRK tracking

TRL Turkey—lira (currency)

TRLR trailer

tRNA transfer RNA

TRO temporary restraining order

troch trochiscus

trop. tropic; tropical

trou trousers

trp. troop

TRPSA transponder assembly

TRR test readiness review

TRT testosterone replacement therapy; thoracic radiotherapy

TRU through (shortwave transmission)

trvl travel

Try tryptophan

ts Tsonga

TS tensile strength; this (shortwave transmission); total solids; transsexual

ts. typescript

t.s. tough shit

TSA Technical Support Alliance; Tourette Syndrome Association

TSC Transportation Systems Center

TSCA Toxic Substances Control Act

TSCATS Toxic Substances Control Act Test Submissions [Database]

TSE Test of Spoken English; Thomas Stearns Eliot

TSgt technical sergeant

TSH thyroid-stimulating hormone

TSH-RF thyroid-stimulating hormone-releasing factor

TSI timber stand improvement; Transportation Safety Institute

TSP trisodium phosphate

tsp. teaspoon; teaspoonful

TSPI time-space-position-information

TSR terminate and stay resident

TSS total suspended solids; toxic shock syndrome; twin-screw steamer

tss. typescripts

T'storm thunderstorm

T-strm thunderstorm

tt Tatar

Tt Titus

TT telegraphic transfer; teletypewriter; that (shortwave transmission); thrombin time; time-tagged; transit time; Trinidad & Tobago (international vehicle ID); trust territory

.tt Trinidad and Tobago

TTAD Telemedicine Technology Area Directorate

TTB [Alcohol and Tobacco] Tax and Trade Bureau; time-tagged buffer

TTBOMK to the best of my knowledge

TTC The Triplet Connection

TTD Trinidad and Tobago—dollar

TTFN ta ta for now

TTH Tuesday/Thursday

TTHMs total trihalomethanes

TTL transistor-transistor logic

TTO transtracheal oxygen

T Town Tulsa

TTP ribothymidine 5c-triphosphate

TTP-HUS thrombotic thrombocytopenic purpura and hemolytic uremic syndrome

TTT that the (shortwave transmission)

TTU Tennessee Technological University

TTX tetrodotoxin

TTY teletypewriter

TTYL talk to you later

TTYS talk to you soon

Tu Tuesday

TU thank you (shortwave transmission); trade union; transmission unit; transport unit

TUC Trades Union Congress; Tucana (constellation)

'tude attitude

Tue. Tuesday

Tues. Tuesday

TUFT transuterine fallopian transfer

TUL Tulsa International Airport

Tun. Tunisia; Tunisian; Tunisian

turbo turbocharger

Turk. Turkey; Turkish; Turkmenistan

TURP transurethral resection of prostate

turps turpentine

TUS Tucson International Airport

TUU transureteroureterostomy

tux tuxedo

TV television; transvestite

.tv Tuvalu

T/V thermal/vacuum

TV-14 strong caution for children under 14 (television rating)

TV-14-D strong caution for children under 14, possible intensely suggestive dialogue (television rating)

TV-14-L strong caution for children under 14, possible strong coarse language (television rating)

TV-14-S strong caution for children under 14, possible intense sexual situations (television rating)

TV-14-V strong caution for children under 14, possible intense violence (television rating)

TVA Tennessee Valley Authority

TVC Cherry Capital Airport (Traverse City, MI)

TVD Tuvalu—dollar

TVG time-varied gain

TV-G for general audience (television rating)

TVH transvaginal hysterectomy

TVI television interference (shortwave transmission)

TV-MA mature audience only (television rating)

TV-MA-L mature audience only, possible crude indecent language (television rating)

TV-MA-S mature audience only, possible explicit sexual activity (television rating)

TV-MA-V mature audience only, possible graphic violence (television rating)

TVP textured vegetable protein

TV-PG parental guidance suggested (television rating)

TV-PG-D parental guidance suggested, possible suggestive dialogue (television rating)

TV-PG-L parental guidance suggested, possible infrequent coarse language (television rating)

TV-PG-S parental guidance suggested, possible sexual situations (television rating)

TV-PG-V parental guidance suggested, possible moderate violence (television rating)

TVS tornado vortex signature

TV-Y for all children (television rating)

TV-Y7 for children age 7 and older (television rating)

TV-Y7-FV for children age 7 and older, possible intense fantasy violence (television rating)

tw Twi

TW tomorrow (shortwave transmission)

.tw Taiwan

T/W thrust to weight ratio

TWA Trans World Airlines

twack twelve pack

TWD Taiwan—dollar

TWI two-way interface

twnhs townhouse

twofer two for [one]

TWoP Television Without Pity

Twp. township

TWTA traveling-wave tube amplifier

TWX teletypewriter exchange

Tx transmit; treatment

TX Texas; transmit

TXR transmitter

TXT text (shortwave transmission)

ty Tahitian; thank you

TY they (shortwave transmission)

tymp. tympanotomy

typ. typographer; typography

typo typographical [error]

typo. typographer; typography

TYS McGhee Tyson Airport (Knoxville, TN)

TYVM thank you very much

.tz Tanzania

TZA Tanzania

TZB Tappan Zee Bridge

TZS Tanzania—shilling

U

u up quark

U internal energy; unit; units; uracil; uranium; you

u. unit; units; upper

U. uncle; University; unsatisfactory

UA Ukraine (international vehicle ID); United Artists; unnum-

bered acknowledgement; uri-
nalysis

.ua Ukraine

UAC user agent client

UAE United Arab Emirates;
United Arab Emirates (international vehicle ID); unrecover-
able application error

UAH Ukraine—hryvnia (currency)

UAPD Union of American
Physicians and Dentists

UAR United Arab Republic

UARS upper atmosphere research satellite

UAS unavailable seconds; user
agent service

UART universal asynchronous
receiver transmitter

uauth user authentication

UAV unmanned aerial vehicle;
unmanned aerospace vehicle

UAW United Automobile Workers

UB uniform billing; upper
bench

UB2 you be too

UBE unsolicited bulk email

UBI United Bar Code Industries

UBIC unrelated business income

uc uppercase (letter)

UC ulcerative colitis; University
of California; University of
Chicago; University of Cincinnati; user community; uterine
contraction

U.C. Upper Canada

UCA University of Central
Arkansas

UCAID University Corporation
for Advanced Internet Development

UCB University of California,
Berkeley; Upright Citizens
Brigade

UCC Uniform Commercial Code

UCCC Uniform Consumer Credit Code

UCCJA Uniform Child Custody
Jurisdiction Act

UCE unsolicited commercial e-
mail

UCF University of Central Florida

UCHI usual childhood illnesses

UCI University of California,
Irvine

UCL University College London; Upper Control Limit

UCLA University of California,
Los Angeles

UCM unresolved complex mixture

UCMJ Uniform Code of Military Justice

UCO University of Central
Oklahoma

UConn University of Connecticut

UCP *Uniform Customs and Practice [for Commercial Documentary Credits]*; User Control
Point

UCPA United Cerebral Palsy Association

UCR Uniform Crime Reports
(compiled by the Federal Bureau of Investigation); University of California, Riverside;
usual, customary, and reasonable

UCS universal character set

UCSB University of California,
Santa Barbara

UCSC University of California,
Santa Cruz

UCSD University of California, San Diego

UCSF University of California, San Francisco

UCT Universal Coordinated Time

UD University of Delaware

UDAG Urban Development Action Grant

UDC universal decimal system

UDEAC *French* Union Douanière des États de l'Afrique Centrale (Central African Customs and Economic Union)

UDITPA The Uniform Division of Income for Tax Purposes Act

UDP uridine 5c-diphosphate; User Datagram Protocol

UDPG uridine diphosphoglucose

UDPGal uridine diphosphogalactose

UDPGlc uridine diphosphoglucose

UE upper extremities

UEF user ephemeris file

UEL upper explosive limit

UFA unesterified free fatty acid

UFC Ultimate Fighting Championship

UFCA Uniform Fraudulent Conveyance Act

UFL upper flammability limit

UFO unidentified flying object

UFTA Uniform Fraudulent Transfer Act

ug Uighur

.ug Uganda

UGA University of Georgia

UGI upper gastrointestinal

UGT urgent

UGX Uganda—shilling

UH University of Hawaii

UHF ultrahigh frequency

UHMS Undersea and Hyperbaric Medical Society

UHR ultra high resolution

UI unemployment insurance; unnumbered information; user interface

UIC underground injection control; University of Illinois at Chicago

UICC International Union Against Cancer

UID user identifier

UIP usual interstitial pneumonia [of Liebow]

UIS Unemployment Insurance Service

UIUC University of Illinois at Urbana-Champaign

uk Ukrainian

UK United Kingdom

uke ukulele

UL unimproved land; urban legend

U.L. Underwriters Laboratories Inc.

U/L uplink

ULA uniform laws or acts

U.L.A. *Uniform Laws Annotated*

ULEV ultralow-emissions vehicle

ULF ultralow frequency

ULP unfair labor practice

ULSI ultra-large-scale integration

ult. ultimate; ultimately; *Latin* ultimo (last month)

ultim. ultimately

.um United States Minor Outlying Islands

UM University of Michigan

UMA upper memory area; Ursa Major

UMass University of Massachusetts

UMB upper memory block

umb. umbilical

UMCC University of Maryland Cancer Center

UMGA Unified Medical Group Association

UMI Ursa Minor

UMKC University of Missouri-Kansas City

UMLS Unified Medical Language System

ump umpire

UMQC unique physician identification number

UMSL University of Missouri-Saint Louis

UMSLG University Medical School Librarians Group

UMTRCA Uranium Mill Tailings Radiation Control Act

UMTS Universal Mobile Telecommunications System; Universal Mobile Telephone Service

UMW United Mine Workers

UMWA United Mine Workers of America

un unit

UN United Nations; until (shortwave transmission)

UNA United Nations Association

UNAIDS [Joint] United Nations Program on HIV/AIDS

UNAMIR United Nations Assistance Mission for Rwanda

unan. unanimous

UNARIUS [Academy of Science] Universal Articulate Interdimensional Understanding of Science

UNAVEM III United Nations Angola Verification Mission III

unb. or **unbd.** unbound

unc. uncirculated

UNCF United Negro College Fund (now called The College FUND/UNCF)

UNCRO United Nations Confidence Restoration Operation in Croatia

UNCTAD United Nations Conference on Trade and Development

UND University of North Dakota

UNDCP United Nations International Drug Control Program

UNDOF United Nations Disengagement Observer Force

UNDP United Nations Development Program

Une unnilennium

UNEP United Nations Environment Program

UNESCO United Nations Educational, Scientific, and Cultural Organization

unexpl. unexplained

UNFCCC United Nations Framework Convention on Climate Change

UNFDAC United Nations Fund for Drug Abuse Control

UNFICYP United Nations Force in Cyprus

UNFPA United Nations Fund for Population Activities

ung *Latin* unguentum (ointment)

UNGA United Nations General Assembly

Unh unnilhexium

UNH University of New Hampshire

UNHCR United Nations Office of the High Commissioner for Refugees

UNI United Nurses International; Univision; User-Network Interface

UNICEF United Nations Children's Fund (formerly United Nations Children's Emergency Fund)

UNIDO United Nations Industrial Development Organization

UNIENET United Nations International Emergency Network

UNIFIL United Nations Interim Force in Lebanon

UNIKOM United Nations Iraq-Kuwait Observation Mission

Unit. Unitarian; Unitarianism

UNITAR United Nations Institute for Training and Research

univ. universal; university

Univ. Universalist

UNIVAC Universal Automatic Computer

unkn. unknown

UNLV University of Nevada, Las Vegas

UNM University of New Mexico

UNMIH United Nations Mission in Haiti

UNMIK United Nations Mission in Kosovo

UNMOGIP United Nations Military Observer Group in India and Pakistan

UNMOT United Nations Mission of Observers in Tajikistan

Uno unniloctium

UNO University of New Orleans

UNOMIG United Nations Observer Mission in Georgia

UNOMIL United Nations Observer Mission in Liberia

UNOMOZ United Nations Operation in Mozambique

UNOMUR United Nations Observer Mission Uganda-Rwanda

UNOSG United Nations Office of the Secretary General

UNOS United Network for Organ Sharing

UNOSOM II United Nations Operation in Somalia II

Unp unnilpentium

unp. unpaged; unpaginated

UNPREDEP United Nations Preventive Deployment [Force]

UNPROFOR United Nations Protection Force

Unq unnilquadium

UNRISD United Nations Research Institute for Social Development

UNRRA United Nations Relief and Rehabilitation Administration

UNRWA United Nations Relief and Works Agency

Uns unnilseptium

uns. unsymmetrical

UNTAC United Nations Transitional Authority in Cambodia

UNTSO United Nations Truce Supervision Organization

UNU United Nations University

U/O urinary output

UOA United Ostomy Association

UOK are you okay?

UP underproof; Upper Peninsula [of Michigan]

up. upper

UP3 uvulopalatopharyngoplasty

UPA Uniform Partnership Act

UPC Universal Product Code; Usage Parameter Control

UPDRS unified Parkinson disease rating scale

upgd. upgrade; upgraded

UPI United Press International

UPIN Unique Physician Identifier Number

UPJ ureteropelvic junction

UPPP uvulopalatopharyngoplasty

UPPR upper

UPR user preferred routing

upr. upper

UPS uninterruptible power supply; United Parcel Service; University of Puget Sound

UPSR unidirectional path switched ring

UPU Universal Postal Union

ur Urdu

UR utilization review; your (shortwave transmission)

U.R. *Latin* uti rogas (be it as you desire)

Ura uracil

URA Urban Renewal Administration

URAC Utilization Review Accreditation Committee

URAQT you are a cutie

Urd uridine

URESA Uniform Reciprocal Enforcement of Divorce Act

URF unidentified reading frame; uterine relaxing factor

URI University of Rhode Island; upper respiratory infection

URL uniform resource locator; *sometimes* universal resource locator

URN universal resource name

urol. urological; urology

URTI upper respiratory tract infection

Uru. Uruguay; Uruguayan

US ultrasound; unconditioned stimulus; Uniform System; United States; United States [highway]

.us United States of America

u.s. *Latin* ubi supra (where mentioned above); *Latin* ut supra (as above)

U.S. Uncle Sam; united service; United States

u/s ultrasound

USA United States Army; United States of America; United States of America (international vehicle ID); USA (cable television network)

USACD United States Arms Control and Disarmament Agency

USACE United States Army Corps of Engineers

USACHPPM United States Army Center for Health Promotion and Preventive Medicine

USADSF United States of America Deaf Sports Federation

USAF United States Air Force

USAFA United States Air Force Academy

USAFE United States Air Forces in Europe

USAFI United States Armed Forces Institute

USAFSAM United States Air Force School of Aerospace Medicine

USAID United States Agency for International Development

USAKF United States of America Karate Federation

USAN United States Adopted Name

USAR United States Army Reserve

USAREUR United States Army, Europe

USARIEM United States Army Research Institute of Environmental Medicine

USB Universal Serial Bus

USBM United States Bureau of Mines

USBOC United States Bureau of the Census

USBR United States Bureau of Reclamation

USBS United States Bureau of Standards

USC. United States Code

USCA United States Croquet Association

USC.A. United States Code Annotated; United States Court of Appeals

USCAP United States and Canadian Academy of Pathology

USC.C. United States Circuit Court

USCG United States Coast Guard

USCIS United States Citizenship and Immigration Services

USCP United States Capitol Police

USCS United States Customs Service

USC.S.C. United States Civil Service Commission

USD United States—dollar; University of South Dakota

USDA United States Department of Agriculture

USDA/APHIS United States Department of Agriculture's Animal and Plant Health Inspection Service

USD.C. United States District Court

USDI United States Department of the Interior

USDW underground source of drinking water

USEAC United States Export Assistance Center

userid [Internet] user identification

USES United States Employment Service

USET United States Equestrian Team

USF University of San Francisco; University of South Florida

USFS United States Forest Service

USFWS United States Fish and Wildlife Service

USG United States government

USGA United States Golf Association

USGPO United States Government Printing Office

USGS United States Geological Survey

USHA United States Handball Association

USHC United Seniors Health Cooperative

USIA United States Information Agency

USITC United States International Trade Commission

USL University of Southwestern Louisiana; Unix System Laboratories

USM United States Mail; United States Mint

USMA United States Military Academy

USMC United States Marine Corps

USMLE United States Medical Licensing Examination

USN United States Navy

USNA United States Naval Academy

USNCB United States National Central Bureau

USNR United States Naval Reserve

USO ultra stable oscillator; United Service Organizations

USP United States Pharmacopoeia

USPHS United States Public Health Service

USPO United States Post Office

USPS United States Postal Service

USPTO United States Patent and Trademark Office

USR. *United States Supreme Court Reports*

USRA United States Railway Association

USR.S. United States Revised Statutes

USRT universal synchronous receiver transmitter

USS United States Senate; United States ship

USSC United States Space Command

USSF United States Soccer Federation

USSR Union of Soviet Socialist Republics

UST underground storage tank

USTA United States Telephone Association; United States Tennis Association

UST.C. United States Tax Cases

USTTA United States Travel and Tourism Administration

USU Utah State University

usu. usually

usw. *German* und so weiter (and so forth)

Ut. Utah

UT universal time; University of Tennessee; University of Texas; Utah

UTA University of Texas at Arlington

UTC Coordinated Universal Time

UTCS universal time coordinate system

ut dict. *Latin* ut dictum (as directed)

ute utility vehicle

uten. utensils

UTEP University of Texas, El Paso

UTF Unicode transformation format

UTI urinary tract infection

util. utilities; utility

utl. utilities

UTM universal Turing machine

UTP uridine 5c-triphosphate

ut sup. *Latin* ut supra (as above)

UTX United Technologies Corp.

UUCP Unix-to-Unix Copy Program

Uun ununnilium

Uuu unununium

UV ultraviolet

UVA ultraviolet, long wave; University of Virginia

UVB ultraviolet, short wave

UVC ultraviolet C

UVCS ultraviolet coronagraph spectrometer

UVEB unifocal ventricular ectopic beat

UVM Universal Voice Module; University of Vermont

UVS ultraviolet spectrometer

UW underwriter; underwritten; University of Washington; University of Wisconsin; University of Wyoming

UWM University of William and Mary

ux. *Latin* uxor (wife)

UXB unexploded bomb

.uy Uruguay

UYU Uruguay—peso

uz Uzbek

UZ Uzbekistan (international vehicle ID)

.uz Uzbekistan

UZS Uzbekistan—som (currency)

V

v. vocals; voice

V 5; potential; vanadium; Vatican City (international vehicle ID); velocity; verb; very; victory; violence (television rating); vocative; volt; volume; vowel

v. verb; verse; version; verso; *Latin* versus (against); *Latin* vide (see); volume

V. venerable; very; viscount; viscountess

V-1 *German* Vergeltungswaffe 1 (vengeance weapon 1)

V-2 *German* Vergeltungswaffe 2 (vengeance weapon 2)

V-6 V-engine with six cylinders

V-8 V-engine with eight cylinders

VA Department of Veterans Affairs (formerly Veterans' Administration); vicar apostolic; Virginia; volt-ampere

Va. Virginia

.va Vatican City State

V/A visual acuity

V-A ventriculoatrial

VAB voice answer back

VAC ventriculoatrial conduction

vac. vacuum

VACM vector averaging current meter

vactor virtual actor

VAD value added dealer; velocity-azimuth display

VADM vice admiral

V.Adm. vice admiral

VAERS Vaccine Adverse Events Reporting System

VAFB Vandenberg Air Force Base

VAFSTF Vaccine Associated Feline Sarcoma Task Force

vag. vagina; vaginal; vagrancy; vagrant

VAI ventilator-assisted individual

val. valentine; value; valued

Val. valley

VAMC Veterans Affairs Medical Center

vamp vampire

van caravan; vanguard

VAN value-added network

V & V verification and validation

VAP value-added process

Va/Q alveolar ventilation/perfusion ratio

VAR value-added reseller; value-added retailer

var. variable; variant; variation; variety; various

vas. vasectomy

VAT value-added tax

Vat. Vatican

VATS video-assisted thoracic surgery; video-assisted thoracoscopic surgery

VAX Virtual Address Extension

VB vertebral body; Visual Basic

vb. verb; verbal

VBG very big grin

vbl verbal

vbln. verbal noun

vBNS very high performance Backbone Network Service

<VBG> very big grin

VBR variable bit rate

VBT vertebral body tenderness

VC vice chancellor; vice consul; Victoria Cross; Vietcong; virtual channel; vital capacity

.vc Saint Vincent and the Grenadines

V/C vector control

VCC virtual channel connection

V.C.C. vice-chancellor's court

VCD video compact disc; virtual circuit descriptor; vocal cord dysfunction

VCE variable cycle engine

VCI virtual channel identifier

VCID virtual channel identification

vCJD variant Creutzfeldt-Jakob disease

VCL virtual channel link

VCN virtual circuit number

VCO Virtual Central Office; voltage controlled oscillator

VCPI virtual control program interface

VCR video cassette recorder

VCS Veterinary Cancer Society

VCU Virginia Commonwealth University

VCUG voiding cystourethrogram

VCXO voltage controlled crystal oscillator

VD venereal disease

v.d. vapor density; various dates

V-day victory day

VDC volts DC

VDE visual development environment

VDISK virtual disk

VDRL Venereal Disease Research Laboratories

VDS virtual data set

VDSL very high bit-rate digital subscriber line

VDT video display terminal

VDU visual display unit

VE virtual environment

.ve Venezuela

V.E. *Latin* venditioni exponas (a sale must be exposed, that is, made)

VEB Venezuela—bolivar (currency)

VEBA voluntary employee benefit account

V-E Day Victory in Europe Day (WWII)

VEE Venezuelan equine encephalomyelitis

veep vice president

VEG very evil grin

veg. vegetable; vegetarian; vegetate

VEGF vascular endothelial growth factor

veggie vegetable; vegetarian
VEL Vela (constellation)
vel. vellum; velocity
Ven. venerable; Venezuela; Venezuelan
Venez. Venezuela
VER visual evoked response
ver. verse; version
Veronica very easy, rodent-oriented netwide index to computerized archives
vers versed sine
vert. vertebrate; vertical
VESA Video Electronics Standards Association
VESL Vocational English as a Second Language
vesp. *Latin* vesper (evening)
vet veteran; veterinarian; veterinary
veter. veterinary
vet. med. veterinary medicine
VETS Veterans' Employment and Training Service
VF variance factor; ventricular fibrillation; very fine; vicar forane; video frequency; visual field
VFD volunteer fire department
V-fib ventricular fibrillation
VFIT visual field intact
VFR visual flight rules
VFW Veterans of Foreign Wars
VG very good; vicar general
.vg [British] Virgin Islands
v.g. *Latin* verbi gratia (for the sake of example)
VGA video graphics array
VGL very good-looking
VGLI Veterans Group Life Insurance
VHA Voluntary Hospitals of America

VHDL very high density lipoprotein
VHF very high frequency
VHPCC very high performance computing and communication
VHRR very high resolution radiometer
VHS video home system
VHSIC very high speed integrated circuit
vi Vietnamese
VI Vancouver Island; Virgin Islands; volume indicator
.vi [U.S.] Virgin Islands
v.i. verb intransitive; *Latin* vide infra (see below)
V.I. Vancouver Island; Virgin Islands
VIA Vaccine Information and Awareness
vibe vibration
vibes vibraphone
VIC voice interface card
vic. vicinity
Vic. Vicar; Victoria
Vict. Victorian
VID vehicle identification [number]
vid. video
videorazzi video camera paparazzi
VIE Schwechat Airport (Vienna, Austria)
Viet. Vietnam; Vietnamese
vig vigorish
VIL vertically integrated liquid
vil. village
VIN vehicle identification number
VINES Virtual Integrated Network Service

VIP very important person
VIR Virgo
VIRGO variability of [solar] irradiance and gravity oscillations
vis. visibility; visible; visual
Vis. viscount; viscountess
Visct. viscount; viscountess
VISSR visible-infrared spin-scan radiometer
VISTA Volunteers in Service to America
vit vitamin
vitals vital signs (pulse rate, temperature, respiratory rate)
viz. *Latin* videlicet (that is, namely)
VJ video jockey
V-J Day Victory over Japan Day (WWII)
VL Vulgar Latin
VLA very large array
VLAN virtual LAN
VLBA very long baseline array
VLBI very long baseline interferometry
VLCC very large crude (oil) carrier
VLDL very low-density lipoprotein
VLF very low frequency
VLMF very low magnetic field
VLR visitor location register
VLSI very large scale integration
VLT very large telescope
VM virtual memory
VMA vanillylmandelic acid; virtual memory address
VMAc virtual media access control
V-mail video mail; voice mail
VMB virtual machine boot
VMC visual meteorological conditions; void metal composite
VMCM vector measuring current meter
VMD *Latin* Veterinariae Medicinae Doctor (Doctor of Veterinary Medicine)
VME virtual memory environment
VMI Virginia Military Institute
V-MI Volpe-Manhold Index
VMM virtual memory manager
VMP Virtual Modem Protocol
VMS vertical motion simulator; virtual memory system
.vn Vietnam
VN Vietnam (international vehicle ID)
VNA Visiting Nurse Association
VNAA Visiting Nurse Associations of America
VNB Verrazano Narrows Bridge
VNC Virtual Nursing College
VND Viet Nam—dong
vo Volapük
VO verbal order; voiceover
vo. verso
VOA Voice of America
VOC volatile organic chemical; volatile organic compound
voc. vocational; vocative
vocab. vocabulary
VOD video on demand
VoIP Voice over Internet Protocol
VOL Volans (constellation)
vol. volcano; volume; volunteer
VOM volt-ohm milliameter
VOR very high frequency omni-directional radio range
VOS verb-object-subject; vessel of opportunity; voluntary observing ship; volunteer

observing ship

vou. voucher

VP variable pitch; venous pressure; verb phrase; vice president

VPD vacuum photo diode

VPDN virtual private data network

VPG virtual proving grounds

VPI virtual path identifier

VPISU Virginia Polytechnic Institute and State University

VPN Virtual Private Network

VPOTUS Vice President of the United States

VPS Valparaiso-Fort Walton Beach [Airport]; volume performance standard

VR virtual reality

VRA very high frequency real-time antenna

VRAM video random access memory

v. refl. reflexive verb

VRTC Vehicle Research Test Center

VRM variable-rate mortgage

VRML virtual reality modeling language

vry very

VS variable block span; very superior; veterinary surgeon; virtual storage; vital signs (pulse rate, temperature, respiratory rate)

vs. verse; *Latin* versus (against)

v.s. vide supra

VSAM Virtual Storage Access Method

VSAT very small aperture terminal

VSCP Vital Statistics Cooperative Program

VSD ventricular septal defect; virtually safe dose

VSM volcano system monitor

VSO verb-subject-object; very superior old

VSOP very superior old pale

VSP Vessel Sanitation Program

VSS vital signs stable

vss. verses; versions

V/STOL vertical short takeoff and landing

VT vacuum tube; variable time; Vermont

Vt. Vermont

v.t. verb transitive

VTB vestibular test battery

VTE venous thromboembolic event

VTF vacuum test fixture

VTHL vertical takeoff, horizontal landing

VTOL vertical takeoff and landing

VTR videotape recorder

VTVL vertical takeoff, vertical landing

VTX very high frequency real-time transmitter

VU volume unit

.vu Vanuatu

VUL Vulpecula (constellation)

Vul. Vulgate

vulg. vulgar

Vulg. Vulgate

VUS views

VUV Vanuatu—vatu (currency)

vv. verbs; verses; violins; volumes

v.v. vice versa

VVSOP very, very superior old pale

VW *German* Volkswagen (people's car)

V/W vaporware

VxD virtual device driver

VY very (shortwave transmission)

VZR varicella zoster (chicken pox)

W

w weight; width; work

W tungsten; watt; Wednesday; week; Welsh; west; western; White (as in personal ads); widowed (as in personal ads); windy; with (shortwave transmission)

w. wife; with

w/ with

WA Washington; with average; word after (shortwave transmission)

WAAC Women's Army Auxiliary Corps

WAAF Women's Auxiliary Air Force

WAC Women's Army Corps

WACMA World Arnold-Chiari Malformation Association

WADB West African Development Bank

WADEM World Association for Disaster and Emergency Medicine

WADR with all due respect

WAF Women in the Air Force

WAFS World Area Forecast System

WAG Gambia (international vehicle ID)

WAGICS Women and Genetics in Contemporary Society

WAHEC World Association of Health, Environment, and Cul-ture

WAIS Wechsler Adult Intelligence Scale; wide area information server

WAL Sierra Leone (international vehicle ID)

WALOC what a load of crap

WAM wave model

WAN Nigeria (international vehicle ID); wide area network

WAP wireless application protocol

WAPA Western Area Power Administration

WAPD World Association of Persons with Disabilities

war. warrant

Ward X the morgue

WARF Wisconsin Alumni Research Foundation

Warks. Warwickshire

WAS Washington Redskins

Wash. Washington

Wasp White Anglo-Saxon Protestant

WASP World Association for Social Psychiatry

Wat. Waterford

WATS Wide Area Telecommunications Service

W. Aust. Western Australia

WAV wavetable synthesis

WAVES Women Accepted for Volunteer Emergency Service

WAW Okecie International Airport (Warsaw, Poland)

Wb weber

WB weather bureau; westbound; word before (shortwave transmission)

w.b. water ballast; waybill

WBA World Boxing Association

WBB Williamsburg Bridge

WBC white blood cell; white blood count; Women's Business Center; World Boxing Council

WBD will be done

WBF wood-burning fireplace; World Bridge Federation

wbfp. wood-burning fireplace

WBG World Bank Group

WBI World Bank Institute

WBMOD wide band [scintillation] model

WbN west by north

WBO Weather Bureau Office

WbS west by south

WBS work breakdown structure; write back soon

WBSP write back soon please

WC water closet; without charge; worker's compensation; workmen's compensation

W-C wind chill

w/c wheelchair

WCA World Chiropractic Alliance

W.C. and Ins. Rep. *Workmen's Compensation and Insurance Reports*

WCB Workers' Compensation Board

WCCFL West Coast Conference on Formal Linguistics

WCE worst-case error

WCF White Christian female

WCI Wound Care Institute

WCL World Confederation of Labor

WCM White Christian male

WCO World Customs Organization

WCS Wireless Communication Services

WCTF World Children's Transplant Fund

WCTU Woman's Christian Temperance Union

wd when distributed

Wd widowed (as in personal ads)

WD Dominica (international vehicle ID); War Department; water damage; well-developed; white dwarf; word (shortwave transmission); would (shortwave transmission)

wd. wood; word

W.D. Western District

W/D washer and dryer

WDC washer/dryer connection; World Data Center

WDCGG World Data Center for Greenhouse Gases

WDDES World Digital Database for Environmental Sciences

WDLL well-differentiated lymphocytic lymphoma

WDM wavelength division multiplexing

WDV water dilution volume

wdy wordy

WDYM what do you mean?

WDYT what do you think?

We Wednesday

webinar web seminar

webisode web episode

Webs world equity benchmark shares

Wed. Wednesday

WEDI Workgroup on Electronic Data Interchange

Wedn. Wednesday

Wednes. Wednesday

WEE western equine encephalomyelitis

WEFAX weather facsimile

WeHo West Hollywood

WEHT whatever happened to

Westm. Westmeath; Westminster; Westmorland
WET Western European Time
WEU Western European Union
Wex. Wexford
Wexf. Wexford
wf wrong font
WF White female; wood floors
.wf Wallis and Futuna Islands
WFC World Food Council
WFCS World's Fair Collectors Society
WFH World Federation of Hemophilia
WFIem. Western Flemish
WFM works for me
WFMH World Federation for Mental Health
WFO Weather Forecast Office
WFP World Food Program
WFQ weighted fair queuing
WFris. West Frisian
WFS Women for Sobriety
WFTC Working Families' Tax Credit
WFTU World Federation of Trade Unions
WFWG Windows for Workgroups
WG Grenada (international vehicle ID); wrong (shortwave transmission)
w.g. wire gauge
WGAS who gives a shit
WGmc West Germanic
WH watt-hour; which (shortwave transmission)
wh. white
WHA World Hockey Association
WHAM! Women's Health Action and Mobilization
WHCA White House Communications Agency

WHERE Women for Healthcare Education, Reform, and Equity
whf. wharf
WHIP walks and hits per innings pitched
WHMIS Workplace Hazardous Materials Information System
WHO World Health Organization
Whodb White House Office Database
WHOI Woods Hole Oceanographic Institution
WHOSIS WHO Statistical Information System
WHPA wellhead protection area
W-hr watt-hour
WHS Washington Headquarters Services
whs. warehouse
whse. warehouse
whsle. wholesale
wht. white
wi when issued
WI will (shortwave transmission); Wisconsin
W.I. West Indian; West Indies
W/I walk-in
WIA weather-impacted airspace; wounded in action
WIBC Women's International Bowling Congress
WIC Women, Infants, and Children (supplemental food program)
Wick. Wicklow
wid. widow; widower
wilco will comply
Wilts. Wiltshire
WiMAX Worldwide Interoperability for Microwave Access
WIMC Women in Managed Care
WIMP window, icon, menu,

pointing [device]; window, icon, mouse, pull-down [menu]

WIN Weight-control Information Network; Whip Inflation Now; within (shortwave transmission); Work Incentive program

wind. windowed

W Indies West Indies

WINK windowed eat-in kitchen

WIPO World Intellectual Property Organization

WIPP [United States] Waste Isolation Pilot Plant

Wis. Wisconsin; Wisdom of Solomon

Wisc. Wisconsin

Wisd. Wisdom

WIT witness (shortwave transmission)

wiz wizard

WK week (shortwave transmission)

wk. weak; week

WKD worked (shortwave transmission)

WKG working (shortwave transmission)

wkly. weekly

WKU Western Kentucky University

wk vb weak verb

WL St. Lucia (international vehicle ID); water line; wavelength; well (shortwave transmission)

WLA wasteload allocation

WLC wavelength calibration

WLU work load unit

WM White male

wm. wattmeter

WMA Windows Media Audio; World Medical Association

WMD weapons of mass destruction

WMF Windows Metafile

wmk. watermark

WML Wireless Markup Language

WMO World Meteorological Organization

WMP waste management plan

WMT Wal-Mart Stores Inc.

WMU Western Michigan University

WMV Windows Media Video

WN well-nourished; when (shortwave transmission)

WNBA Women's National Basketball Association

WNL within normal limits

WNRC Washington National Records Center

WNW west-northwest

WNWD well-nourished and well-developed

wo Wolof

WO warrant officer; who (shortwave transmission)

w/o without

WO3DC World Ozone Data Center

w.o.c. without compensation

WOCN Wound, Ostomy, and Continence Nurses Society

WODC World Ozone Data Center

WoMS World of Multiple Sclerosis

WONCA World Organization of Family Doctors

WONDER Wide-ranging Online Data for Epidemiologic Research

WORM write once, read many [times]

WOSB woman-owned small business

WOTAM waste of time and money

WOTAN weather observation through ambient noise

WOW World Ocean Watch

WP weather permitting; whirlpool; wild pitch; word processing; word processor

WPA Work Projects Administration; World Psychiatric Association

WPBA World Professional Billiards Association

wpc watts per channel

WPF White professional female

WPI Wholesale Price Index

WPL Wave Propagation Laboratory

wpm words per minute

WPM White professional male

wpn. weapon

WPT World Poker Tour

WR were (shortwave transmission); western range; wide receiver

W.r. Wassermann reaction

Wra Wright antigens

WRAC Women's Royal Army Corps

WRAF Women's Royal Air Force

WRAMC Walter Reed Army Medical Center

WRAPD World Rehabilitation Association for the Psycho-Socially Disabled

WRDA Water Resources Development Act

WRED weighted random early detection

writ. writer; written by

WRIPS Wave Rider Information Processing System

WRNS Women's Royal Naval Service

wrnt. warrant

WROS with rights of survivorship

WRT with respect to

WRVS Women's Royal Voluntary Service

WS was (shortwave transmission); West Saxon; William Shakespeare; Wisdom of Solomon; working storage; workstation

.ws Samoa

WSA wilderness study area; Williams Syndrome Association

WSFO Weather Service Forecast Office

WSMR White Sands Missile Range

WSP [Federal] Witness Security Program

WSTA World Societies for Technology in Anaesthesia

WSU Washington State University; Wayne State University; Wichita State University

WSW west-southwest

WSX Wessex

wt warrant

WT watertight; what (shortwave transmission)

wt. weight

WTC World Trade Center

wtd wanted

WTF what the fuck

WTFIGO What the fuck is going on?

WTG way to go

WTGP Want to go private? (that is, to a private chatroom)

WTH what the hell

WTO World Tourism Organization; World Trade Organization formerly **GATT**

WToO World Tourism Organization

WTrO World Trade Organization

WTTM without thinking too much

WU Washington University

W/U workup

WUD would (shortwave transmission)

WUWT What's up with that?

WV St. Vincent & the Grenadines (international vehicle ID); West Virginia

W.Va. West Virginia

WVI World Veterinary Index

WVR Within Visual Range

WVS Women's Voluntary Service

WVU West Virginia University

w/w wall-to-wall

WW widowed (as in personal ads)

WWAF widowed Asian female

WWAM widowed Asian male

WWBF widowed Black female

WWBM widowed Black male

WWF World Wildlife Fund

WWHF widowed Hispanic female

WWHM widowed Hispanic male

WWI World War I

WWII World War II

WWJD What Would Jesus Do

WWJF widowed Jewish female

WWJM widowed Jewish male

WWMCCS Worldwide Military Command and Control System

WWNWS Worldwide Navigational Warning Service

WWU Western Washington University

WWW [United Nations] World Weather Watch; World Wide Web

WWWF widowed White female

WWWM widowed White male

WX weather

WY why (shortwave transmission); Wyoming

WYCM Will you call me?

Wyo. Wyoming

WYRN What's your real name?

WYSIAYG what you see is all you get

WYSIWYG what you see is what you get

X

x abscissa; by; times (that is, multiplication)

X adult audiences only; Christ; Christian; experimental; extra; reactance; 10

x. *Latin* ex (not including, without)

XA extended architecture

XAF Communauté Financière Africaine (CFA)—franc

XAG Silver Ounces (currency)

Xan xanthine

XAU Gold Ounces (currency)

XBH extra base hits

XBT expendable bathythermograph

XC cross-country

XCD East Caribbean dollar

XCP expendable current profiler

XD ex dividend

x-div. ex dividend

XDR external data

representation; extreme data rate

Xe xenon

Xerox PARC Xerox Palo Alto Research Center

XF extra fine; extremely fine

XFER transfer

XFCN external function

XGA extended graphics array

xh Xhosa

XHTML Extensible Hypertext Markup Language

XI ex interest

XID exchange identification

XIDB extended integrated data base

XING crossing

XIY Xi'an Xianyang Airport

XL ex-library; extra large; extra long

Xmas Christmas

XML Extensible Markup Language

XMM x-ray multi mirror

XMP xanthosine 5c-monophosphate

XMS extended memory specification

XMT transmit

XMTR transmitter

Xn. Christian

Xnty. Christianity

XO executive officer; extra old

XOM Exxon Mobil Corp.

XPD Palladium Ounces (currency)

XPF CFP franc (currency)

XPNDR transponder

XPS Xeroderma Pigmentosum Society

XPT Platinum Ounces (currency)

Xref cross-reference

XRF x-ray fluorescence

xrt x-ray therapy

XS extra small

x-sect cross section

XSL Extensible Stylesheet Language

XSU cross strap unit

XT crosstalk; extended technology

xtal crystal

XTAL crystal (shortwave transmission)

XTP xanthosine 5c-triphosphate

xtr extra

XUV extreme ultraviolet

XW ex warrants

XX double strength ale; 20

XXL extra extra large

XXX pornographic; triple strength ale

Xy xylose

Xyl xylose

XYL wife (shortwave transmission)

Y

y yen

Y admittance; hypercharge; year; YMCA; YMHA; YWCA; YWHA; young; yttrium

y. year

Y2K (the year) 2000

YA yesterday (shortwave transmission); yet another; young adult

YAC yeast artificial chromosome

YAFIYGI you asked for it, you got it

YAG yttrium aluminum garnet

YAP young aspiring

professional
YAR Yemen Arab Republic
YATB you are the best
Yb ytterbium
YB yearbook
YC yellow card (soccer)
YCC Youth Conservation Corps
yd. yard
YDT Yukon Daylight Time
.ye Yemen
yel. yellow
yeo. yeoman; yeomanry
YER Yemen—rial (currency)
YF yeast free
YGBK you gotta be kiddin'
YGWYPF you get what you pay for
YHBT you have been trolled
YHBTTYFPHAND you have been trolled, thank you for playing, have a nice day
YHBW you have been warned
YHVH Jehovah; Yahweh
YHWH Jehovah; Yahweh
YHz yottahertz
YHZ Halifax International Airport
yi Yiddish
Yinglish Yiddish influenced English
yippie Youth International Party [member]
YKWIM You know what I mean?
YL young lady (shortwave transmission)
YMCA Young Men's Christian Association
YMHA Young Men's Hebrew Association
YMMD you've made my day
YMMV your mileage may vary
yng. young

yo Yoruba; year-old
YO years old
YOB year of birth
Yorks. Yorkshire
YOW Macdonald-Cartier International Airport (Ottawa, Canada)
YOYO you're on your own
YP Yellow Pages
YPLL years of potential life lost
YQB Québec International Airport
yr. year; your
yrbk. yearbook
YRBS Youth Risk Behavior Survey
yrd yard
yrly. yearly
Yrs. Yours
ys yoctasecond
ysec yoctasecond
YSL Youth Soccer League
YSO young stellar object
YST Yukon Standard Time
YSU Youngstown State University
.yt Mayotte
Y.T. Yukon Territory
YTD year to date
YTM yield to maturity
YU Yugoslavia (international vehicle ID)
.yu Yugoslavia
Yug. Yugoslavia; Yugoslavian
Yugo. Yugoslavian
YUL Dorval International Airport (Montreal, Canada)
YUN Yugoslavia—new dinar (currency)
yuppie young urban professional
YV Venezuela (international vehicle ID)

YVR Vancouver [BC] International Airport
yw you're welcome
YWCA Young Women's Christian Association
YWHA Young Women's Hebrew Association
YWIA you're welcome in advance
YYC Calgary International Airport
YY4U two wise for you
YYSSW yeah, yeah, sure, sure, whatever
YYZ Lester B. Pearson International Airport (Toronto, Canada)

Z

Z atomic number; impedance; zenith distance
z. zero; zone
za pizza; Zhuang
ZA South Africa (international vehicle ID)
.za South Africa
Zach. Zacharias
ZAF South Africa
ZAN we can receive absolutely nothing (shortwave transmission)
ZAP acknowledge please (shortwave transmission)
ZAR South Africa—rand (currency)
ZB zero beat
ZBB zero-based budgeting
ZBR zone bit recording
Zc Zechariah
ZC zoning change
Z-CAV zoned constant angular velocity

ZCG local receiving conditions good (shortwave transmission)
ZCP local receiving conditions poor (shortwave transmission)
ZCS cease sending (shortwave transmission)
ZD zenith distance; zero defect
ZDV Denver Air Route Traffic Control Center; zidovudine
Zec Zechariah
Zech. Zechariah
ZEEP zero end-expiratory pressure
Zeph. Zephaniah
ZETA zero energy thermonuclear assembly
ZEV zero-emission vehicle
ZFB your signals are fading badly (shortwave transmission)
ZFS your signals are fading slightly (shortwave transmission)
ZFW Fort Worth Air Route Traffic Control Center
ZG zero gravity
ZGS your signals are getting stronger (shortwave transmission)
ZGW your signals are getting weaker (shortwave transmission)
zh Chinese
ZHC how are your receiving conditions? (shortwave transmission)
ZHz zettahertz
ZI zonal index; zone of interior
ZID zone of initial dilution
ZIF zero insertion force
ZIFT zygote intrafallopian transfer
zin zinfandel
'zine an inexpensively

produced, usually underground, fan magazine (from "magazine")

zip compressed file

ZIP zone improvement plan; Zone Information Protocol

Zl zloty

ZLB give long breaks (shortwave transmission)

ZLS we are suffering from a lightning storm (shortwave transmission)

zm. zeptometer

.zm Zambia

ZMK Zambia—kwacha (currency)

ZMO stand by a moment (shortwave transmission)

ZMQ stand by for... (shortwave transmission)

Zn zinc

ZOC zone of contribution

ZOI zone of influence

ZOK we are receiving OK (shortwave transmission)

zoo zoological garden

zool. zoological; zoologist; zoology

ZOT zone of transport

Zp Zephaniah

ZPG zero population growth

ZPRSN Zurich Provisional Relative Sunspot Number

Zr zirconium

ZRE Congo (former Zaire) (international vehicle ID)

ZRH Zurich-Kloten Airport

ZRL zero risk level

ZRO are you receiving OK? (shortwave transmission)

zs zeptosecond

Z's sleep

zsec zeptosecond

ZSF send faster (shortwave transmission)

ZSH static is heavy here (shortwave transmission)

ZSR your sigs strong readable (shortwave transmission); zeta sedimentation ratio

ZSS send slower (shortwave transmission)

ZST zone standard time

ZSU your signals are unreadable (shortwave transmission)

ZT zone time

ZTH send by hand (shortwave transmission)

zu Zulu

ZVS signals varying in intensity (shortwave transmission)

.zw Zimbabwe

ZW Zimbabwe (international vehicle ID)

ZWD Zimbabwe—Zimbabwe dollar

ZWO send words once (shortwave transmission)

ZWR your sigs weak but readable (shortwave transmission)

ZWT send words twice (shortwave transmission)

zzz sleep

zzzz snore